OUTWITTING
TODDLERS

OUTWITTING TODDLERS

BILL ADLER, JR. and PEGGY ROBIN

KENSINGTON BOOKS
http://www.kensingtonbooks.com

KENSINGTON BOOKS are published by

Kensington Publishing Corp.
850 Third Avenue
New York, NY 10022

All Kensington titles, imprints and distributed lines are available at special quantity discounts for bulk purchases for sales promotion, premiums, fund raising, educational or institutional use.

Special book excerpts or customized printings can also be created to fit specific needs. For details, write or phone the office of the Kensington Special Sales Manager: Kensington Publishing Corp., 850 Third Avenue, New York, NY, Attn. Special Sales Department. Phone: 1-800-221-2647.

Kensington and the K logo Reg. U.S. Pat. & TM Off.

ISBN 1-57566-646-4

First Kensington Trade Paperback Printing: March, 2001
10 9 8 7 6 5 4 3 2 1

Printed in the United States of America

To our parents:
Gloria and Bill Adler (Bill's parents) and
Florence and Fred Robin (Peggy's parents),
who actually knew a thing or two about parenting.

C O N T E N T S

Introduction
Why Do Toddlers Need
to Be Outwitted?

Here's the problem with toddlers: They're just old enough to have formed a separate identity from their parents, and just strong enough to begin to exercise that identity by doing the opposite of what their parents want. So the parents, who until now might have thought they had a sweet, good-natured, and relatively helpless baby on their hands, are suddenly faced with a small but determined adversary whose main word seems to be "NO!"—and who can run and kick and throw things.

Once they get over the shock of the first-time confrontation with their headstrong toddler, parents quickly realize they need to take action. If they're of the old school of parenting, they use their authority, issuing orders and punishing disobedience. However, most of today's childcare experts warn against that approach, telling parents that too many rules and punishments will squelch their children's spirit and make them feel put down, unimportant, and afraid to try new things.

The standard parenting guides these days tell you to *explain* things to your toddler, try to get them to understand *why* they can't take their pants off at the grocery store or stay up until two in the morning. That sounds good in theory, but parents quickly discover that logic and reasoning will take you only so far with a twenty-month-old who is lying on the floor and screaming at the top of his lungs, "NO DOCTOR!"—when the appointment for his checkup is in fifteen minutes.

Then there are those parents who decide not to challenge their toddler's contrariness; they just give in to every demand—and usually end up with children so spoiled that even after the toddler years are long past, they're still behaving like two-year-olds.

If it's wrong to force obedience, useless to reason with them, and dangerous to surrender to them, what can a parent do? *Outwit them!* Use your superior brain and adult resourcefulness to come up with a way to get your child to go along with what you want.

The trick is to make your child believe that this is what he or she really wants, anyway. If you can get your toddler to cooperate without threats, punishments, or tears, you will give the child a sense of accomplishment and pride. You will reinforce your toddler's budding spirit, not crush it—and without spoiling your child by giving in.

But *how* do you outwit them? They may have little experience of the world, but they *are* smart, and inventive, and unpredictable. That's why you need *Outwitting Toddlers*.

Where did we get all these bright ideas about how to outwit toddlers? From other parents, mainly. When we first conceived of this guide, we decided the best way to find out what works and what doesn't is to talk to parents of toddlers and compile their collective wisdom. We asked our friends and relatives for their best ideas, and we asked them to ask *their* friends and relatives. Just to be sure we were not limited by geography, we put out queries over various parenting forums on the Internet.

Of course, our own experience as parents of toddlers helped enormously, too. We look at our own two girls, now years beyond toddlerhood, and conclude that we did a pretty good job. They presented us with the usual problems—they refused to go to bed on time, they were hard to toilet train, they had their share of tantrums—plus one was seriously hooked on thumbsucking, while the other went through a phase of refusing to take a bath. With a little ingenuity and a lot of patience, we managed to work through these (as well as many other) problems.

We just wish we could have had a book like this on hand at the time, so that we could have solved the problems a lot faster, and with far fewer mistakes along the way.

We also consulted plenty of parenting guides. We had books by Penelope Leach, Dr. Spock, T. Berry Brazelton, and quite a few others. What bothered us in these tomes by such esteemed experts is how cocksure they all were that their suggested techniques would work on every sort of child.

To take just one quick example, in her book *Your Baby and Child from Birth to Age Five*, Penelope Leach issues the decree, "Always tell your child why." She goes on to add, "It is an insult to your child's intelligence to tell him to do something without telling him why." "Because I said so," she argues, is a terrible parental response which should *never* be used. Let's say you find your child playing with a shovel. If you tell him to put it down without giving a reason, Leach says the child "cannot fit this particular instruction into the general pattern of 'how to behave' that he is building up in his mind." The *only* way to get a child to accept and follow your commands, in Leach's view of the situation, is to provide the rationale: Is it because the shovel is dirty? Or it belongs to someone else? Or because it's breakable? Or because you want to be sure of finding it when you need it later?*

We think few toddlers would actually put the shovel down promptly after receiving one of those explanations. Here's what we think would actually happen (depending on the type of toddler involved):

1. A series of unending questions follows: "*Why* is the shovel dirty? Does that make it bad to play with? *Why?* Why can't we just wash it off in the bathroom? Why can't I just have a bath after playing with it?" ... and so on and so on, endlessly—all with shovel in hand.
2. As you launch into your explanation of what's wrong with playing with a shovel, your toddler has already grabbed the shovel and run off, and is about to clobber another child with it.
3. Your child just locks his two hands around the handle and refuses to drop the shovel, and begins screaming, "NO! I WANT SHOBBLE!"
4. Your child simply ignores you and goes on playing with the shovel.

What makes *Outwitting Toddlers* quite different from most other parenting books is that we understand that toddlers are *not* all alike.

* Leach, Penelope. *Your Baby and Child from Birth to Age Five.* New York: Knopf, 1990, p. 457.

What works with one type of toddler may backfire with a different sort of child. For some children the only thing that gets immediate action is the no-nonsense response "BECAUSE I SAID SO," which makes clear that there is no time for argument. For others, a simple explanation may be useful. For still others, the best course of action is simply to go over to the child and yank the shovel out of his little hands before he has a chance to think twice about his options. You have to know your child.

Recognizing this reality, we will never give only a single answer to the problems we tackle, but will offer two—and sometimes three or four—different strategies to try out.

We also understand that not every parent is suited to the use of every type of technique, and so the book considers how various styles of parenting match up with the different *Outwitting* techniques described. For example, a parent who is normally strict might get better results with a technique that requires the child to act promptly, while a permissive parent might be better off trying a solution that allows the child to do the required action at a later time, or in a more interesting and more fun way.

We encourage you to take a results-oriented approach to parenting, to ask yourselves, when considering the solution to any potential problem, "Do I think this will work with my child? Or do I think it could end up doing more harm than good to try it?"

We're not pushing any theory to account for why your toddler can be headstrong and difficult. You can get that from plenty of other books. Each child psychologist has his or her own take on how nature or nurture leads inexorably to certain parenting problems—although we've also noticed that many of these books end up blaming the mom for a lot of what can go wrong. Social critics, on the other hand, tend to focus on some fault in the structure of society: Feminists blame the patriarchal system; antifeminists blame working mothers; moralists point to a decline in social values. Because these experts focus on the big picture, they have little advice of value for the day-to-day problems of parents and toddlers.

Instead, *Outwitting Toddlers* presents ideas and suggestions from all kinds of parents of all kinds of children. Our goal is to be as "hands-on" as possible. To the extent that we have any ideology at all, our predisposition is that parenting should be *fun*—at least much of the time. In addition to offering advice for many common parental dilemmas, we'll also present some funny stories about toddlers who simply could not be outwitted.

One final thought, for those of you who suspect that your child may turn out to be one of those tough cases with a turn of mind so devious that it can defeat any adult-conceived plan: Keep in mind, *everything* is outgrown eventually. So keep the long, *long* view—and keep your sense of humor, too. For the day *will* come when your toddler is grown and has his or her own toddler, who is every bit as impossible as your child is today. Your grown-up child will turn to you for your sage parenting advice, and you can simply nod mysteriously and say, "I *could* tell you, but it's much better for you to work out the answer on your own . . ."

There you have your revenge for all those times your toddler simply would *not* do what you wanted, no matter what clever trick you devised. But in the meantime, keep trying! Because in 99.9 percent of cases, adults can outwit their little ones if they put their older, more experienced minds to work! Good luck in your efforts!

Bill Adler
Peggy Robin
www.adlerbooks.com

OUTWITTING
TODDLERS

Clothing Wars and Battles Over Appearance

Nobody expects much from babies when it comes to appearance. They can go out in public with drool all over their faces and spit-up stains all over their clothing, and they can lie around naked except for a diaper—all without embarrassment to them or their parents. But what a difference a year makes! Somewhere in toddlerhood the child starts to be aware that clothing isn't just something your parents put on you—it's something they expect you to start being able to put on by yourself—and that it matters to them what pieces of apparel you choose. And even more significantly, it starts to matter to you—the toddler—too. But what parents think is important about clothing (size, weather-appropriateness, cleanliness) is rarely the same as what their toddler thinks is important (having the right Pokémon characters printed on the fabric).

How should these conflicts of opinion be resolved? Can it be done without leaving everyone feeling like tearing their hair out (leading to yet another popular question: How do I tame my toddler's tangled tresses)?

Some of the specific questions and some possible solutions follow.

You can't imagine the fuss we go through every time it's cold outside. For some reason, my son just won't wear a jacket. It can be ten degrees out, and he says he's not cold. I just know it can't be good for him to be so exposed—besides which, I don't want him making these kinds of decisions for himself. On the other hand, I hate to keep fighting a major battle each time the temperature dips below fifty. Any recommendations?

I'm going to assume that you've already heard that standard bit of parenting advice, the "blue coat/red coat option offering." You tried it out, and discovered it didn't work for you. (For those of you who haven't, it goes like this: You give your child a choice—not about whether to wear a coat or not, but about *"which* coat to wear, the long, blue one . . . or how about this short, red jacket?" The idea is that if your child gets to pick something to wear by himself—even if it's not exactly the plan he had in mind at first—he will feel he's having his say, and will cooperate by selecting one of your two permitted choices.)

The trouble with this is that any child who can talk and is the least bit stubborn will figure out that there's a third choice—no coat—that he wasn't offered, leading him to feel even more exasperated as he insists: "I don't want to wear *any* coat because I'M NOT COLD!"

So, assuming you're not going to forcibly wrestle him into your chosen garment, you'll need a few other strategies. We don't recommend trying every one but, rather, carefully selecting the best one to start out with, based on your own appreciation of your child's personality and your own priorities for the lessons you'd like him to learn. If the main thing you're out to teach him is that he must live with the consequences of his own decisions, then go with Strategy 2 (page 3), but if you think he's so stubborn he'd never admit that he was cold, even to the point of minor frostbite, then try anything *but* 2.

Strategy 1: Find him a coat that he really *wants* to wear.

Just at the start of the cold weather season, take him shopping and let him choose a warm coat he really loves—on the condition that he *will* wear it whenever you say it's cold enough outside for him to need it. Don't object to color or styling or materials or any factor of practicality or styling. Don't object to price either (just take him to the sort of store that carries merchandise within your budget). Okay, so he'll probably pick out the most ridiculous thing the store has, with fake leather and fringes that remind you of something that would have been too tacky to be seen on the old *Sonny & Cher* show, but whatever it is, it's still better than having him go out in the snow half-naked, isn't it?

Strategy 2: So let him be cold—what's the big deal?

Call his bluff. Let him go out without a coat. Then one of the following three things will happen:

1. He will get cold and say, "Mommy, can I have my coat now?" and you'll say, "You told me you didn't want it, so I left it at home—I guess we'll just have to go home now," and you'll cut his outdoor playtime short, which will teach him the consequences of ignoring your parental wisdom the next time.

2. He will get cold and say, "Mommy, can I have my coat now?" and you'll say, "I *thought* you'd be cold, so I brought it along." You'll pull the coat out of the trunk of the car or out of the stroller bag—and your child won't really have suffered any negative consequences . . . but then, learning to choose the right clothing for the weather isn't all that essential a skill for a toddler anyway. He'll have plenty of time to develop a more weather-sensible attitude when he's older. In the meantime, it's no great burden on you to carry his coat around for him, so that he'll have it when he finally realizes that you were right—it's coat-wearing weather.

3. He really won't feel too cold, and never will ask you for that coat. In that case, he probably was right—he didn't need it after all.

Little kids can usually manage to keep themselves warm enough just by the body heat they generate from running and jumping and playing. However, you do have to exercise some adult control and caution. Playing in subzero weather without sufficient covering can be dangerous. Little fingers and ears and other extremities can get frostbitten, so any time the temperature is hovering near or below the 40°F mark, hold your ground!

Strategy 3: Keep warm with layers.

Maybe the trouble is just with the *idea* of a coat, not with the concept of dressing to stay warm. Your little boy may be perfectly willing to put on a few layers of other, more comfortable, types of clothing: a cotton turtleneck, with a fuzzy sweatshirt over it, and maybe a down vest on top of that. With a polar fleece hat and a good pair of mittens, he can be just as protected from the cold as he would be in the average winter coat. In fact, since the majority of body heat is lost through the head, a warm hat is actually more helpful than a poorly insulated coat, so if you're going to insist upon any one article of clothing for cold weather protection, let it be a hat.

Strategy 4: Be creative!

Take one of your own woolly sweaters and shrink it down to size; most toddlers love the idea of wearing something that belonged to Daddy or Mommy. If it's mittens he disdains, let him wear socks on his hands. Or hand puppets. Think Clint Eastwood in *The Good, The Bad, and the Ugly*—try a serape. Think Phantom of the Opera, or Superman, or Count Dracula—try a cape. What about the gear associated with some admired profession? Firefighters never go out without their protective outerwear. Police officers have their bulletproof vests. If you can find a similar-looking jacket and sell your child on the idea of wearing it to be like one of his heroes, you'll both be happy. (But a few years from now, when he still insists on wearing his fireman coat, even though it's torn and looks ridiculous on a five-year-old instead of a two-year-old, check the questions and answers on page 86 in Chapter Four, "Giving Things Up," for some possible solutions to this dilemma.)

> ## TIP TO MAKE WINTER GEAR WEARABLE
>
> When you buy winter clothes, go for comfort (that is, your child's idea of comfort, not yours) above all. Avoid anything stiff, hard to put on, hard to take off, or confining to move around in. (Whoever designed those bulky, stifling, all-in-one snowsuits anyway? It sure wasn't a kid—or the parent of one!) Watch out for and avoid: scratchy inner linings, tight elastic at the cuffs (adjustable Velcro closings are much better), inside drawstrings (especially if they're knotted at the ends), and metal buckles or fasteners.

My daughter loved her bath when she was an infant. She's turned one, and now, suddenly, right before a bath, she cries and acts like she hates it. What's going on, and more important, how do I get her back to loving the bath?

With a one-year-old who's preverbal, who knows? Maybe the last time you bathed her, the water was a touch too hot, or maybe she got water up her nose and hated the feeling, or maybe it's just that now her imagination is sufficiently developed for her to be afraid of slipping, or drowning, or monsters coming into the water. Maybe she just wants to be in control over something, and has discovered that avoiding a bath is her new arena of independence.

We may not be able to explain the reason for her fear, but we can offer a few pointers for getting her back into the tub.

The old reliable method that's done the trick for years is the bribe (or to use more pedagogically correct jargon, the reward). Get your daughter the most wonderful bath toy you've ever seen. Set it up in the tub. It should be something that needs water to work completely, like a paddlewheel activity board or a rubber elephant with a trunk that acts as a sprinkler. First, let her play with it in the bath while dry. Now tell her you are going to put in an inch or two of warm water, to make the toy work better. (If the noise from the faucet is the problem, then let her leave the room while you fill the tub.)

For many children, that will be all you need to do to get them playing and splashing happily again. Once she enjoys the idea of a bath once more, then over the next several baths, try gradually increasing the water level until you have enough to make the job of getting her clean faster and easier on you, the child scrubber.

Here are some other ideas to try if the toy-in-the-tub trick proves less than effective.

If it's summer, try a wading pool outdoors. Many a toddler who has balked at sitting down in a cold, hard, gleaming white tub has happily jumped into a rainbow-colored plastic pool decorated with pictures of baby whales and starfish. Once you've successfully reintroduced the concept of water fun outdoors, you should be able to make progress toward the parallel concept of water fun indoors— especially if you take some of the best pool toys inside with you.

Offer to take a bath with her. For some toddlers it's the idea of the separation behind a wall of porcelain that's scary, rather than being in water. Caution: Use this technique once, or at most two or three times, to coax a fearful child back into the tub. You don't want to create an expectation on her part that she'll always have parental company in the bath, and end up with a pattern that's hard to break when she's older.

Try sponge baths outside the tub with wet washcloths. This is a good temporary solution to keep her relatively clean while you look for ways to ease her transition back to the tub. Just don't make the washcloth activities too much fun (no washcloth puppet shows, no long, comfy massages) or else you'll find it hard to make a tub bath seem the winner by comparison.

Forget about tub bathing and teach her to enjoy a shower. Standing up under a warm, gentle, rainlike spray may be more appealing, especially if you have a separate shower cubicle rather than a tub with a high shower head. You may find it easier to teach your child to wash herself in a shower and not want to go back to tub bathing.

Bubbles to the rescue. Bubble baths have won back many a child who swore never to enter a tub again. Gentle, hypoallergenic kids' bubble solutions are available in a seemingly endless variety of colors, scents, and types—including bath foams and "silly string"—and they're nontoxic, so you don't have to worry when your child gets the idea to taste the yummy-smelling bathwater.

Try magic sponges. We guarantee your child will want to see more of these intriguing bath items, which you can find in some toy stores or novelty shops. When dry they look like small capsules; they come in plastic packets of three to five for a few dollars per packet. Toss them into the tub as it's filling with warm water, and within a minute or two the hard capsule coating will dissolve and a tiny sponge shape will emerge from each capsule and begin to un-curl itself. Another minute more and you see two- or three-inch sponge versions of animals or circus performers or spaceships. Even adults want to get in and play when they see what pops out from the magic sponge capsules.

Make your tub look and feel more kid-friendly. Take your little bath-hater to the bed-and-bath discount store and let her pick out a fun-looking bath mat, with duckies or fishies on it. Get a *Little Mermaid* shower curtain. Cover the tub spout with a rubber slipover hippo head (you can order this product from the One Step Ahead baby products catalog, or get one in the shape of a dolphin from The Right Start catalog—see the Resource Guide at the back of this book for contact information). You can install a handheld sprayer in the shape of an elephant's trunk. You can decorate your tub tiles with alphabet stick-ons. Or buy a set of bath paints to turn tub time into an art party. Listen to your child's ideas about what *she* thinks would transform the tub into the place she wants it to be.

Equip your toddler for life underwater. Sometimes it's not the tub that needs a little something extra, it's the child. She might take to the bath like a frog to a mud puddle if only she felt properly prepared. Let her wear a set of no-slip aqua shoes in the tub to give her a sense of groundedness. How about a tot-sized scuba mask—that works if she's afraid of getting soap in her eyes. What about a pair of water wings? Or a snorkel? Sometimes all a child really wants is some small token of evidence that her parents understand how scared she feels. Once the child has that sign, then things can go back to the way they were, without further fuss.

Conquer the fear of going down the drain. Here's a good strategy to try if her bath time fear stems from this cause: Invite her to watch you play a bathtub game with a doll. Get a medium-to-small doll—one she'll have no trouble understanding is much, much smaller than she is. Make sure it's solid and heavy enough not to get swept under when the tub starts draining (that would be *very* counterproductive, so be sure to test out your model privately first, if you're not positive of the result). Sit the doll in the tub in water up to its tummy. Give it a few bath toys and then try letting your daughter bubble it up with soap. She can do this without getting in herself, if she likes. Let her play happily for five or ten minutes. Then let the water drain.

"See!" you say. "Dolly has had a bath and now the water is going down the drain—just the water—and Dolly is sitting here in the tub, no problem." If your child still looks dubious about the demonstration, don't urge her to get back in the tub right away, but repeat the scene a few times over the course of the next few weeks. Each time you give the doll a bath, have your daughter participate in more of the activities. Have her help you fill the tub. Have her use a washcloth to help you wash the doll. Have her pull the plug or flip the bath drain lever. Be prepared to repeat the doll-bathing demonstration three or four times before suggesting that your child get into the tub to take a bath with the doll.

What not to do. Do not give up and let your child go more than a half a week without some sort of washing. The longer you delay dealing with the issue, the more firmly cemented in the toddler mind is the message, "Hey, this works! All I have to do is keep up a fuss, and I'll never have to put up with being bathed again!"

Don't worry too much about further traumatizing your child with your efforts. Your persistence proves that you care about her feelings and will go to any *reasonable* lengths to gain her cooperation—but on the question of "Do I have to be cleaned regularly by some method?" you will only take "yes" for an answer.

My son will splash in the bath happily for hours on end—until the instant he sees me go for the shampoo bottle. Then he starts to shriek and tries to jump out of the tub. How can I convince him that shampooing is not some especially diabolical form of toddler torture?

The trouble is, he's already had proof, as far as he's concerned, that it *is* torture. On some previous hairwash, he got shampoo in his eyes and he hated it. Now his fear of shampooing is based on experience, and so is quite a rational thing. He already knows what most parents don't realize: *There ain't no such thing as a tear-free shampoo.*

It's not that the soap bubbles sting, but having water or *anything* dripping into the eyes feels very uncomfortable to a child.

So the parents' job is to do whatever it takes to make sure that the eyes stay dry. Here are some ways to accomplish this:

- Train your child to look up at the ceiling during the hairwash. You can say, "Point your chin up as high as you can" or you can simply pull your child's forehead back parallel with the ceiling before you start to rinse.
- Pour the rinse water from a pitcher or a large measuring cup that has a narrow spout, allowing you to control the flow of the water. If your tub is equipped with a hand-held shower hose, that's even better to get control of the direction of the water and keep it running backward, away from the child's eyes.

- Tell your child to keep his eyes shut, or better still, hand him a washcloth to cover his eyes with during the rinsing.
- For even more protection (or for a child who can't seem to sit with his head tilted in the right position) try a shampoo visor. (The One Step Ahead catalog sells one for $6.95—see the Resource Guide for further information.)

Some homes have a laundry basin that is the right height for use in hair washing. Have your child sit on a chair with the back of his head resting on the front edge of the sink, just as you do in a hair salon. Use the laundry sprayer (if you have one) to wash his hair neatly in the sink. If your basin lacks the sprayer, it's easy to rig one up by buying one of those rubber-hose-ended types that you simply slip over the length of the basin spout.

FREQUENTLY ASKED SHAMPOO QUESTIONS

How often should I wash my child's hair?

Unless your child plays every day in the mud, twice a week is fine.

Should I use a conditioner on my child's hair?

There's really no need to, unless your child's hair is especially fine and dry, or prone to tangles. Also, many popular children's shampoos contain detangling and conditioning ingredients, so that you clean and condition in one step.

Is it safe to use a dandruff shampoo on my two-year-old?

Yes, but you must be sure to keep it out of your child's eyes. Your best bet is to buy a dandruff shampoo specially formulated for children. If the problem persists even after using the shampoo twice a week for more than two weeks, ask your pediatrician to advise you further.

The label on my children's shampoo bottle says "Lather, rinse, repeat." Is this really necessary?

We'll clue you in on a little secret that will save you time and help your budget, too: You can skip that second lather and rinse without qualms. Unless your child's been dipping her hair in glue, or paint, or bubblegum, or something else extraordinarily hard to remove (in which case, you may need a scissors, not a second round of shampoo), a single lathering and rinsing should be perfectly adequate.

Help! I feel like my son's valet. Dan won't even try to learn to dress himself. He's two now and I'm wondering if I'm going to have to dress him until he's twenty-two. How can I get him interested in learning this essential skill?

By being patient, that's how. There aren't many two-year-olds—girls or boys, but our guess is, especially boys—who are interested in handling clothing and putting it on properly. Actually, you should count yourself lucky, when you consider that some kids at this age develop a sudden hostility to the idea of wearing clothes, and want to experiment with being naked all day. Now *that* really is a problem!

Your main task with a two-year-old, and quite possibly with a three-year-old as well, is to stay calm and cheerful while you subtly put across the idea that getting dressed is a normal everyday thing that anyone can learn to do. You can make things easier by buying only the simplest and easiest-to-manipulate style of clothes. Nothing that ties, buckles, or has complicated fastenings. Elastic-waist pants, a bit on the loose side, without elastic cuffs, are what your toddler needs if you want him to be able to pull them up all by himself. Big T-shirts with large neck openings are the top covering of choice.

For his feet, choose socks with no-slip treads on the bottom and different colored heels and toes to help him keep an eye on what part of the foot goes where. Velcro shoes, in our opinion, are the greatest invention since sliced bread. Skills involved in shoe tying remain out of reach of most children until about midway through the kindergarten year (and if your child is in a school with a well-designed curriculum, you can let the professional teachers teach this skill; they're good at it and can probably do it with far less struggle than you'll need to get the concept across). Velcroing is about right for a two-year-old, who will still need an adult's help holding the shoe's tongue up straight and pulling the strap to the right level of tightness.

Each time you help your child put on clothes, show and explain what you are doing. For two-year-olds, repetition is the key to almost everything they can hope to master.

One thing to watch out for when it comes to T-shirts: Toddlers naturally try to stick their face (as opposed to the top of the head) through the head opening—which doesn't work. They're naturally afraid of having their eyes covered during the brief moment of pulling the shirt over. Then they get their chin stuck and yell for help. The parent rushes into the room to see this scene, only to complain that the child isn't even trying. After having an irritable parent pull the shirt down for him, the child gets the message, "This is too hard and it just gets my parents mad when I try"—so next time he won't even try to put on his shirt at all.

To avoid this syndrome, try stretching the shirt's head opening for your child before you let him try. Show him that it's large enough for him to look through to the ceiling—that should help to convince him that there's room enough for his head to fit through. Guide him the first few times so that he doesn't stick his chin in first but lets the opening fall to the top of his head, and then show him how to place his hands at the bottom of the shirt in order to jerk the shirt down and let his head pop through in one efficient motion. He shouldn't try to put his arms through the sleeves until he's got his head through successfully.

You mustn't expect him to master all these movements in his first couple of tries . . . or even his first dozen tries. It really is a lot more complicated (to him) than it looks to you.

To teach putting pants on: Have him start in a sitting position. The edge of the bed is good because his legs will naturally be dangling down. Sitting on the floor also works as a starting position, if the child is instructed to keep his legs out straight and his toes pointed. (If it's a girl, you may want to say, "Point your toes like a ballerina." For a boy, try this: "Point your toes so they look like arrows," and show what you mean by pointing your own toes.)

The first time he tries to pull the pants up, he may find his feet get stuck in the same place in the pant legs or he may hit a fold partway down. You say, "No problem," and you pull the pants back off and set him up to start over, with a bit more parental help to guide the pants on this time.

Once each leg is mostly inside the correct section of the pants, the child stands up and into the pants, and he's done it!

After your child has mastered the basics of putting on clothes by himself, there are a couple of tips that might help make the process easier and more fun:

Let him listen to a weather forecast for the coming day. Dial your local weather service on the telephone or get a forecast over your computer and let him hear it, adding whatever simple explanations he may need. ("Precipitation" is a long, fancy word for "rain.")

Then have him help you pick out a weather-appropriate outfit to wear the next morning. Lay all the pieces out on the floor in the outline of a boy lying faceup. That way, he won't have any difficulty figuring out what goes where, and what needs to be put on first, second, and third.

Here's a product that might help: a kid's clothing organizer. One Step Ahead sells a set of canvas shelves that hangs from a closet rod. There is one shelf for each day of the week, plus a couple of bins for shoes. At the beginning of the week, the adult lays out each day's clothing on the correct shelf—ending all whining and arguing over what the child will put on each morning. Getting ready for preschool goes so much faster when the child finds everything together: socks, underwear, shirt, pants, any other pieces of clothing needed to complete the look for that day.

Other items that could speed up the dressing process include:

- Clothing hooks installed along the wall within a child's reach.
- A child-size coat tree in the front hall.
- A shoe organizer downstairs to keep toddler shoes together and near the front door.
- Keeping like pieces of clothing together. Use mitten clips to keep mittens attached to jackets. Buy jackets with hoods instead of trying to keep hats and jackets together. Use combined skirt-and-blouse hangers to keep matching parts of an outfit together in the closet.
- Organizing all hairstyling accessories in one drawer (see the box following).

FORWARD OR BACKWARD?

Here's an easy way to help any toddler answer this tricky question. Take a laundry marker and draw a big red dot on the inside waistband of the back of all the pants and underwear your toddler possesses. Draw a green dot on the inside of the waistband in the front. Always keep the color coding the same: Green means front, red means back. With T-shirts the rule is that the design goes in front and the back side is blank (but it's up to you, the parent, to remember this rule and only buy those T-shirts that conform!).

THE HAIR DRAWER

So much to do, so little time to do it all! Having a toddler with long hair can make you feel that way every single morning. You've got to brush it, then braid it, or put it into twin buns, or try to copy whatever new hairstyle your little fashion plate has suddenly decided she absolutely must have. And then there's all that paraphernalia! The hairbands, the bobby pins, the hair clips, the scrunchies, the bows, and those elastic-band-thingies with little plastic balls at the ends (we call them hair "bobblies" but we've heard lots of other names for them). How do you find them when you need them?

Bill came up with a brilliant solution. He calls it "The Hair Drawer." He emptied a kitchen drawer of corkscrews and fondue forks and other adult utensils that we never seem to use much anymore, and turned it into the one place to find children's hair accessories. After our daughters are done with their milk and cereal, but are still seated at the breakfast table, it's the perfect time to do their hair. No more wondering, "Where's my purple lace bow with Esmeralda on it?"

Also, it makes straightening up simpler, because we no longer have to bother about sorting out which hair supplies go on which girl's dresser. Now everything is communal, mingling together happily in a single, easily accessible drawer in the kitchen, where both girls know their hair will be brushed and styled each morning before they go out the kitchen door to the car.

Toddler Appearance: What not *to worry about*

• *Tucking shirts in.* Attempting to get them to keep their shirt-tails inside their pants is a waste of time. Within ten minutes the shirt-tail will be out again.

• *Oddly matched tops and bottoms.* Any successful self-dressing should earn praise, and a little detail like mismatched colors or styles should pass without comment. (Exception to this rule: For a special occasion when you really need your toddler to look tidy, lay out the outfit you have in mind ahead of time and provide full assistance in putting it on.)

• *Misaligned buttons on sweaters or shirts.* The very fact that a small child can button a button at all is remarkable. If he's only missed one, the sweater is still very wearable; he won't be bothered by the mistake. If the alignment is off by two, three, or more buttons and you want to redo it, then say, "That's very good, but let me just straighten it out a little bit for you," and, as quickly as possible, rebutton the ones necessary.

What doesn't *work as a teaching tool:* Those soft cloth books that have pages with shoelaces to learn to tie, zippers to learn to pull, snaps to snap, and buttons to button. Why don't they work? Because the experience of pushing a button through a buttonhole is completely different when it's on a flat page in front of you, rather than on something that runs in a line down your wiggly little belly. Your child may enjoy playing with the buttons and snaps in those cloth books, and may even get good at them, without being any further along when it comes to dealing with real clothing—leading parents to feel that their kids aren't trying very hard. We recommend starting with, and staying with, the real thing, on real children.

Tip to help you keep your sanity in the interim: If getting dressed takes a good, long while for your child to learn, then accept the fact, and plan for it in the months to come. The main reason clothing battles are so often worse than they need to be is that the parent has an adult view of the time it *should* take to get ready to go somewhere. He (okay, we're stereotyping some dads unfairly here) thinks to himself, "It doesn't take forty-five minutes to put on a T-shirt and a pair of pants," and so he figures the kid ought to be ready to go out the door by a certain time . . . and then when that time comes around and the kid is still sitting on the floor with one sock half on and a half-dozen other pieces of clothing littered all over the floor, he starts to yell. The key to avoiding this scene is not to keep trying to teach the kid to get dressed faster, but simply to allot a full forty-five minutes for the dressing and getting ready process—no matter how simple the clothing. Give it a full hour if brushing and braiding of long hair are involved.

Do "The Flip"

Here's the quickest, surest way to teach your toddler to put on her own coat or jacket. It's called "The Flip" and most preschools teach it, but it's just as easy to learn at home.

First, lay your child's jacket or coat down on the floor, arms spread out, with the open front facing up. Have your child stand with her feet pointed at the collar or the hood of the garment. The coat will appear upside-down to the child.

Now tell the child to bend down so that she can stick her arms into the sleeves (which are still upside-down to her).

While your child is in this position, pick up the coat by the bottom hem and flip it over her head. It will now be on her right-side-up and ready to be zipped or buttoned.

With one or two more practices, you won't have to help her anymore; she'll flip the coat over her head all by herself.

Every morning I try to brush my three-year-old daughter's long, thick hair, and every morning she runs screaming from the room the instant she sees the hairbrush. How can I get her to sit still long enough for me to make her look presentable—or at least not look like a character from The Bride of Frankenstein?

The simplest approach is the pixie haircut. This one works best if your child knows and loves the play *Peter Pan*. Wanting to look like Cathy Rigby or Mary Martin in the title role (depending on which version of the play/video your child may have seen) could be the incentive she needs to shed those long, tangle-prone locks. Tell her that once she's shorn, hair dressing will be a breeze, and your problems may be over in a snip-snip-snap.

But what if your little girl's favorite character is Rapunzel? Learn to brush in a kinder, gentler way, following this multistep process:

• First, you need to wash your little girl's hair fairly frequently—every other day is best, but at a minimum twice a week, using a detangling conditioner as soon as the shampoo has been rinsed out. Rinse again after the time indicated on the conditioner label, and then, *even before you get your child out of the tub*, comb through her hair with a wide-toothed comb or a slightly rounded brush with widely spaced bristles. This should be very easy to do, requiring no tugging at all.

• The best time for the hair wash is just before bedtime. Tuck a towel around your child's pillow if she doesn't like sleeping on a damp pillow. The next morning your child's hair should still be fairly smooth and easy to brush through.

What about those days when everything your child did on the playground has left her hair in an impenetrable snarl? The thing you need is a little help in a bottle—in the form of a detangling spray such as Johnson & Johnson's "No More Tears" or some other brand of comb-through conditioning spray. They really do help.

Still, they won't just make the tangles melt away on their own. All parents of long-haired girls should learn the right brushing technique. You can't just brush as you did before (pull-pull-ow!). And you do need to have the right equipment: not one brush, but two. First, you need to use a very soft, natural boar-bristle brush on the hair; later in the process you'll use a hard, plastic styling brush with nylon-tipped bristles.

Start by separating a small section of hair from the front and hold it out so that you can brush just the ends of that section. Do the underside of that section, too. Now, on the same section, start again, but this time from a little higher up, brushing gently downward to the ends, but stopping and restarting if your brush gets caught, so that you're never pulling too hard. Repeat the procedure for the underside of the hair you've just brushed. Only after you've brushed through all the lower parts of that section should you do any brushing from the top.

When you've finished your first section, select another section and repeat all these steps.

If you encounter any tangles that won't yield painlessly to the soft-bristled brush, don't try to work on them. Leave them alone for now. Wait until you've soft-bristle-brushed all the hair and *loosened* the major tangles before you switch to your second, hard styling brush. The kind that works best is one with widely spaced bristles, each with rounded-nylon tips, set in uneven rows on a curved (but not round) surface. Start as you did with the soft brush, with one section of hair, just a few inches from the bottom. Brush the hair through to the ends, remembering to get to the underside too, and then start over from higher up on that same section, till you can easily brush that whole section smoothly from top to bottom. Then move on to the next section. When you've done all the sections, you're finished.

During this second brush-through, you may still encounter some tangles. Using your fingers, not the styling brush, separate the tangled hair from the rest of the section. Give it an extra spritz of the detangling spray. Now make sure you're holding the tangled piece of hair from a point *above* the knotty part. That way, when you apply pressure with the brush, you won't be yanking the hair from its roots. It's still best not to jerk the brush through the knot. Better to go at it slowly and patiently, till the knot finally yields to the even pressure of the brush.

This soft-brush/hard-brush method is, admittedly, twice as time-consuming as the way you've been brushing before, but once you've mastered it, you and your child should find the morning hair brushing stress-free, even relaxing. Just remember to add another ten minutes to your getting-dressed time in the morning.

For those children who want long hair but can't manage to sit still for ten minutes each morning (even if it means pain-free brushing), we have a solution: braids! Detangle your child's hair with a silkening conditioner after a hair wash, comb it through (which should be easy now that it's been rinsed), and then immediately put it into neat, tight braids, securing the ends tightly with coated elastic bands.

You can leave the braids in several days running, until the next hair wash, in most cases. Unless your child gets paint or glue in her braids while doing an art project at preschool, you may not have to brush her hair at all, except for twice a week, right after her hair is washed.

Okay, but what about the child who hates having her hair in braids, but also hates having to sit still for a long but gentle hair brushing? We say: For you there's no choice but to get out those Cathy Rigby pictures, and sell the kid on that pixie haircut!

THE TANGLE FAIRIES

My two-and-a-half-year-old daughter used to cry and yell that she didn't want her hair brushed, even after I bought a soft brush and did my best to detangle with gentle strokes. She was still afraid that it *might* hurt. Then I had an idea to make the whole ritual more fun. I told her a story about the Tangle Fairies. These are tiny, invisible mischief-makers who fly into the rooms of sleeping girls at night and love to play in long hair. They dance around, holding the strands of hair like Maypole strings, and have their fun until morning when, just before the child awakens, they fly away. If a child doesn't brush her hair smooth, but leaves it tangled all day, the Tangle Fairies won't visit her, because they'll have nothing to do with hair that's already a mess. They're friendly fairies, and they really do like the little girls whose hair they've chosen as their playground, even if their visit means more hair brushing work the next morning. My little girl loved this story, and it made her more patient and more willing to have her hair brushed and styled, if only to see if she could get a glimpse of the fairies who would be sure to return that night to make more tangles.

—Billie J.
Bethesda, MD

Help! My child was sent home from preschool today with a case of head lice! Yuuuuchh! I feel like burning everything in the house!

Don't reach for the blowtorch yet! First double-check your child to make sure the problem hasn't been misdiagnosed. Given the fact that head lice spreads easily and can be hard to eradicate once it takes hold, many school and daycare centers have become hyper-vigilant, and are sending children home on the mere suspicion of nits in their hair.

We know of at least three cases in which a child was sent home when dandruff was mistaken for nits (louse eggs). School nurses say this mistake rarely happens, because the oval-shaped, sticky nits are easily distinguishable from irregular dandruff flakes, which can be flicked away by a fingernail. However, when one school nurse is responsible for checking the heads of two hundred children in the course of a morning, or when untrained teachers' aides and parent volunteers are asked to screen heads, mistakes can and do happen. In one case we know about, the mother had to take her child to the pediatrician to have him certify in writing that the child was lice-free before the school would let the child return.

In another case, a parent was summoned to pick up her supposedly lice-infested three-year-old. She brought along her old high school microscope and asked the daycare center director to show her the evidence under the lens. The director plucked what she said was a nit out from the child's head . . . but upon 60-power magnification, had to admit it was just a rounded flaked-off bit of scalp tissue. And so it went with the other "nits" that were discovered.

So don't just take the school's word for it: Be sure you have seen the proof.

Here's a good way for untrained eyes to learn to tell the difference between nits and dandruff. Call the National Pediculosis Association at 617-449-NITS, or visit the organization's web site at www.headlice.org to order the "critter card," a laminated card showing an actual preserved nit and an actual preserved louse.

Once you've confirmed that lice are actually present, you do need to take immediate action. You need one method to eliminate all visible lice right away and another method to deal with any eggs that may hatch during the next two weeks. As soon as you begin to do any research into this topic, you will discover that you've stepped into a hotbed of controversy.

There are two diametrically opposed schools of thought. The mainstream approach is to use a pesticidal shampoo, such as Rid or Nix, to name two of the more popular brands. If that doesn't do the trick, then try again with an even stronger prescription-only pesticide called lindane.

The opposing view is that pesticidal products are harmful to children and should be banned. Advocates for this position say that there are other, nontoxic ways to eliminate the nasty critters. For example, you can suffocate them by coating the child's head with petroleum jelly and then covering with a shower cap overnight. (But be warned that it may take four or five shampoos to completely wash the petroleum jelly out of the hair!) Or you can go after them one by one, combing through every strand of hair with a fine-toothed metal comb, picking out each nit as you find it, and squashing it between your fingernails.

We urge you to read as much as you can about the pros and cons of both approaches before proceeding. The World Wide Web is a great resource in this regard. Almost any search engine will pull up dozens of web sites with articles, research papers, and links to parent discussion groups, in response to the keyword "lice." Tips, strategies, and lice-combating techniques abound, and new ones are coming out every day.

We were especially encouraged to hear about a patent recently granted to an invention that makes it possible for the parent to find nits easily. It's a fluorescent dye that you put on your child's hair, which binds to *chitin*, the organic material that forms the outer coating of lice eggs (nits). You shine a black light on your child in the dark, and you instantly see all the nits lit up, enabling you to pick them out without missing a single one.

After you've treated your child's head by whatever method you've chosen for safety and effectiveness, you must also treat anything that may have come in contact with your child's head. That means tons and tons of washing, drying, vacuuming, and bagging. First of all, wash all hats, scarves, and coats in hot water in the washing machine. Then use your dryer's hottest cycle to dry them. For wool or other non-machine-washable fabrics, send out for chemical dry-cleaning.

Wash all sheets, blankets, and pillowcases.

Vacuum everything else you can think of that your child's head may have touched: the car seat, car seat cover, and all carpeting in your house and in your car.

About bagging: You may have heard that it's necessary to seal all stuffed animals inside a plastic trash bag for two full weeks. This may be more trouble than you need to go through—and more than your child can stand if the thought of sleeping just one night without her special Pooh bear has her in tears. In that case, just put the crevice-tool on the end of your vacuum cleaner hose and go over each special furry toy thoroughly, until you're sure you've covered all the surfaces. Repeat a few days later, and again a week later, and do a final vacuuming at the end of the two-week period and you should feel confident that nothing's coming back.

Our final thoughts on this unpleasant subject: When it comes to lice, prevention is always better than any of the cures.

- Never let children share or trade combs, brushes, pony tail holders, or other hair accessories.
- During lice outbreaks, keep your child's long hair neatly braided or keep short hair trimmed very close, to reduce the chance that your child's hair will brush up against any other child's hair.
- Ask your preschool or daycare center to install separate cubbies, so that the children's jackets and hats aren't kept together on a coatrack.
- Children's nap mats or cots should be made of an impervious material and cleaned after each use, or else assigned and used by only one child during the school year.

IF YOU *Must* THINK ABOUT LICE (UGH!), THEN KEEP THESE FACTS IN MIND

- Short hair will not be any less inviting to lice, but there will be far less hair to pick through. Finding and eliminating the lice by the hand-picking method will be far easier than with long hair.
- Lice don't jump from one surface to another. They can only crawl, so if there's no physical contact between a lice-infested object and a lice-free one, you don't need to treat the lice-free one.
- Lice are found just as often in children from clean, well-kept homes as from sloppy homes—so there's no need to feel ashamed if you're told your child has lice.

My son needs a haircut, but I have an easier time taking my poodle to the dog groomer's than getting my son to sit still at the barber's. Do you have any good ideas?

How about letting the dog groomer do the cutting? Except your kid would probably end up with one of those funny little top-knot styles with a red bow—so scratch that idea.

Okay, how about yourself as the stylist? He trusts you, doesn't he? And you can bet it's easier for him to sit still at home in a comfortable, familiar chair than in that huge, black barber's chair, surrounded by strangers. Once he gets used to the idea of letting someone accomplish this quick and painless procedure, and once he's got a few months or years of experience behind him to help him understand how simple and ordinary the act of haircutting is, he should do much better when he's taken out to have the job done.

Use the proverbial bowl, if that helps you to cut an even line. Until he's at least twelve, he won't care and probably won't even notice that he looks like Davy Jones of the Monkees.

If you're unsure about undertaking this responsibility, avail yourself of any of several handbooks or videos available through the Internet. Amazon.com carries a book called *How to Cut Your Child's Hair at Home* by Laura Derosa, or you can order an entire home haircutting set (booklet and barber supplies) from www. cuttinghair.com. If you're not online, then call 800-671-HAIR to order the video *6 Simple Cuts for Kids* from HairOutlet.com.

When you feel he's finally ready to try to sit in the elevator chair, here are some tips to help things along:

Take him with a friend who doesn't cry at the barber shop. Ask the parent of that friend to go with you and let her son go first. Your son will doubtless be reassured by seeing his friend smiling as his hair is trimmed.

Find out whether it's something specific about the haircutting process that he dislikes. It could be he doesn't like the feeling of the nylon smock that keeps the hair off his clothing. In that case, all you need to do is *bring along your own big, soft, familiar towel* and pin it around him.

Use a haircutter who comes recommended as being wonderful with kids. The barber you've chosen may strike *you* as the sweetest guy, but your child is less than wowed by him. You might do better at one of those shops that does nothing but kids' hair all day long. They show videos like *Blue's Clues* while your child is undergoing the procedure, and they have a hair shampooing station that looks like Noah's Ark, with friendly animals grinning down as the "rain" falls from the shower head. The waiting area is stocked with toys, and best of all (from the child's point of view), when he's all done, he gets to pick a little reward (like a lollipop or a sticker) from a prize box on his way out the door.

Sometimes what scares children the most is the idea of some part of them being lost forever. One way to deal with this fear is by letting him keep the cuttings in a plastic baggie. (But talk to the barber about this possibility in advance: You don't want to promise him something that turns out to be forbidden by the public health rules in your area.) If you don't like the idea of taking home a baggie full up swept-up hair clippings, *try asking for one snippet of hair,* which your child will get to place in a special keepsake box in his room. Maybe if he places the bagged bit of hair under his pillow, the Hair Fairy will come and take it away, leaving him with a shiny coin in its place.

Now that my twins can dress themselves, we seem to spend a half hour or more each morning arguing over what they can go out in. They invariably choose something which, to my way of thinking, is totally inappropriate. One day one twin is insisting on wearing a pair of old, patched jeans to the Easter church service; the next day we're off to the playground but the other one has put on her Halloween kitty costume with a long dangling tail that I worry will get tangled up in the monkey bars. The worst fight came when they thought they could wear their bathing suits to Sunday dinner at Grandma's house. My husband doesn't back me up in these arguments either. He says there's no harm in letting them have their way when they're so young, and that there's plenty of time for them to learn to conform to society's dress code.

Well, that's *not* what your twins are learning, actually. The chief lesson they're absorbing is that they don't have to care about what Grandma thinks, and that Mommy's fuss about playground safety is less important than her toddler's sense of style.

Clothing *does* matter—especially when poorly chosen clothing presents a risk of injury or will be taken as a mark of disrespect.

That doesn't mean you need to engage in a shouting match every time you and your girls have a difference of opinion. Outwitting your girls is definitely what's called for here (and that will help ease the tension with your spouse as well). We have some strategies we think will work for you.

- First, try a delaying tactic. Say, "Yes, of *course* you can wear your favorite old blue jeans—right after we get home from church."
- Second, try sweet reason: "No, the kitty suit isn't good at the playground. Think what might happen if the tail got caught in the see-saw or got wrapped around the monkey bars. It would probably get ripped and ruined, and then you could never wear it again." (Note: Your most effective appeal is not to the child's fear of getting hurt, but to her love of the costume and her desire to protect *it* from damage.)
- Third, use the opportunity to teach a lesson about respect: Say, "Well, you *could* wear your bathing suit to Grandma's house for dinner, but I'm worried how that would make Grandma feel. She was brought up to think that when you go someplace very nice, you always put on your nicest clothes to show how special you think it is to go there. I'm sure she would never understand why you would come to her house if you're dressed for the pool."

Having thwarted their choice of dress—even with a good rationale for doing so—you want to do what you can to reassure your children that you don't find all of their sartorial ideas worthless. Offer a compromise whenever you can. If your kids can wear the bathing suit under the fancy dress without anyone being the wiser, that's fine. As for the kitty costume at the playground, maybe a part will suffice for the whole.

Use your imagination to craft a compromise; the effort you put in will certainly be worth it if the result is averting a lengthy duel.

For example, let's suppose your child insists on wearing a favorite superhero's cape to preschool: Try to work with the school to set parameters of when and where the cape may be worn. Perhaps as a mat cover during nap time. Perhaps your child can wear it to and from preschool but leave it hanging in his cubby the rest of the day. The class may have a dress-up corner or regular time set aside when children are permitted to become different figures in their imaginations. Unless the school administration is utterly inflexible, a solution that leaves all satisfied should soon be forthcoming. (And if it isn't, that tells you something disturbing about the nature of the school where your child spends much of his day).

Some Guidelines for the Clothing Wars

- Don't give in when there's a safety issue involved. (Never allow children to play in anything with dangling strings that could end up around their necks.)
- Give due consideration to how your child's style of dress will be interpreted by others. (Grandma's standards may seem old-fashioned, but they're important to her. Make clear to your toddler that because you care about the way she feels, you will dress to please her whenever you visit her house.)
- In most instances it's okay for toddlers to look silly or funny. They don't need to feel dignified by their clothing, and you shouldn't try to feel dignified for them by proxy.
- At those times and places where dignified dress is expected, toddlers usually aren't welcome. Toddlers don't belong at a formal concert, at the funeral of a distant relative, or any other solemn religious service. What you need for those occasions is a babysitter, not a clothing battle.

CHAPTER

2

The Nightmare of the New Situation

Toddlers are natural conservatives. They always want to keep the status quo. It's cute when they look up at you adoringly and say, "Mommy, I want you to live with me forever," and "Daddy, promise me you'll always be here to tuck me in at night," but it's maddening when they cling to you, screaming, as you try to go off to your new job, or refuse to be tucked into the new, full-sized (and expensive!) bed you've bought for them. Yet both the cuteness and the terror result from the same longing for an assurance of sameness, of predictability, and with it, some hope of control.

You'd think that we adults could sympathize, but what often throws us about the way our toddlers resist change is the seemingly benign nature (to us) of the things they so desperately fear. Perhaps an analogy will help you see things through your child's eyes. Imagine yourself in a foreign country. You're just beginning to learn a few things about the customs of the people there—maybe you've learned a little bit of the language—but you still find yourself confused and overwhelmed. Then, all of a sudden, you're plunked down in the middle of a formal dinner reception. You don't know a thing about the type of food being served, you don't know the rules for the proper handling of the strange new utensils the other guests are using with ease; you don't even know which of the things on the dinner table are food and which are decorations. All the others around you, including your boss, your friends, your family seem to know just what to do.

You try to communicate your distress to them, but the more you try to get across what's bothering you, the more they all seem out of patience with you. They act as if you should already know your as-signed role. The more you try to copy their behavior, the more you're aware of being hopelessly out of your depth. You'd like to leave, but for some reason (you don't quite understand why) you *cannot* get out of there. You start feeling trapped, panicky. Maybe if you were sick (you think desperately), or if you were to have a seizure, then someone would take you away from this nightmarish place. So you fall to the floor, clutching your heart, or you start flailing about, unable to stop yourself.

Now, of course, *everyone* is noticing you. Then someone acts at last . . . and you are carried out, safe, in that helpful person's arms. It hardly matters to you now, in your feeling of relief, that the per-son who is taking you away is angry at you for causing such a scene.

This is what it's like, in your toddler's mind, to be left for the first time at a daycare center, or with a strange, new sitter, or even to be left to spend the day at the home of grandparents who are not regular visitors.

Of course, not all children find new situations so difficult. Many of us are born with a sense of adventure, a joy in exploring new places, and we will even seek out new people to meet, new places to go. Psychologists who have studied personality tell us such an out-going nature is most likely an intrinsic part of the personality, as is the opposite condition, shyness.

These two different traits can appear in siblings born to the same parents, just as two outgoing, adventurous parents may find that they have a child who is timid and slow to adjust.

A child's nature may be inborn, but coping skills are learned. Once you know you have a child who doesn't take quickly and eas-ily to new places and people, you must be extrasensitive to your child's feelings and take things slowly. You ease transitions by

preparation; you introduce all changes in the tiniest possible increments. You do lots of talking, giving constant reassurance at every
step of the way. And you still expect lots of crying, and you never
snap, "Stop that noise!" (Well, that's your goal, at least.)

But no matter how cautiously you move things along, it seems
that nothing you do is working, and that your child will never adjust . . . until one day the sun comes out and your child is smiling
again. You've done it, you've guided your child out of yet another
scary situation, and from now on, everything will be easier.

How do we know this? We're parents of two of the greatest little
champions of sameness the world has ever seen. They're up in arms
right now at the very idea that we might change the paint colors of
our house. And yet, these same two children, during their toddler
years, successfully got through room changes, nanny changes, the
arrival of visiting hordes of relatives, not to mention that ultimate
challenge to the timid: the first day of preschool (though not without one hell of a fight—see the boxed story on page 39). If our two
survived all this, we promise you that yours will too, no matter how
dismal the prospect seems right now.

Some years ago when our daughter Kayley was about three,
I was driving her to the daycare center when I noticed that
she was in a quiet, pensive mood. There had been a great
many changes in her life, and I was aware that she had been
feeling harried and pressured lately. She'd just learned to
use the big toilet, and we'd changed childcare situations recently, and she'd just started a new gymnastics class. But I
had no idea what she was worrying about as I maneuvered
the car around the tight parking lot underneath the daycare
center building.

But then she blurted it out: "You're not going to make
me learn to drive, are you? It looks *hard!*" At that moment
I suddenly saw how things had been going from her point of
view: new this, new that, dress yourself, use a fork and
knife, learn this or that skill and learn it fast. What would
we ask of her next, she'd been worrying, to learn to drive a
car and go to work and pay taxes?

"No," I replied, "that's one thing I'm not about to make you do anytime soon!"

"Promise?" she asked, and brightened instantly to hear me unhesitatingly give my word.

—Bonnie D.
Woodstock, NY

*D*oria *used to be such a happy, carefree thing, that is, before I went back to work. Now, every morning she clings to my leg and screams, "Don't go! Mommy, don't go!" as I struggle to get out the door. I'm in tears myself by the time I reach the end of the driveway. How long can I expect this to go on?*

She can probably dish this treatment out longer than you can take it, unless you do something soon to keep her from turning this obstructionist act into a permanent morning ritual. Here's what we suggest:

Get dressed for work as usual. Get her dressed to go out, too. Say, "Today, you're going to get a special treat. You get to visit Mommy's office and see the place where I work all day."

Very important: Do not phrase this in the form of a question. Never ask, "Do you want to visit Mommy's office today?" because that gives her the opportunity to say no, which she certainly will choose (or to put it more accurately, "NOOOOO! I don't wanna goooooo!").

In fact, let us pause at this point to go over a general principle of human relations that comes up in a great many walks of life, which goes as follows: "Never ask a question to which you don't already know the answer." Lawyers learn this dictum in their first year of law school. You don't want to give the witness the opportunity to introduce new facts or alternative theories into evidence. Translated into parent-ese, this means if you want to be the one to say what you do and when you do it, you don't give the other party (that is, your child) the chance to bring up other choices. Encourage independent thinking, but only when you're confident that the product of that independent thinking will likely meet your approval.

The worst possible course is to encourage a young child to express an opinion that you then have absolutely no interest in carrying out. That's confusing to a toddler, who won't be able to determine those times when it's reasonable and worthwhile to express a preference, and those times when only the grown-up gets to say what's going to happen next.

Now, back to the take-the-child-to-work scenario. Rather than disappearing at 8 A.M., make clear that today, things will be different, and that your child will be going to work with you. Arrange ahead of a time for your babysitter to meet you later on at your office. Give yourself and your child a good half hour to an hour there, just the two of you, to show the child around the place where you spend your working day.

If your boss and your coworkers don't object, take your child around to see the rest of your workplace. Let her run a drawing through the copying machine. Let her sit in your swivel chair and spin around a few times, and then go to get a cup of water in one of those funny triangular paper cups at the water cooler. Show her the picture of her on your desk and the telephone you use to call and talk to her from work. Let her ask questions about the work you do and how and where you do it, and give simple answers.

If you think your job is too complicated for a toddler to understand, take some time to work on how to make the essence of your occupation clear. Explaining what you do can actually help you to realize what's good about your job and what's not so good—and maybe get you thinking about ways to improve your life at work.

Now ask your child to leave you a drawing or a handprint. Make sure she knows that you think of her often while you're at work, that she's always in your heart, in your thoughts. That's the easy part.

Here comes the hard part. At the conclusion of this tour, the babysitter will take your child home. That separation will probably prompt a new, office-based version of the clinging and crying that you usually experience at home. To avoid such a scene in your workplace, walk them down to the bus stop or to the car.

The next morning, as you get your child ready for your departure, remind her of everything you did together at the office and everything you'll be doing again at work today. Promise to call—and be sure to remember to follow through—if you're sure that your child would get real comfort from a phone call. As with most *Outwitting Toddler* techniques, give a thought to your child's personality and temperament before deciding which suggestions to try out.

Don't expect the clinginess to evaporate just because your child now has some connection to your workplace. You may need to keep repeating the same facts about what you will be doing at work, day after day, until your child memorizes your lines like a poem or a catechism. Then you say bye-bye and go out the door, closing it quickly behind you. (You might ask your spouse to hold your child while you say good-bye, so she can't run after you.)

If you're going back to work after a period of staying home, it's essential for your child to bond well with the babysitter in the days or even weeks before your first day of work. Hiring of the sitter ideally should take place about a month in advance, not only to give your child time to get used to this new person but also to give you time to find out just how good a sitter you've hired, and make a change if necessary.

The absolute biggest "Don't" in our minds is to allow the sitter's first day of work to coincide with your own first day away from home. You never want your child to face two separate adjustments at the same time; that's beyond the capacity of all but the most extroverted, independent-spirited toddler.

For the first few days, maybe even the first few weeks that you're at your new job, it's a good idea to have the sitter really work hard to make your child's time without you as pleasant as she can. Arrange in advance for the babysitter to do special things with your child, such as a visit to a new playground. These outings should begin as soon after the sitter's morning arrival as possible, to get your child engaged in pleasant diversion and quickly take her mind off the fact that you're not there.

Cautionary note for the parents of extremely introverted kids: You are probably best advised to instruct the sitter to preserve and maintain the child's normal schedule to the greatest extent possible. You need to consider your own child's personality and reaction to your absence when deciding whether interesting excursions with the sitter would help more than they would hurt.

One thing that is almost always helpful is the "transitional" object—a blanket, teddy bear, or other toy that your child finds especially comforting in a time of stress. Encourage your child to hold on to this object during your daily leave-taking. Talk to it yourself, and treat it with respect. Tell it, "You have a good time with Doria today, and be waiting for me when I get back!" Give it a good-bye kiss, to show your child you value whatever she loves, just as you value all her feelings.

Now is definitely not the time to start weaning your child away from any habit or activity she finds comforting. That means no potty training during your first weeks at work, no push to get rid of a pacifier, no discouragement of thumb sucking, and if she wants to wear the same ratty knit cap every day—even if it's the hottest part of July—let her.

Even though you might want to schedule some varied morning activities, the rest of the day should follow the child's normal schedule. The sitter should make sure your child naps at the same time as usual. She should also prepare the same sort of lunches your child is used to having, with her favorite foods on the menu the first few days. Don't let the sitter introduce any new rules or restrictions. It's so much harder to get used to Mommy being at work if the substitute Mommy scolds the sort of behavior that Mommy didn't mind. Tell the sitter what's allowed and what isn't, to make sure there's no misunderstanding in this area.

For nervous parents who worry that their child will not easily settle down after a hard morning's separation, it's fine to call home for a quick check-in the moment you arrive at work.

Assuming your sitter is doing a reasonably good job of helping your child accept the transition, you just need to be patient. Things *will* get better. You should probably figure on about two weeks before you'll be able to get out the door without tears, but the crying should start to decrease soon. If nearly a month goes by and you haven't seen much improvement, then you know it's time to change your tactics.

Try this for a radically different approach: Get up in the morning about an hour earlier than usual, get dressed, and leave for work before your child is awake. That way your child has no opportunity to force you to view a heartrending, guilt-tripping scene, but instead awakes to a changed reality, which she must accept.

Perhaps you will conclude that your sitter lacks the creativity and experience to help your child make the transition. If there is a good childcare center near your workplace, you might be better off taking the child with you to delay the separation until she's at a place where other parents are dropping off their children, too, and the setting is designed for transitions. You may also be able to find a childcare center that will permit you to visit at lunchtime or other times during the day, which may be of particular importance to those moms who are breastfeeding toddlers, and for whom going back to work would otherwise mean abrupt weaning.

Another advantage to the daycare center approach is that the child's day will be structured, with trained childcare professionals and an emphasis on learning and developmentally appropriate activities. Joining a daycare group can be presented to the child as a step up, out of the house, out of babyhood. If you think your child would take to the notion of becoming a big girl who goes out for the day, just like Mommy and Daddy go to work, then hunt carefully for the daycare center you think will provide the most nurturing and beneficial environment.

If your child still experiences separation anxiety, read on.

Christopher had no trouble adjusting to the fact that I'm not at home during the workday anymore. He was fine when I left him at home with the nanny. What's not going well is the start of nursery school. Each time I drop him off, it's like the very first time. I'm considering pulling him out, and waiting another year. Is this a good idea?

We thought of doing that with our own daughter, Karen, in her first weeks of preschool at age three and a half. We're wondering if your child, or any child, was ever as adamant as ours about not going to school. To find out more about how it went for us, see the box on page 39. As you'll see, she managed to get over her fear, and we ended up not only certain that we'd made the right choice in making her stick it out, but extremely pleased with her progress at school. Her adjustment to many other new situations was easier because of the confidence she gained when she realized she could cope with leaving home every day.

One important thing we learned from our experience was to trust the judgment of the professionals who ran the preschool we picked. They were right when they urged us to do the seemingly callous thing and walk away quickly, even while she cried for us. The faster we left the building, her teacher reported, the faster she got over her tears, and the easier it was for the staff to get her involved in group activities and distract her. When we sneaked back around the outside of the building to catch a glimpse of Karen through the window shades, we could see for ourselves that that was how it went. Karen would be up off the floor, no longer crying, but playing happily with her classmates, within a minute or two of our departure.

Find a good school, check it out thoroughly, and then trust the professional teachers to ease your child's transitions for you. This is not a do-it-yourself project, and if you try to make it into one, you could make the situation even worse.

That's not to say that there's nothing you can do in the meantime. Here are a few things you can do to complement the teachers' efforts to help your little Christopher or Karen adjust to the new routine.

1. Follow the same, *brief* good-bye ritual from today forward. You can give him a hug and a kiss in the carpool line or walk him to the door, and maybe add "Have a fun day!" but that should be it. Avoid the temptation to respond to requests for "just one more kiss," or to "stay just one more minute" so your child doesn't have the hope that he can prolong his time with you.

2. Let the school be more fun than home in some important ways. If your home is an unmatched toy paradise, if it's Artworld, or Petworld, how can any school possibly compete? In our case, it helped that we had never bought our three-year-old an easel or a set of brushes. Painting her own picture was a wonderful new thrill, something she could do only at school. For the whole first month at school, the very first thing she did in the morning (the instant we went out the door) was to go for her smock and take her place at an easel. We saw other children comforting themselves with different diversions that the school had to offer: One chose the large, springy rocking horse every day, while another always went to the dress-up trunk; and still others congregated at the fully equipped child-sized kitchen to play house. A well-run school or daycare center will have a wide range of tempting activities that will soon make your little one glad he's there.

3. Let your toddler take a "transition object" (that is to say, a teddy bear, a blanket, or some other plaything that he takes to his bed at nap time and at night). Not all preschools permit children to do so. Some childcare experts believe that these objects belong to the world of infancy, and the start of preschool is the time that they should be left behind. Many, perhaps even most preschools, ban pacifiers and try to discourage thumbsucking at nap time. When first researching school choices, be sure to bring up this subject with the school's director, and if you find the school's policy out of line with your child's needs, keep looking. At the start of the school year, make sure your child's teacher is aware of your child's beloved object, and that your child can get hold of it when it's most needed. Many times all the child really needs to know is that Blankie is in the cubby or that Ruff-pup is in his backpack, to feel reassured in a stressful situation.

4. Introduce your toddler ahead of time to as many of the faces and spaces of his new preschool as possible. Your child should get at least one chance to play in the classroom and on the playground before school opens, ideally not too many months ahead of time (because he'll forget all about it if it's too far in advance) but not so close to the first day that he has no time to get used to the idea of becoming a schoolchild. Try to get a class list and invite one or two

of the children who will be in class for a playdate at your house or at a nearby playground.

5. Talk to your child about school every day for a week or more before the first day. Don't try to reassure your child about being there without Mommy or Daddy; that will just plant the notion in his mind that this is a subject that requires a high level of reassurance. Your comforting words and phrases on that score will be needed *after* he discovers on his own that it's scary to be left in a new place. Instead, talk about what children do in preschool, with as much specific detail as you can include. If the class has a pet bunny or hamster, for example, talk about that. (Preschool classes with pets have a real advantage, we think, over those without them.) Keep your tone cheerful and confident, to convey the sense that school is a place every child belongs. Talk about how much you loved your own school as a small child (and if you hated it, see page 123 in Chapter Five on the value of creative storytelling).

6. When and if separation anxiety first strikes and the crying begins, suppress, suppress, suppress all your natural maternal/paternal instincts to come to the child's aid. Do *not* tell your child you will come for an earlier than normal pickup. Do not let the child tug on your hand, try to pull you back into the room, or in any other way impede your exit. Do not hang around watching the classroom any longer than your child's teacher considers wise. If the school is good, then trust in its staff. And if it isn't good and you find yourself losing confidence in the staff members' ability to ease your child's separation anxiety, then you probably should start looking for a different, better-run school.

7. Don't jump to the conclusion that your child is not ready for the preschool experience, but if you'd like a qualified, professional opinion on that issue, you may want to take your child to an early education consultant or preschool testing center, where staff members are specially trained to evaluate a child's readiness for preschool. Your child will take a test composed of many separate elements—ball playing, listening to a story, drawing a picture, stacking blocks, and other "games" that are fun and easy to do. Taken together, they provide a full portrait of your child's range of skills and abilities, including emotional maturity. If it should turn

out that your child has some special adjustment problem or developmental delay, the education counselor will be able to direct you to a preschool with the resources to address your child's needs or may advise you about in-home programs to help prepare your toddler for preschool at a later date.

8. Read one or all of the following three books about preschool: *Preschool for Parents: What Every Parent Needs to Know About Preschool,* by our friend and neighbor Toni S. Bickart and Diane Trister Dodge; *Smart Start: The Parent's Complete Guide to Preschool Education,* by Marian Edelman Borden; and *Preschool Primer for Parents: A Question and Answer Guide to Your Child's First School Experience,* by Doris Herman. (All three books are in print and readily available in bookstores or by ordering on-line.)

KAREN GOES TO PRESCHOOL: A SORROWFUL TALE (BUT WITH A HAPPY ENDING)

Here's our story. Our daughter Karen started preschool at age two and three-quarters. The first morning she got up bright and early, we got her dressed, and we cheerfully told her it was time for her to go to her new preschool. We had taken her there to see the place some weeks earlier and she'd had a great time. She was very enthusiastic about going back, even babbling with excitement. This is great, we thought, as we walked her in: There were happy kids everywhere, scrambling over the indoor play equipment, climbing, bouncing. She smiled in delight, and found a place on a teeter-totter amid a group of kids and started to play. She fit right in, so well that she hardly noticed when we said good-bye and left.

This is wonderful! we thought—and amazing. There's no separation anxiety at all! It's easier than we had any right to expect. We must have prepared her well, we congratulated ourselves.

The next morning, we woke Karen up, and told her it was time to get ready for preschool again. This time, instead of bouncing out of bed, she cried, "NO!" and grabbed onto slats in the headboard of her bed with a death grip so tight that it took both of us using all our strength to pry her fingers from around them. After a ten-minute struggle, we finally had her up and out of her bed and managed to wrestle her into her clothing. We had to carry her kicking and screaming down to the car and pin her with down with a clinch hold in order to buckle her into her car seat. Once we arrived at the school, we practically had to drag her into the building and down the hall to her classroom.

What was behind all this resistance? Apparently, she had thought all our talk about school before it started and all the times we'd visited it over the summer had been preparation for a one-day event. She'd been there, she'd had fun, and that was the end of it. She'd never imagined that she'd be expected to do it all over again! We'd never warned her that she would be going back the next day, and the day after that, and every weekday thereafter! Now, as we moved toward the door after saying good-bye, she threw herself down on the floor and began flailing her arms, while her legs thrashed the carpet. She was inconsolable.

We stood there stunned and helpless, not sure what to do, only certain that we couldn't leave her there that way. But her teachers, having seen this all before, had no doubt as to what we should do next. "She'll be fine," they assured us. "Just say good-bye and go quickly, and she'll perk up pretty fast. They always do."

So we were ushered out to the "tea and tissues" room, which was set up especially for parents who find it tough to leave a crying child. The school director was there, and she told us we could creep around the back of the building to get a peek at our daughter through the darkened glass of the rear window.

So we did, and we found her, no longer on the floor, but standing at an easel, wearing a painting smock. She was somber, but she was painting intently. Satisfied that she would be all right, we left for work.

When we picked her up that afternoon, she had her painting with her. We ooohed and aaahed over it like a masterpiece (which, of course, it was. We've saved it for her and we intend to keep it forever).

But the next morning was just as bad as the one before. And the one after that was no better. For the next week and a half, it was the same thing, day after miserable day. We had to pull her out of bed every morning and tussle with her to get her ready, and then carry her into the classroom. Each time we left to the sound of protests and sobs. Each time we'd sneak a look into the classroom and see that a minute or two after she believed we were gone, she'd stand up, go over to an art easel, and start to paint. Then she'd be okay.

At the end of the first week, we seriously asked ourselves, Is she ready for preschool? Maybe we should pull her out, wait until she's more accepting of the idea. . . . This daily drama of struggle and coercion couldn't be doing her any good. . . .

In our confusion and anxiety over the long-term consequences, we failed to notice the subtle but sure signs of short-term improvement. Day by day she was protesting less, crying for shorter periods. By the middle of the second week of school she was no longer crying at all when she woke in the morning. By the end of that week, we dropped her off at the classroom and realized that she hadn't shed a tear as we said good-bye. By the end of the third week she was even smiling in the morning. By the end of the fourth week, she was saying she loved her school to anyone who asked her about it.

Now, seven years later, we might have forgotten about our struggles with her, and our doubts that she would ever adjust, except for the fact that remembering—and telling this story—might help other parents through the crisis of getting used to preschool for the very first time.

We've been interviewing nannies with the plan of hiring one full-time. We've met several excellent prospects, but I'm afraid my three-year-old Kevin doesn't see any of them in quite the same light. My main worry is that he'll be so difficult the first few weeks that he'll scare anyone we hire out of sticking with the job.

If you've got someone who's top quality, she'll be up to the challenge of even the most intransigent tot. The key thing here is to be sure that the nanny you hire has the experience, temperament, and self-confidence to melt your little nanny-hater's heart.

For a comprehensive guide to everything you need to know to match your family with the right kind of childcare provider, we have no hesitation about recommending one of our own guides, *The Safe Nanny Handbook: Everything You Need to Know to Have Peace of Mind While Your Child Is in Someone Else's Care* (William Morrow and Company, 1998), by Peggy Robin. The book completely covers every aspect of the subject from the wording of your nanny advertisements to conducting informative interviews to doing a background check and calling references, through negotiating the employment agreement, to training the nanny to meet the requirements of your unique household. See pages 94–96 for guidelines about staging the meeting between your nanny and your child to get things off to the most positive start.

One very useful tip discussed in the book is a way to give the nanny a secret little assist to enable her to win your child over quickly. Sit down with her ahead of time and familiarize her with your child's personality, his particular foibles, his likes and dislikes. Suppose he's a Tigger fanatic, and has seen *The Tigger Movie* at least five times. Then make sure she's had an opportunity to see the video herself, and maybe learn to sing Tigger's song. At their first meeting, she says, "You know, you're so cute and bouncy, you remind me of Tigger from *Winnie the Pooh*, then she sings the song. Your child will be thrilled to meet someone who shares his passion and thinks he resembles that mutually admired figure.

She should also know from the very first what games he likes best, and what he considers the yummiest dessert. It's always a good idea to have her serve his favorite foods at the very first meal she prepares for him.

You definitely want to stick around for the first several days your new nanny is on the job. Hiring should always include a training period, during which one or both parents will be available to familiarize the nanny with your home and the way you want things handled. If time off from work is not obtainable, then pay the nanny to start work on the weekend, when you can be there. During this time you will steadily gain confidence that you've made the right choice and can trust the nanny with your child, before you go back to work. (If after the end of your supervisory period you don't have such a feeling, it's back to the interview process to start your search anew!) The training time also doubles as an adjustment period for your child, who doesn't have to struggle with separation anxiety at the same time as stranger anxiety. Your reassuring presence tells him that this new person has your approval; she's okay for him to like, too.

Even the best babysitters sometimes experience rejection at the start. Some children need a very long time to get used to being left with anyone but a parent. If that's the case, you need to be sure your sitter isn't the type to get rattled by rejection, but will have a few additional tricks of her own to try to win your child over. If she's loving and creative and energetic and bright (all qualities you should have been probing for by use of deft interview questions), then she will succeed faster than you would have thought possible.

But it might speed things up even more if during those first few rough days, she were the bearer of a few great gifts. Of course, you should pay for them, but let her wrap them and present them to your child as her own thoughtful gestures. Be careful not to prolong this strategy beyond the first week—otherwise you'll quickly condition your child to expect a present every time she arrives, and to feel disappointed the first time she arrives empty-handed.

More than presents, what works best to impress your child is your own attitude toward the nanny. If he sees that you regard her as a second-rate substitute for parental care, he will unconsciously absorb that attitude, and he's sure to reject her. But treat her as a wonderful addition to your family right from the start—give her your respect and, once you get to know and like her, your affection. He can't help but mirror your feelings.

One thing to put out of your mind: that infernal Disney movie *Mary Poppins!* It's the bane of great nannies everywhere, because no one can live up to the magical, fictional nanny's standard. After all, a real nanny can't make the kids' mess straighten itself up, and even with a spoonful of sugar, sometimes the medicine is going to be thrown back up. So do remember, your nanny is only human, just as your child is, and allow her the time and patience she needs to grow into the job (just as you show patience and allow your child the time he needs to adjust to this new situation).

I'm having a baby in just a few months. I've tried to discuss it with my two-and-a-half-year-old daughter in a positive way, but every time I bring the subject up, she cries, "But I'm your baby!" Should I just trust that her feelings will change once the new baby is actually here?

Oh, her feelings will change, all right—for the worse, unless you find a way to start turning things around. There are a few standard fears that toddlers have about becoming an older sibling that you might want to start working on now, before her imagination has a chance to start magnifying them.

First of all, you want to make sure she understands that she is not being replaced. You can't tell her too often, "You'll always be my baby," and "You're my firstborn, and that makes you special."

When you talk about the new baby, you want to make clear that this is a wonderful event for the whole family. It's not just that *you* are having a baby but that all of you are having a baby. She's having a sister (or brother) and eventually gaining a playmate, which means, in a way, that it's her baby, too. Let her know the names you are considering (though don't give her the final say!). Let her see the crib where the new baby will sleep. Let her help you fold and put away all the tiny baby clothes. Talk about how you'll be feeding the baby. If you'll be using bottles at any point, tell her that she'll be able to hold the bottle for the baby. Show her the tiny clothes and let her hold them up and compare them to her own clothes.

In all your talk about the baby, you do need to be careful to give a realistic idea of what having a newborn will be like. Here's how we explained it to our own two-and-a-half-year-old: "Your new baby sister won't be able to do much of anything for a long, long time. All she really knows how to do right now is sleep, cry, suck, pee, and poop. That's it. She'll have to learn to sit, to stand, to crawl, to walk, to talk. You already know how to do all these things, so the new baby will really look up to you. You'll be able to teach her so much." That cautionary speech not only prevented Karen from expecting a fully developed playmate (and from being disappointed at getting less than that for most of the first full year) but it also reassured her that she held a strategic advantage over the baby, who was so far behind her in so many ways.

Another helpful thing to do right away is to sit down together and look over your toddler's newborn pictures. Show her how cute she was, what she was like at a day old, a week old, a month old, and so on. You let her see how wonderful it was having one new child, and you may give her a bit of appreciation for your desire to have another.

Of course, once the baby is home, you won't be able to hide the fact that you'll be much busier than you've ever been before—so warn her of that part of the deal. But quickly add that, busy as you'll be, you will always make time for her. You'll still do the important things that you did before. You'll tuck her in at night. You'll read her stories. There will still be time when you'll go places together, just the two of you.

One of your main goals as you near your due date is to plan to make the time of the birth go as smoothly as possible for your daughter. Make sure that her caregiver during the time that you're away is someone she really loves to be with. If she's never had anyone but you taking care of her overnight, then you should consider going away with your spouse for a weekend *now*, to give your appointed substitute a night's practice.

Your caregiver during delivery ideally should be someone who is willing and able to spoil your child for that time, showering her with attention, praise, and presents. She should be made to feel like the center of the universe.

By the way, you shouldn't worry about the effects of this short-term spoiling. If there's ever a time for a child to be overindulged, it's the day that she loses her only-child status. For most children the quickest, simplest way to their hearts is through a few well-chosen presents, labeled as if they come from the new baby. None of them needs to be expensive—a toddler can be as happy with a tiny stuffed animal from the dollar store than some exquisitely hand-sewn collectible bear. Also, many of the baby toys people give you as shower presents can go straight to your toddler. Your newborn won't know they're for her or even have the ability to play with them for at least six or seven months. In the meantime your toddler will love them—and associate them with having a baby in the house, and get the idea right from the start that this change is, on the whole, a very good thing.

PEGGY'S MOTHER'S STORY

When I first brought Peggy home from the hospital as a newborn, her brother Richard, who was then nearly three, was curiously calm about the big change in our household. I had hired a baby nurse to help me out for the first few weeks, which I supposed was why he wasn't jealous; the nurse took over enough of the routine infant care that I was able to spend a good deal of time with my older child. It was only on the nurse's last day of work that I discovered the real reason Richard had been so blasé. As the nurse said her good-byes and headed up the street, he ran after her, yelling, "Wait! Wait! You forgot to take your baby with you!"

—Florence Isbell
Chevy Chase, MD

WARNING: BEWARE OF MOST "NEW SIBLING" BOOKS

One thing you may be tempted to do for your child while expecting a baby is to read her a book about the arrival of the new baby. In the months before our second daughter was born, we went to a bookstore to see what was available as a picture book with a new-baby-in-the-house theme, and we found a great variety of choices. We started perusing the pages with the thought of buying one or two, but came away with none. The trouble was, all the books at some point or another concluded that having a new baby was not all to the good. In every book we picked up we found a line that went something like this: "Sure, there will be times you feel left out and sad and angry at the new baby—but that's okay."

What a bad idea, we thought then (and still think) to start out even before the new baby has arrived predicting such negative emotions. Before the child has even had a chance to experience both the good and the bad of being a sibling in real life, the books all identified the downside. Why put such thoughts in the child's head before they arise on their own? If and when the child starts to feel left out, the parents can and should be alert to their child's mood and respond appropriately, but don't start telling the child *ahead of time* how miserable she's going to be!

*S*am, my thirteen-month-old, reacts with horror to his own grand-parents. My husband's parents live far away and they can visit only twice a year, but each time they come, it's awful. Sam screams and hides the minute he catches a glimpse of them coming toward the house. They're hurt, of course, but worse, when I don't bring Sam out of his hiding space under the bed, they accuse us of not letting them have time to get to know him better. They say if we'd just leave and let them babysit, he'd be fine. But he's so panic-stricken, I just know it would be wrong to abandon him right *away. Those first few minutes set the whole tone of the visit, which I've wanted to cut short to save us all from further tension. My husband thinks his parents are right, that I'm being too overprotective. I tell you flatly, I'm not expecting your advice to help, since I don't think it's possible to outwit a child into loving people who scare him.*

That's probably true . . . but how about trying to outwit the grandparents into changing their behavior? They just might be open to change if you approach them in the right way, emphasizing the fact that you're all after the same thing, to help them develop a warm, comfortable relationship with their grandchild.

Ask them humbly for their advice and ideas for ways to help Sam become more familiar with them. One thing that they should be able to do right away is increase contact between themselves and Sam in advance of their visit. Starting a few weeks before their planned arrival, ask them to call to talk to Sam on the telephone every few days. Even if Sam isn't talking much yet, it will be good for him to get used to hearing their voices. Ask Grandma or Grandpa to sing him a familiar lullaby, or read to him from his favorite picture book while you turn the pages of your own copy at home. Videotaped messages are also a godsend in these situations.

Talk to them yourself about your worries over Sam's shyness. Let them be the ones to hit upon the solution of giving your son some additional time to get used to being around people he doesn't see every day. That's the key—the lack of daily contact. You never want to imply that their own grandchild views them as strangers (even if that's exactly the way it seems to Sam). Once they think they're the ones with the wisdom to hang back (and it's not their daughter-in-law ordering them how to behave) they will transform themselves (or so we hope!) from hit-and-run huggers into the very souls of sensitivity.

On second thought, it might be better if you hand over the job of explaining your son's shyness to your husband. They'll have an easier time, we think, being guided to the desired conclusion if their own son is leading up to it, rather than their daughter-in-law. You and your husband, however, should work out with each other in advance how he's going to broach the topic and map out the dialogue he hopes to elicit. He should begin by simply making some factual observations about Sam's response to them in the past. He then goes on to remark that Sam is invariably that way with people he sees less frequently than once a week, but that when he does have a chance to get comfortable with a person, he can and does get over his shyness, and even becomes warm and charming. Then let them be the ones to suggest some ways to let his natural friendliness emerge.

Retraining older people works best when it's a team effort. Before the start of the visit, work out with your husband just what activities you think Sam could do along with his extended family, and then with his grandparents alone.

Once they see that they can have a hand in crafting a solution, we believe (well, we hope!) that they will be enthusiastic about implementing their new go-slow approach.

How should that new approach work? What they need to do is step back about ten giant steps, starting from the time they arrive at your house. They should not ask that Sam come out to greet them. The last thing a boy like Sam wants is a pair of older, unfamiliar people swooping down on him the minute they step onto his turf.

A good starting point for the grandparent get-together might be while Sam is secure in his high chair, enjoying a meal. If he's using a bottle or a sippy cup, give him a small amount to start out with, and when he's drained the container, let Grandma be the one who brings him his refill. Let Grandpa be the giver of that special dessert at the end of the meal—the delicious treat you rarely allow Sam to have but know he loves best. (But make sure Grandpa doesn't have any plans to introduce some new, untested food. If Sam ends up hating it, he'll immediately link that unpleasant taste experience with Grandpa.)

One possible factor in this equation could be your child's heightened sense of smell. If Grandma always comes soaked in a powerful perfume, that can send a sensitive child running the other way. If Grandpa smokes cigars, make sure he doesn't do it around Sam.

Once your in-laws have gained some insight into how and why Sam reacts to them as he does, they should have an easier time learning what works and what doesn't in each of their carefully managed encounters with your child. Once they see the first signs of progress—though they may well think it's Sam who's improving, not they—let them continue to build up their points of contact in gentle increments.

What if, after all your efforts, you still can't get them to agree to a more low-key greeting? You and your husband can still protect Sam from overly intensive contact by keeping control over the time and place of that first encounter. Make arrangements for Sam to be away from the house at the time they come in, and when he does arrive, let it be when they're already busy doing something, so he won't be the immediate focus of their attention. Alternatively, you could time their arrival to Sam's usual afternoon nap—or think of some other way to get them into the house without letting them throw themselves upon your child, first thing.

While waiting for the situation to get better, it's important to try to stay calm and collected whenever Sam does react badly to his grandparents' actions. Remember, you should never punish a child for being clingy or not wanting to give someone a hug. Just let him see you acting warmly and lovingly toward your in-laws—that should help.

It's important to let your child have a break for some of the time of their stay. Visits that involve frequent outings and disruptions of his schedule can be hard on a child. Even as the grandparents are developing into better companions for him, you'll still want to spend some time alone with him, just as you did before the visit began. That way he'll be less likely to suffer from "grandparent overload" or "burnout."

Be sure to reward them whenever they've had some quiet, non-stressful time with Sam by letting them spend more time with him alone. Show them how he likes his diaper changed, and then trust them to do it right. Let them tell him stories and put him down for a nap. When you think they're ready, let them have him overnight (we think they'll do you proud).

Also, keep in mind that stranger anxiety typically peaks around one year to eighteen months, so as Sam ages, the situation will naturally get better on its own.

CHAPTER

3

Getting Them to Eat—But Something Other Than Junk Food

Is there a toddler on earth who has that wonderful, well-rounded diet that all the parenting experts tell you is so important? We haven't met one yet. Either a child is too picky and doesn't eat enough, or is voracious and doesn't know when to quit. Some parenting guides are quick to reassure you that despite this or that quirk in taste, your toddler won't starve but will find a way to get more or less all the nutrition he or she really needs. Yes, but their short-term survival is not what you're worried about. It's the long-term consequences: eating habits formed in childhood affect adults for the rest of their lives.

If your two-year-old girl turns her nose up at practically everything you offer, could that foretell an eating disorder at fifteen or sixteen? (We'll give you the reassuring answer right now, which is no, not at all.) If your four-year-old son seems to devour everything in his path and he weighs sixty pounds, will he grow up to be the size of a Sumo wrestler? (The answer to that one is less resoundingly clear, and it's probably wise to take precautionary measures. There's certainly no harm starting now, when he's too young to open the refrigerator by himself, substituting healthy snacks for high-sugar, high-fat ones.)

When toddler nutrition veers too far in one extreme or the other, causing parents more than the everyday quotient of anxiety, it's time to turn to a trusted pediatrician for help—but for parents of the average toddler with less-than-ideal eating habits (and that's about 95 percent of them), the answers to the following questions ought to provide both reassurance and relief.

How do I convince my kid that vegetables aren't poison? The way he reacts when I put broccoli in front of him, you'd think I was making him eat hemlock! Meanwhile, my sister-in-law's kids eat everything on their plates without a word of complaint. What's she doing right? What am I doing wrong?

Aaah, those perfect nephews and nieces. You do know, don't you, that they're only like that when they're at your house? At home they're just as picky and obnoxious as your own kids (maybe not about eating, but about some other issue—something that drives your sister-in-law completely around the bend). And besides that, your sister-in-law may not be doing anything different; it could be that she's just blessed with kids with cooperative taste buds. Or maybe she has terrorized them into eating whatever she puts in front ot them.

The point is, whatever the reason that other kids eat healthily, don't worry about *them*. Your job as a parent is limited—happily for you—to stewing about the situation inside your own household. Here are some possible ways to work on that.

1. *Forget about vegetables for a while.* There is no First Law of Nutritional Health dictating that all children must eat vegetables. There are plenty of other, better-tasting sources of the same essential vitamins and minerals. Fruits, for example. Most kids love fruit. Melons have many of the same nutritional benefits as yellow vegetables like squash. Bananas are loaded with potassium, strawberries are full of vitamin C, and the calcium and iron found in spinach and kale can be ingested just as easily (actually, for most toddlers, way more easily) in the form of string cheese, yogurt, or

ice cream. (One caution about applying this strategy: Some of these recommended substitutes for vegetables are high in sugar content, so be sure that your toddler gets a good toothbrushing after eating to guard against cavities, and do introduce the practice of flossing now, to make it a daily habit.)

2. *Find vegetables they do like.* Experiment with different kinds of vegetables and with new and enticing presentations. Make vegetable faces. Come up with some fun and creative vegetable recipes, like the one in the box on page 55.

3. *Get a whole book's worth of advice* on this subject by reading *Coping with a Picky Eater: A Guide for the Perplexed Parent* by William G. Wilkoff. If your child is a fan of the *Arthur* TV show, he might like to listen to you read him *D.W. the Picky Eater* by Marc Brown (about Arthur's little sister). And both parents and children will delight in the pictures of funny vegetables in *How Are You Peeling?* by Saxton Freymann and Joost Elffers. We enthusiastically recommend this book for toddlers because you don't need to be able to read a word to understand it. You can flip through its colorful pictures of funny foods and really pique their interest in a great many different types of vegetables. If this book doesn't leave you loving vegetables, then you're really in a pickle!

4. *Try kids' chewable vitamins.* Now, don't think we're saying that you can let your kid eat junk food all day long and then hand them a vitamin pill, and think to yourself, "Fine, I've taken care of a hundred percent of their nutritional needs." But if you're doing the best you can to try to get them to expand their limited palates, but you know that they're still not getting a full five servings of vegetables and fruits each day, then relax, and let Flintstones Chewables, Bugs Bunny, or Shamu the Killer Whale and His Friends put your mind somewhat at rest. You may have to experiment with brands (color and shape being as important to a toddler as taste—maybe more important) to find a supplement your toddler will accept. And be careful to limit them to one vitamin a day and make it clear that vitamins are like medicine: They must be taken properly, only when a grown-up says to do so.

5. *Get them to drink their vegetables.* V-8 Juice is a good choice for a drink once or twice a day—and way better than soda or

so-called "fruit" drinks that have little or no actual juice in them. So is orange juice fortified with calcium. Of course, milk (or soy milk for those with dairy digestion problems) should be the mainstay beverage.

6. *Be persistent but not insistent.* Keep offering vegetables with each meal, and introduce new ones from time to time, but don't punish them for refusing after that first trial bite. We call this the "No Thank You Bite" and say that, for politeness' sake, you at least have to try whatever the cook went to the trouble to prepare. It's good for children to learn early on that they must appreciate the effort that went into making a balanced meal, and that they can't turn down food with "yuck" faces, rude noises, or gestures of disgust. This type of training does need continual reinforcement (especially since they'll soon be visiting other houses where the kids are allowed to get away with murder at the dinner table) but it has a long-term payoff. We speak from experience, not as parents, but as former picky eaters ourselves. Peggy ate virtually nothing but cold cereal and occasional tuna fish sandwiches as a child but suddenly, in college, discovered the full range of foods, including nearly all the vegetables and fresh fish. Our good friend Alice as a child used to eat ketchup sandwiches (yes, it is what you think it is: two pieces of white bread with nothing but ketchup in between) and she, too, went on to develop into a healthy, varied eater as an adult. So we say, take the long view, and don't fight now over every meal or you'll send the message that mealtime is meant to be a battleground—and so it will be.

ANTS ON LOGS

Here's a quick and easy favorite of my vegetable-hating former toddler Claire (she's now six, but was introduced to this snack food in nursery school, and she loves it still):

Ingredients:

Celery stalks
Light cream cheese
Raisins

Wash celery stalks and cut off the leaves and ends. Spread light cream cheese down the tube-like length of each stalk. Dot the top of the cream cheese with raisins—they're the "ants"—and serve. Or if you prefer, leave the celery leaves on and stand the stalk up, creating a variant: Ants Climb Tree.

After every meal my kitchen looks like a splatter painting by some Expressionist artist. Is there any way to get a toddler to eat more neatly?

The short answer is no. The long answer is yes, you should start working now on teaching simple concepts like "Food goes in your mouth, not on the floor" and "That's applesauce, not finger-paint"—but don't start expecting these lessons to sink in for at least another year or two. Sometime before the start of kindergarten your child will learn to make the majority of whatever's on the plate end up inside her stomach (as opposed to, say, in her hair).

In the meantime, however, you need to make things easier on yourself in terms of cleanup. The following are some ideas designed to shorten the amount of time you spend mopping, wiping up, and otherwise capturing bits of toddler meals that somehow went astray.

First, protect your floor. Some like to put down a plastic protective mat; others say, "What's the point, since you just have to clean the mat each time?" One trick we've seen for quick and easy cleanups is the use of a round, plastic wading pool. Place the high chair in the middle and let it catch everything that falls. At the end of the day, if it's really grungy, just take it outside and hose it off. Otherwise, you can give it a quick sweeping-out with a broom or a handheld cordless vacuum, or simply shake out all the debris over a large trash can.

Next, try reducing the "drop zone"—the amount of free space surrounding the eating surface within your toddler's reach. One way to accomplish this is to have the child eat right at the table, instead of in a high chair. Place the child on a booster (one that has a secure seat belt) on top of one of your regular dining or kitchen chairs and pull that chair up as tight to the table as it will go. Use a wipe-clean vinyl tablecloth on the table, or an extra-large plastic placemat. Not only will you reduce the gap between your child and the eating surface, but you will also have your child seated more like the other members of the family. That should help your child to learn to copy others as they enjoy their meal together. Children set apart in their high chairs are more apt to become bored with their meals and start playing with their food as a way to amuse themselves.

Coupled with this strategy, you will also want to release your child from the booster (or high chair) as soon as the child's interest in eating appears to be waning. Most toddlers have very short attention spans, as well as limited-capacity stomachs. When they stop being interested in opening their mouths to let food in and start looking around for other places to put it, take that as a sign that the mealtime is over for them, and let them go on to something else. If the rest of your family is still eating, a playpen stocked with toys may provide the toddler with safe entertainment for the next ten or fifteen minutes. With small children, parents almost never get a chance to linger pleasantly at the table. For active toddlers who are not the playpen-accepting type, the best thing is usually to let the toddler have a nearby, gated-off, baby-safe area to run around in (an adjacent family room, if you have one, or perhaps just a part of the kitchen fenced off with a removable pressure-mounted barrier), while the rest of you finish off your meal in a relatively civilized fashion.

For those who, for scheduling convenience, prefer to feed the toddler separately, it's useful to have a high chair with a super-sized, close-fitting tray. You may not want to bother to use plates or utensils at all. Just cut all food into toddler-sized bits and put it directly on the tray for your child to self-feed. You'll save yourself countless hours that would otherwise be spent holding the fork up, saying inane things like "Open wiiiide, and let the melons come inside." With all foods made graspable, your child will eat what he wants and ignore what he wouldn't eat anyway. (For parents who are afraid that their child won't be getting enough nutrition, given so much freedom, be sure to read the question and answer about picky eaters immediately following.) Once you realize that your child isn't eating something you've put out, whisk it away before he gets the idea to make it disappear to the floor, or find out what it would look like if flung against the kitchen wall.

Now for what *never* works: those suction-to-the-tray plates and bowls you can buy at baby product stores. We had them in many different makes and models when our two girls were at the high-chair stage of dining. We never found one that a determined toddler of average strength could not dislodge within twenty seconds. Perhaps if you used Krazy Glue® to bond them to the tray top, they'd stay . . . but then you'd have a cleanup problem of a different sort.

Another thing you mustn't count on to prevent messes is the bib. Do food spills *ever* go where the bib is? There are basically two ways of dealing with the food-on-the-clothing problem, and they're complete opposites. One is Don't Worry Be Happy. Just buy cheap, easily washable clothing, and try to wash out what washes out, and put up with the stains that don't. With most brightly patterned prints, no one will ever notice. The other way is Total Prevention. Have your child wear a terrycloth beach cover-up or a painter's smock during meals. Or throw an adult-sized T-shirt over your child. You may want to clip it at the back with a large alligator clip (the kind you use to clip an eighty-page report together) to make it tighter-fitting around the neck. Or you can try to find one of those super-sized bibs that cover the whole front. One mom we know used to cut a head-sized hole in her old towels and drape them over her messy eater before each meal.

Even with all these efforts and more, however, eating with the average two-year-old is never going to be an experience in fine dining. In our fantasies of a perfect world we'd like to see a national restaurant franchise that would promise to take the mess out of feeding your toddler once and for all. It would go like this: You take the family out to this specially designed restaurant that is divided into two sections, one for those members of the family who can appreciate fine cuisine served on tables nicely set with table-

cloths and china, the other where everything is plastic and disposable and the menu is just pizza, chicken nuggets, spaghetti, and rice
crackers. On the messy-eater side the waiters and waitresses all
double as babysitters, bottle-holders and spoon-feeders; on the fine
dining side they're trained in elegant, European-style service. There
is a partition between the two sides of the restaurant made of one-
way mirrored glass (so that the adults can see in, but the kids can't
see out), and the kids' side is totally soundproofed. When the kids
are done on their side, they're ushered out into a cleaning-off area,
where they're hosed down rather like cars passing through a car-
wash, and then on to the blow-drying, hair-combing, and clothes-
straightening room, after which they may enter the waiting room to
be picked up by their parents and taken home—all well fed, neat,
and happy—parents and children alike.

Y*ou've heard of picky eaters, I'm sure, but maybe none as picky
as my son Danny. He only eats one food. That's right, one. It's
packaged chicken nuggets that are shaped like dinosaurs. He has
them for breakfast, lunch, and dinner. I've read magazine articles
and other advice books that say, "Put out a variety of foods for
him, and let him pick and choose what he wants—he'll soon discover new tastes." Well, I did just that—and guess what?—he
didn't. He really will go several days at a time not eating more
than a nibble at each meal. What should I do?*

Keep yourself well stocked with chicken nuggets—at least for
the time being. We know *exactly* how things are over at your house,
because our older child for a long time existed entirely on spaghetti,
with a slight coating of margarine on it. Like you, we tried following the advice we found in other parenting books (yes, parenting
experts have their own problems, and we do consult our competi-
tors' books!)—but the "take it or leave it" approach didn't work
for us either.

We got our daughter to branch out in her food choices bit by bit,
offering, in addition to her usual meal of spaghetti, a bowl of some
other type of pasta, in a more interesting shape. The first sign of

progress came when she decided she liked wagon wheel–shaped noodles as much as spaghetti. From there we experimented further, until eventually a number of other shapes were deemed acceptable: first elbow noodles, then penne, then seashells, and later on, even some whimsical specialty shapes, like tennis racquets and Christmas trees. But still, no marinara sauce—just margarine.

Still, she didn't starve. Fortunately, she liked to drink milk, which is a good source of some important nutrients, and she liked those children's chewable vitamins, so we knew she wasn't missing out on vitamin C and some other essentials that milk and pasta lack. That's important: If your son is drinking only fruit juice, or worse, soda, then you *do* have a potentially serious problem, and you should definitely have your pediatrician check to make sure your son isn't at risk for any disorders caused by vitamin or mineral deficiency. But if he checks out fine and is growing and developing at a normal rate, then stop worrying, and at your leisure, you may want to try out any or all of the following techniques:

Introduce similar tastes. You know he likes things with a fried, breaded coating. Find others and introduce them as "cousins" or "daddies" of his beloved dinosaur nuggets. You can buy breading-coated fishsticks in different shapes—and chances are fair to good that he'll take to them. Onion rings could be tempting, too. Put the dinosaurs inside the rings and tell him they're floating in their ring floats. Or try introducing breaded cheese fingers as the fallen tree trunks of dinosaurland.

If that doesn't get you anywhere, then try introducing a different taste, not for a regular meal (where he seems to have trouble accepting the concept of variety) but during snack time—when kids are sometimes more likely to accept new things, because snack means "special treat" and they understand that "special" means both "different" and "good." Ice cream is a fairly nutritious snack food, and it's so sweet that even the pickiest of eaters tend to go for it. (And if he doesn't, maybe all you need to do is try out another flavor. If you started with vanilla, try chocolate the next time you offer it. If that doesn't go over well, then consider what other desserts—if any—your child does like. Oreo cookies? Then what about Oreo ice cream?)

Once you've got them eating ice cream, you've got a wedge to introduce other dairy foods. Yogurt is like ice cream except that it isn't frozen. You can buy it in those kid-friendly miniservings, the kind that come with sprinkles or "magic crystals" that you mix into the yogurt to make it change colors as you're eating it. Pretty cool!

From yogurt it's a short hop to the creamy variety of cottage cheese, which could bring you to whipped cream cheese, which tastes good on a bagel, and once they like bagels, they may move on to other breads with stuff on them, and now you're slowly working your way over to real foods, like peanut butter and jelly sandwiches.

Or another way to work within that snack time window of opportunity is to begin sneaking in a few fruits. Even if your child rejected cut-up or mushed-up banana as a baby, try it again, but this time monkey-style. Lop off the top with a knife and just barely initiate the peeling process. If your toddler is the exploring, let-me-get-at-every-hidden-thing personality type, he'll immediately want to solve the puzzle of how to peel and eat this thing all by himself.

Apples can be made more interesting if you slice them. Since tiny teeth may find the peel difficult to chew, your best bet is to serve apples with the skin cut off. Flat, circular slices of apple can be arranged on a plate in ascending size to look like a snowman. Dot the face with two raisins for eyes and one for a nose, with a cut sliver of celery for the smiley mouth, more raisins for buttons, and maybe some carrot shavings for hair, some thin carrot sticks for arms, and you've got a character more interesting than a whole Jurassic Park full of dinosaur nuggets.

Of course, the truly picky eater, while he may appreciate your food artistry, still may not be ready to actually *eat* your creation. So it helps if you do voices. "Don't eat me, don't eat me!" your snowman-apple character can shriek in a cartoonishly obnoxious voice. This may be just the incentive your contrary-minded child needs to do exactly that.

Excellent edible characters, who can also serve to introduce new tastes to your picky child, may be created out of sliced cheese (the bright orange variety, like Velveeta, tends to have good toddler appeal and can be made into virtually any shape that you can find as a cookie cutter), sliced lunch meats (like ham, turkey, or bologna) or soft white bread, all of which can be quickly turned into a human or animal shape using a cookie cutter. Our own two picky eaters liked to eat cheese or bread when it was cut into rocking horses, kangaroos, squirrels, and bunnies. Once our younger daughter was a little older (that is to say, three or four, instead of one or two), she invented the idea of combining the sliced cheese and the lunch meat into a single entity—a sandwich! We didn't have the heart to tell her someone had already laid claim to this novelty. By the ripe old age of five, she had to have a sandwich in every bag lunch she took to day camp—but at least she was getting some variety in her lunch meats from day to day. And yes, we still do have to cut the bread for her into certain shapes. Animals and people are out (too babyish for our big first-grader); triangles and crustless quarter-pieces are in.

So, speaking from experience, we say, just wait. A broader palate *is* in your son's future. In the meantime stock up your freezer on dinosaur nuggets and be glad that his one staple food is something simple, and not something obscure or difficult to prepare. We know of one little girl who liked only a certain brand and flavor of toaster Pop-Tarts, and then the company stopped making them! Another little boy we heard of would eat tuna salad, but it had to be mixed with seven or eight different ingredients—celery, onions, green pepper, mayonnaise, pickle relish, a touch of mustard, plus a few more odds and ends we forget—mixed in just the right proportions, and it took a good twenty minutes to make. Worse, still, he would reject it if the mixture was just a shade off in any direction. He, too, has changed (he's now fifteen) and is the typical all-devouring teenager.

So if nothing else helps, relax, and wait for time to supply the cure.

The French Way

We have relatives who live in France, and their three children (boy-girl twins and a daughter fourteen months older than the twins) eat virtually everything: all kinds of vegetables, meats, seafood, soufflés, even escargot! They say they've never heard of a child who would only eat one food—and if there was such a child, what parent would allow the situation to persist? We've spent a little time in France ourselves, and seen firsthand the French difference when it comes to attitudes about child feeding. Parents serve everything to their children from an early age (three months!) and just assume their children will like everything, if it's made from fresh ingredients and is well prepared (and what French food isn't?).

Although we took quite an opposite attitude when it came to our own children (we chose not to push our children to eat things they didn't like), we put forth the French way of dealing with picky eaters as an alternative for those parents who either lack the time to prepare food according to the picky eater's whims, or who believe, as a general principle of life, that toddlers should have to eat whatever is being served.

First, you need to cook for your children just as you would for someone with the most sophisticated palate. Shop with care, not skimping on quality of produce and insisting upon freshness. Regard your cooking as an art form. Serve each dish with the expectation that your child *will* like it. In addition, children in France are taught table manners while still in their high chairs. They must at least try what is served to them, eat without making faces or protests, and if they don't like it, they still have to show some polite appreciation for the cook's effort. Parents may not force their children to eat all of a food they don't like, but they certainly wouldn't make anything special for that one child who doesn't like a particular dish.

Parental strictness about meals means that for the first few years of life, the naturally picky eater may feel harassed and uncomfortable at the table, constantly being scolded about this or that, but by about the age of six or seven the child has developed into someone who dines with an ease and sophistication that most Americans manage to attain—if indeed they ever do—only after they reach early middle age.

*M*y *child never stops eating. He'd eat all day if I let him. He eats a good variety of foods at mealtimes, but the rest of the time it seems that he's always whining, "I'm hungry!" Should I let him have a snack every time he wants one or try to cut back on all this snacking?*

Before we get to that, let's get to work on teaching him the right way to ask for food. Whining "I'm hungry" isn't it, and you shouldn't have to jump to his commands. It's never too early for him to hear, "This isn't a restaurant, and I'm not the waitress!" Then say, "Do you mean, 'Mommy, could I please have a snack?'"

After you get the question phrased in the form you prefer, then you can answer it in a variety of ways:

1. Introduce the concept of "It's too close to dinnertime [lunchtime, whatever]." It's an age-old line, and it's stuck around because it works. Once your child gets used to hearing it, he'll start to accept the idea of certain times of the day not being eating times—that is, unless you actually don't mind being the on-call short-order cook. You can point to the clock (and it's helpful if your kitchen has a big, round-faced clocks with easy-to-read numbers on the wall) to show him what number the little hand must reach before it's time to eat. The Delay-Until-the-Clock-Says-OK method is one of the handiest of our regular *Outwitting Toddlers* techniques, one we'll be suggesting in a wide variety of contexts. Getting your children used to the idea of waiting until a certain time arrives will teach them that the world doesn't revolve around their wants, and that there is a time and a place for everything. Keeping to a schedule not only helps the adult to maintain a reasonable order to the day, but also helps the toddler to feel that life runs according to a predictable rhythm, rather than being haphazard, scary, out of control.

2. Take into account your child's metabolism. Some kids have a faster metabolism, which means that they get hungry sooner after a meal. If that's the case, rather than plan for three large meals a day, you might be better off serving four or five very light meals, with appropriate snacks spaced out evenly throughout your child's wak-

ing hours. The downside to this solution is that the at-home parent or caregiver must spend more time in the kitchen and take time to plan snacks that are healthy. You don't want to just shove a bag of chips at a hungry child and say, "Here's your snack." You'll also need to keep an eye on serving sizes at mealtimes, to make sure that your child's light meals are indeed smaller than before; otherwise your child could easily end up having three big meals a day, plus two more light ones, plus frequent snacks. The transition to a lighter but more frequent eating schedule should be made in slow increments, so that the child doesn't feel suddenly deprived or jolted by the change.

3. Assuming you can cure a child of whining for between-meal snacks (by not responding positively to his demand to be fed), then go ahead and provide food upon request—but retain control of what the snack will be. Whenever your child says, "I want candy" or "I want ice cream," you reply, "Okay, you can have a little something now. Here is what we have"—and then you name only a few choices that are nutritionally sound. We recommend offering those big, flat, round, rice crackers—they're low-fat, with a decent amount of fiber, are reasonably filling, and you can get them in a wide variety of flavors, one of which your toddler is bound to like. Another good choice is popcorn without butter or with just a few squirts of a low-fat spray margarine. Keep bags of those pre-washed baby carrots on hand. (You can never eat too many carrots! And here's an added tip: When frozen, they make good teething objects for sore gums.) Or trying giving your toddler a clementine, which you've started to peel. He'll have fun tearing the rest of the peel off, and separating the sections. Clementines are not only nutritious but they're seedless, juicy, and sweet. Or how about an apple cheese sandwich? Just cut two full-circle slices off an apple, cut the peel off the edges, and put a slice of American cheese in between. Just as important as offering yummy, healthy food is making sure that the unacceptable choices are hidden away. You don't want your toddler rejecting the apple you've just washed and cut in favor of the box of cookies left plainly in view.

4. Always offer a healthy drink with the snack. Milk is good (2 percent or lower for children over age one). Chocolate milk is a bet-

ter bet than fruit juice, and fruit juice is better than soda. Water drinking is a good habit to encourage when the weather is hot, because it hydrates without filling your child up with empty calories. In general, drinking while eating is a good practice, because it helps your body to recognize the "full" feeling sooner, instead of wanting to eat and eat and eat.

5. Very important—make sure your child is not asking for food out of boredom. Active kids don't have time to sit and snack all day. The worst habit to get into is to serve snacks to kids who are parked in front of the TV or VCR. That gets them in the habit of expecting to eat while seated for long periods of time. A good rule is that snacks or meals must always be consumed in the kitchen or dining room. That way eating brings about a break in an activity, and most children have to be really hungry to interrupt their playtime for food. Keeping eating confined to the table also makes it easier for the grown-ups to keep the house clean.

If none of these ideas helps your child to cut down on snacking, or complaining about hunger, then a talk with your child's pediatrician is in order. He or she will probably run some tests to rule out some physical cause for his constant hunger.

What *not* to do: *Never attempt to put your child on a diet without your pediatrician's explicit instructions.* A toddler's electrolyte levels can all too easily get out of balance when food intake changes abruptly.

Tonya's not yet three, but she's already too big for her high chair. Still, I don't think she's ready to sit in a regular chair at the table. She's just too fidgety to sit still, and she just ends up getting down and wandering off. What other options should I try?

The obvious answer is a booster on a regular chair, but be sure to get one that has a safety strap to prevent her from sliding off onto the floor. The strap also reinforces the idea that the child is not in control of when to leave the table; the adults are. However, you should keep in mind that once your child is done eating and has started to squirm and try to extract herself from the booster, she's probably reached her limit of table-sitting time, and you should release her to a safe play area. There's nothing to be gained from forcing a toddler to last the length of an adult meal in a seated position. It just means frustration for the toddler and constant scolding from the adults.

You may not need to go out and buy a separate booster if your high chair is adjustable for height. Look under the seat where the legs attach to see if you can lower the seat level and then remove the tray and pull your toddler right up to the table.

A different, but equally workable approach is to increase the separateness of your toddler's seating arrangement, rather than include her at the grown-ups' table. That is, buy her a toddler-sized table and chair set. Parents who do this tend to serve their small children a separate, earlier meal. For example, you could set the toddler's dinnertime at 5:30, with a simple, quick main course of bow tie pasta with butter and parmesan cheese, while the adults sit down at 8:00 for a meal of pasta primavera (made from the bow ties set aside from the batch cooked earlier, and mixed with vegetables in a primavera sauce). The advantages of such an arrangement are threefold:

1. Your toddler will enjoy a greater sense of independence during dinner.
2. The adults' dinner can be slower-paced and uninterrupted by the need to correct the toddler's behavior at the table, deferring battles over table manners until the toddler years are past and children are school-age and motivated to learn so that they do not appear awkward and uncool in front of their friends.
3. One spouse can get the toddler ready for bed while the other prepares the adult meal. If both of you are efficient at your jobs, your toddler may even be down for the night by the time you are ready to eat at 8:00.

What *never* works: the old telephone-book-on-the-chair means of boosting the toddler up to adult table height. Your Yellow Pages directory may be thick enough, but its paper cover is too slick to be safe.

A GREAT DINING TIME-SAVER FOR TWO-CAREER PARENTS

When neither parent has time to cook a creative meal for themselves, let alone think up tempting recipes for their kids, it's time for outside help. More and more meal services these days are available for time-squeezed working parents. You may hire a personal chef who comes to your house two or three times a week and prepares several days' worth of meals that need only be microwaved before serving. Or you may prefer a home-cooked meal delivery service that lets you order precooked, reheatable dinners to be delivered at a fixed time daily, selected from a menu faxed to you a week in advance. Your meal-time relief may be simply to call for pizza delivery on Mondays, and Chinese food on Thursdays. Your city or town may also have a company such as Take-Out Taxi or The Butlers that provides you with a multipaged booklet of menus from many different types of restaurants; you call the company to order the meals you prefer, and a delivery person goes to the restaurant to pick up the food and bring it to your door. With Internet access, you can get the same service online in many major metropolitan areas through Food.com or Kozmo.com, among others. This is a burgeoning field of business, and new choices are becoming available everyday.

All of these options are more expensive than cooking a meal yourself, but if time is money and you have too little of the former but are making a sufficient amount of the latter, then we say great! Enjoy playing with your little ones for a while instead of shooing them out from under your feet as you juggle hot pots and dishes.

I'm sorry to say it, but my child has already got the junk food habit. He thinks the three major food groups are candy, chips, and soda. Should I try to wean him slowly off the junk food habit, or cut him off cold turkey?

Neither one. There's a third option, which is to continue to offer these items, but judiciously, meaning at the right time and in the right place. We think it's fine to enjoy a special treat now and again. Not everything has to be good for you. Some things are just yummier than others, and there's no use trying to pretend otherwise. You must make clear, however, that a child can't have cake instead of a balanced meal, but he may have it for dessert—after he has eaten a fair portion of his main course.

Outings may be another time to loosen up, nutritionally speaking. It's easier to pick up a bag of chips from a vendor at the zoo than to have to pack cut-up vegetables in baggies. Of course, snack-sized boxes of raisins are easy to grab and stick in a diaper bag, and if your toddler loves them, by all means, try that first.

When you enter a convenience store or come upon a vendor's cart and your child asks for a treat, try this: "How about an ice cream or a frozen fruit bar?" The first choice has some calcium and protein, while the second choice is lower in fat than most other goodies, and may even have a few vitamins in it. If the answer is, "No, I want a bag of chips," then offer to buy pretzels instead (they're not as fatty, and many toddlers like them as well or better than chips). When soda is the request, offer to buy an orange juice or a milk shake.

Note: If your children haven't yet tried soda, we say your best course is to pretend that it's an illegal drug. We see no reason to let toddlers have even a taste. Soda has zero nutritional benefit, and takes them away from other drinks that really are good for them (mainly milk), and the fizziness may upset their tummies. Even worse, many sodas contain caffeine, a stimulant that does nothing good for young bodies and may do some harm. Soda also contains phosphorus, which interferes with the absorption of calcium.

Since a toddler can't pop the top of a can by himself, the only way he'll get started on the soda habit is if an adult pours it for him;

so let your friends and relatives know right away that you have a no-soda-for-kids policy.

Once your child has a taste for soda and junk food, he will chafe at not being allowed to have it on demand. Here's where you get sneaky. You start setting what sound like reasonable conditions. You say, "Sure, you can have a candy bar," in exchange for a promise to go to bed on time. The toddler of course promises, but when bedtime comes around, will forget all about it. Then you bring up the fact that you paid him in advance with a candy bar, and that serves as a spur to keeping his part of the bargain.

Some child psychologists say that using special treats can be very effective, both as a reward after-the-fact for specific good behavior, or as something to be withheld in case the child fails to follow through. Many parents, too, say they would never have accomplished toilet training without the promise of M&M's as an incentive (a handful for each time a child makes pee-pee, a whole packet for a poop). Others argue that junk food is a poor motivator, and that children are better off learning to do what's expected of them for its own sake, because it's the right thing to do. You may want to discuss these issues with your spouse first before deciding whether or not to use candy and other treats as a reward. In addition, we urge you to consider your own child's personality and attitudes toward special snacks so that if you decide to go ahead, you can dole out the reward in the way your child finds most motivating.

If you take your child off junk food completely and try to ban it from your house, you must be prepared to get rid of your TV, ban visits to other houses, and move to an ascetic commune in the middle of nowhere. For everyone else in Middle America, junk food is here to stay—so the sooner we learn to exercise judgment and moderation about it, the better for our health.

THREE TIPS TO HELP YOU TAME THE JUNK FOOD MONSTER

• Let the dentist be the junk food police officer. The first time you take your child in to see the dentist, ask your dentist to explain in clear, simple language the harm that too many sweets can do to small teeth. Children tend to take seriously what they hear from authority figures in white coats.

• Don't take toddlers shopping with you if you can possibly avoid it. And when you have no alternative (no spouse or sitter to keep an eye on them while you shop), keep completely away from the candy aisle, the sugared cereal aisle, the cookie aisle, the chips and packaged snacks aisle. Wave your shopping list under their noses and insist that you have time only to look for the specific things you came to buy. When checking out, get in the lane with the CANDY-FREE CHECKOUT sign hanging overhead (many supermarkets these days now offer parents at least one such lane per store).

• Get your kids hooked on some nutritious snack that they can have every time they ask for it, without a fight. String cheese, raisins, grapes (cut in half vertically for kids younger than four), dried fruit-and-nut mix, yogurt in single kid-sized servings, cinnamon toast or low-fat toasted bagel bits are some of the choices that may convert your junk food addict into a better, healthier snacker.

CHAPTER

4

Giving Things Up

Thumbs, pacifiers, bottles, blankies, and stuffed bears—they're so cute and so loved, and they make our children feel so warm and fuzzy inside. Why should we even think of making them give up these things? A few possible reasons:

- Because it's easier to get them to give up something now, at two, than later at, say, six or seven . . . or seventeen.
- Because a baby at eleven months with a thumb in its mouth may be adorable, but at eleven years, it's pathetic.
- Because sooner or later your child is going to be in a setting where someone else makes the rules, and one of those rules is going to be "No teddy bears in school."
- Because your child's dentist has warned you that if you continue to allow your child to fall asleep with a bottle of milk or juice, he'll lose all his baby teeth to "nursing bottle caries."
- Because you're sick and tired of hearing your mother-in-law say, "When are you going to take that plug out of her mouth?"
- Because her preschool teacher suggested that your child would become more verbal if she gave up her pacifier.

So now you've decided to wean your child away from the beloved habit—how are you going to do it? Cold turkey? That seems so cruel. In small, subtle increments? But will that really work? And what should you say to your child about the changes you have in store? Or should you say nothing, and wait until the child first notices that the pacifier is missing?

We have some answers to these and other questions from parents who have managed to make their own children give up something with success—and from some who barely survived some terribly trying times.

My daughter is four and she still needs her "passy." Relatives say, "When are you going to take that plug out of her mouth?" We're really afraid when she starts kindergarten next year she'll still have it. Last year she was in half-day nursery school, just three hours a day, and was okay without it, but next year she'll be in school till 3 o'clock, with a midday nap time, and she's never even tried to lie down to rest without it.

There are two possible approaches you can take. Which you choose depends on how much time you have and how well you think your child would fare under one or the other. They are: *Cold Turkey* and *Slow, Incremental Steps*.

Cold Turkey works when a child is self-motivated, or can become motivated with a little encouragement from adults, to give up the pacifier for a logical reason. It's most likely to succeed with an adventurous child who isn't afraid of being a big girl, who has already taken some other important steps toward independence (such as successful toilet training or learning to dress herself). A prerequisite is a child who can talk well—at least well enough to express her basic thoughts and feelings, and listen to and understand a logical explanation.

With a child fitting this description, you do a lot of explaining before the arrival of the big day (you could call it "I Don't Need a Passy Day"). You pick a date that has some significance to your child (if you can manage it). It may be a half-birthday—say, four and a half. Or Valentine's Day—because that's a day you get candy to suck on and give up sucking on a rubber plug—or try Arbor Day, and turn that into the day that you plant the pacifier in a hole in the ground, and then plant a new tree over it. Start talking about the day you've picked about two weeks ahead of time.

Work up a number of rousing festivities for the big day. You could start with some special music—a John Philip Sousa march around the house with band instruments playing. Then make breakfast a super-special treat: try whipped cream on the strawberries on her cereal, or special pancakes. After a fun morning out someplace your child suggests, lunch can be yet another child-picked delight.

But at some point during the afternoon of this special day you get to the main event: The Handing Off of the Pacifier. She gives, you receive. In exchange you bestow upon her a Certificate of Graduation from the Pacifier-Dependent School of Thought, printed in fine calligraphic style on a piece of yellowed parchment and bound with satin ribbon (or some similar token that you have devised).

Optional: For those who think a paper scroll or a homemade trophy won't be enough of an incentive, go ahead and give her a more substantial material reward as well (that is to say, a nice, big toy).

Now you take the pacifier you've been given and you put it in a box. You may do something special with it, such as bury it in a tree-planting hole or put it in a keepsake box with her first pair of shoes and a lock from her first haircut. Don't throw it out. When you trash something that you know has meant a great deal to your child, you send the message that her feelings for the surrendered item were trash to you, too. No amount of logic or attempts to explain will convince her otherwise.

On that long, hard first night without her "passy," you might want to let her stay up later than normal, doing something exciting, something that will tire her out. Instead of putting her to bed in the usual way, try rocking her to sleep, just this once. (But don't ever rock a child to sleep three or more nights in a row: it's entirely too habit-forming!)

Let her verbalize how much she misses it (okay, we actually mean, "let her whine about it"), without once reminding her that it was a baby thing. Just nod and say you know how hard it is to give up something so special, but add, you've done it yourself, and you know she can, too. Name a few other children you know who have done it, as well; if you don't know them personally, they can be hypothetical, based on your knowledge of the fact that every year lots of children give up pacifiers, just as she's has done this day.

But don't listen endlessly, or she'll think it's all right to stay stuck on the subject, day after day. After the first five or six times, change the subject, or look bored. Try to keep her distracted, too busy to obsess about her loss. Get her involved in a discussion on some other topic of special interest to her. One of the main handicaps for the pacifier-using child is that she can't speak freely with a perpetually plugged mouth. Now is the time for her to discover that she can talk, sing, and play games with you unobstructed, as she could never do before.

Now, if you don't think your child is emotionally tough enough to make a clean break, or if she's not verbal enough to understand the greater purpose being served, then follow the second method.

Cut back on pacifier use in *Slow, Incremental Steps*. This approach is designed to cause minimal disturbance, and is best suited to a child too young to notice (or at least verbalize objections to) your gradual introduction of restrictive rules.

The first rule to introduce is that pacifiers are for home use, not for outings. You may give a reason for the new rule if you think it will be understood; that is, because the pacifier keeps dropping and there's no place to wash it off. In the beginning you may keep an exception for times when the child has to take a nap someplace other than home, or suffers an especially nasty cut, scrape, or other misfortune.

Go a couple of weeks to a month with the new rule in place, until she can't remember what things were like back when she had that pacifier available to her, twenty-four/seven.

Now you're ready for Rule Number 2: No sucking while walking around. The pacifier is only for when she's lying down, at naptime and at bedtime. Again, come up with some half-brained reason to help convince her to resign herself to her fate. You can tell her that it's important for her to be able to answer quickly sometimes, and therefore she should not have a pacifier in her mouth, blocking her speech.

Let a few more weeks pass. You're not under much outside pressure anymore, because no one sees your child sucking on the pacifier, except the few who put her down for naps or put her to bed at night.

Now for the third and final step: taking the pacifier away altogether. There are three common ways to accomplish the deed. The easy way out is to find a relative or friend willing to do it for you. If there's a grandparent who's been nagging you about your child's pacifier habit, let him or her be the bad guy. Send the child for a sleepover visit, but "forget" to pack her pacifier. Once she's there and realizes she doesn't have it, she'll accept the fact that there's nothing that can be done. Because sleeping at the grandparents' house is already such a strange, different experience, she'll have much to occupy her thoughts besides the absence of her sucking device. She may well have a hard time falling asleep—but at least she won't associate the difficulties exclusively with the loss of her pacifier. When you've got her back home, tell her how proud you are of her for sleeping without her "passy," and that you're sure she can keep it up. Hold a firm line when she dissents.

To accomplish the same end without sending your child away from home, arrange for the pacifier to drop from sight. Wait until your child goes to find it, and then say these lines: "Gee, where did it go? You know, I was pretty sure I saw it here a short while ago . . . Well, why don't you try going to bed without it? I bet you can do it."

To increase the odds that she'll accept your challenge, you might want to mention—and have on hand—a prize to offer her if she wins. (Winning means falling asleep without a pacifier and waking up in the morning in one piece.) Do your best to choose something you know will be a strong incentive for your child to try to win, and you'll certainly help to ease the pain of the loss.

Our third and final option relies on the cooperation of your child's dentist. Some pediatric specialists keep a bin bearing the label: LEAVE PACIFIERS HERE. Others are willing to play the anti-pacifier role when parents request it. Discuss the problem in advance with your child's dentist to find out whether you are in sync on both the timing and the explanation your child will receive about the visit. Then set up an appointment, which for the pacifier will be a one-way trip. You may find that your child can adjust far more easily to something an outside expert says is necessary than to that same instruction coming from you, the loving parent.

What *not* to do: Never let a dentist spring the "Leave Pacifier Here" bit on your unsuspecting child without discussing the whole plan carefully with you in advance. There are dentists who figure it's up to them to protect kids' teeth, and that parents will thank them afterward for their intervention. We think that may be a quick, sure way to get rid of a pacifier, but the cost, in terms of loss of parental authority, is simply too high.

One final question answered: If you're worried that your child will quickly substitute thumbsucking for the missing pacifier, we say don't be. A child over age two will generally find the feel of a thumb too different to make the switch. If a child under age two is forced to give up his pacifier, he may discover the joys of thumb-sucking, but then, he's still young enough to have a strong, instinctive need to suck. We believe there's value in that. It's only after the permanent teeth start to come in, at age five or six, that strong, regular sucking may have ill effects. If that's the case, you'll be interested in the question-and-answer set that follows.

*A*lison *is three and sucks her thumb so hard every night she has a thick ridge around the joint. Should we start discouraging this activity, and if so, how?*

Don't worry about that ridge, it's perfectly normal, and it will go away when she quits being a thumbsucker. (If it looks really raw and has breaks in the skin, that's different, and in that case, let her pediatrician have a look at it.)

Now as to whether and when to discourage thumbsucking: We understand well why parents worry about it, because we had a four-year-old daughter who was a confirmed thumb addict, and we were worried, too. But an older, wiser couple we met on the playground advised us not to make a big deal about it, because in most cases (so they said) kids will give it up on their own. And true to those words, Karen did give up the thumb, shortly before her fifth birthday.

However, you probably have seen (as we have) older kids, age six and seven, and even eight or nine, who walk around with their thumbs in their mouths. And you can't help but think: What if my child *doesn't* stop sucking at four, or at five? What if she's the exception. . . .

So, if the prospect of having a thumbsucker in the midchildhood years seriously unhinges you, you might want start by gently planting the idea that thumbsucking isn't the most attractive behavioral trait, and that it's better confined to private time, like just before bedtime.

Your daughter probably has a tendency to suck when she's hurt, tired, or cranky, and so be extra patient and understanding when the circumstances warrant. You definitely do *not* want to scold or tease her when she puts her thumb in her mouth, but do try to engage her in conversation, and then when she replies with her thumb in her mouth, say: "Sweetie, nobody can understand you when you talk with your thumb in your mouth. You have to take it out to tell me what's wrong."

Make sure she understands, too, that she can come to you or other adults in her life for a comforting hug and kiss whenever she's upset about something. Of course, she'll need to put *both* of her arms around you for a real hug, which requires her, again, to take her thumb out of her mouth.

If your child's dentist has a light, engaging manner with young patients, you can also enlist him or her to provide additional, medical reasons for cutting back on thumbsucking. As soon as the baby teeth start to loosen, the permanent teeth, even before they're visible, are already inside the gum, lining up in their positions. The constant action of the thumb against the roof of the mouth does affect the way they come in. A small child can't really digest the significance of thumbsucking or care that much into the future about her bite alignment, but just to have the dentist raise the concern tells the child there's a real reason not to suck. It's not just a weird grown-up notion that somebody invented to trick children out of a good thing.

At three, and at four, these occasional observations should be enough for your child to absorb the idea that thumbsucking eventually should be abandoned—and it will be, in due course.

Past age five, you might want to step up your campaign just a notch. Require your child to confine thumbsucking to the house, and later on, just at bedtime. (Follow the Slow, Incremental Steps approach used to end pacifier use.)

Past the age of six you have a school-age child, subject to murderous peer pressure about anything perceived as babyish, which thumbsucking indisputably is. You have very little control over the situation at this point, because despite the best efforts of teachers to put a stop to the teasing and torment that other children dish out, there will always be a few meanies who reject the message. If your child is old enough to be the object of schoolyard bullies but still won't give up the thumbsucking that sets them off, your concern goes far beyond the fact that your child still has this habit; you'll want to seek help in dealing with your child's overall social situation, and soon. A child psychologist can help you discover whether your child is feeling isolated and threatened by the larger world around her, and if that turns out to be the case, work on the more serious, underlying adjustment issues (of which continued thumbsucking is undoubtedly just a symptom).

You notice we did *not* recommend the Cold Turkey method that we suggested for giving up pacifiers. That's because it won't work in this case: Thumbs are always there, and no trick will enable you to hide them or render them inaccessible.

What about coating the thumb with a nasty-tasting substance or covering it with a bandage? We say don't. These measures are mainly punitive, and turn the thumb into a sort of forbidden drug. As soon as the bad stuff is gone, the allure is even more intense. Also, now you've made the thumb into a battleground, and since she has the home field advantage (it is, after all, part of her body), she's bound to win.

What might help: incentives and rewards for giving up thumb-sucking. For little girls who like dressing fancy and looking grown-up, promise to do her nails as soon as she shows she can go a week without thumbsucking. You have a clear rationale for this plan, because nail polish always flakes off, and even small amounts can be harmful if they ended up in the mouth of a thumbsucker. (Never paint the nails of a child under age three, except with nontoxic play nail polish.) Let your daughter pick a glittery polish or even ten different shades, one for each finger—or buy those kids nail-art books that include stickers and ornaments for your child's fingernails.

For boys or for girls who don't care about looking fancy, think about what sort of incentive might work best, given your own child's personality and motivations. Rewards generally work best when they bear some obvious relation to the problem to be solved. So, for example, if you think your child might like a set of finger paints, you could say, "I'd like to get you a set of finger paints, but you need to be done with thumbsucking first. Just let me know when you think you're ready to try to give it up, and I'll have the paints waiting for you."

My son is getting ready to start preschool. He's been really nervous about it, and we were doing our best to reassure him that it would be fun, when we received a letter from the school detailing their policies about lunch, the car line, nap time, and various other matters—among them, the request that children leave their favorite toys at home. But Zack has never been anywhere new without his old standby, Kangy-Kangaroo, to keep him company. How do I break the sad news to him that he's going, but Kangy isn't?

We're thinking you might be better off to break the sad news to the director of the school that you're withdrawing your application. We strongly believe that where children younger than four are concerned, these "transitional objects" (child psych-speak for teddy bears, blankies, and other "loveys") do far more good than harm. They provide reassurance, continuity, and a feeling of being loved and protected that help children cope when they're in a new situation. But that's not just our personal opinion. The April 2000 issue of the *Journal of Consulting and Clinical Psychology* published a study showing that children who had a favorite blanket with them during a doctor visit were noticeably calmer and less anxious than those who did not. In fact, children who had a blanket to hold but did not have a parent present during the examination were as calm as those who had a parent, but no blanket.* So why shouldn't your son have the benefit of his Kangy?

Definitely raise these concerns with the director of the school. Find out the reasoning behind the school's policy, and then work to come up with a compromise that would meet both the school's and your son's needs. Maybe the children can be told that their special toys may accompany them to school but must remain safely inside their backpacks. Perhaps the kids could be allowed to take the toy out and give it a hug whenever they get a boo-boo.

If you make it clear to the director of the school how important it is to your child to have his stuffed animal on hand—and that it's even more important to you to have your son's feelings acknowledged—the "no stuffed animals" rule may be bent in your son's favor.

However, if the reason given for the ban is that preschool-age children are too old to need to lug a toy around all day, then you may not get anywhere with your efforts to compromise, and in that case, you must make a decision: Is this the right preschool for your child? Assuming you conclude that it has other benefits that more than compensate for this rule—for example, it's located in the same building where you work, or you've been given a tuition subsidy for that school only, or you simply can't afford to lose the deposit that you had to put down upon acceptance—then you need to find a way to ease the blow for your son.

One approach that might work well is to suggest to him that Kangy is just too special to be put at risk for getting lost between school and home. You might add that the other children would be sure to see how wonderful Kangy is, and want to hold him and even

---

* Study results summarized in *The New York Times,* May 2, 2000.

take him home themselves. They might feel jealous if they didn't have such a special animal themselves. This sort of logic should be within the comprehension of even a two-year-old.

Part of the morning ritual before going to school should be to have him give Kangy a good-bye kiss and place him lovingly in a special spot to wait for his master's return—guarding the door to your son's room, or perhaps safe on his pillow in his bed. You may be surprised to find how receptive he is to the idea of having a special good-bye ritual with Kangy each day.

On the other hand, he may still balk at spending a full school day or half-day without the protective presence that he's grown used to. In that case a Kangy substitute may do the trick. Try this: Take a very clear close-up photo of his love object and have it laminated for longer wear. Give it to him to keep in his jacket pocket or in his backpack. The school should have no objection, and he will be able to take it out and sleep with the picture during nap time or touch it for reassurance whenever he feels stressed.

One thing *not* to do: Blame the preschool for the separation. Don't say something like, "It would be okay with me if you brought Kangy to school, but the teacher said you can't." That will only give him negative feelings about his teacher, or about the school.

Whatever solutions you try, it's important for your son to see how hard you *are* trying. Then, regardless of the outcome, your child will be reassured that you understand the intensity of his feelings and take them seriously. He'll believe you're on his side, and are not part of an effort to deprive him arbitrarily of something that he loves, which in turn will help him to be open to your suggestions for ways to get through the school day without the love object. If, on the other hand, you appear to belittle his attachment—if you call the stuffed animal a "baby thing" and suggest it's no big deal to do without—he'll get the message that you are clueless, that you just don't "get" it. He'll reject any solutions you come up with, just as an astronomer would reject an observation about the solar system from someone who believed that the world was flat.

I know we should have started training our daughter to use a cup much earlier, but, well, at the time it seemed so messy and inefficient . . . watching my one-year-old struggle to drink (even when we put on a "sippy" lid) just made me wonder whether it was worth the hassle . . . so, to make a long story short, here she is, just past her third birthday and still drinking (quite happily, on her part—unhappily for my part) from a bottle. Now every time I hand her a cup, she just pushes it away and says, "No cups! I want my bottle!" So, to avoid a long, drawn-out argument, I usually give in. Meanwhile, my neighbor's daughter (the one who was toilet-trained before two!) is already drinking from a cup with no sippy lid at all! Any ideas for how to get out of this cycle?

First of all, ignore that neighbor with the precocious youngster! Stop focusing on what somebody else's kid can do. It'll just drive you crazy, and for all you know, that kid by the age of thirteen will be a total burnout from having to be the first and best at everything since infancy, while yours will just be coming into her own.

But as for the problem of the here-and-now: You are right not to fight a battle over every drink she takes. Still, you do want to win this war eventually, so there has to come a time when you stand firm.

We speak from personal experience here (and we are among the very few parenting "experts" humble enough to admit that our own children for a time had us hog-tied over simple things such as bottle devotion and night waking). But we did eventually prevail, and with no lasting trauma to any of us—at least that's what we're thinking right now. Who knows what recriminations may pour out on a therapist's couch many years on—but then that will be grist for some future book! Anyway, here's what worked for us:

First, we decided upon the approach to take. Since our daughter was, like yours, also over three, she was old enough to have some concept of time and dates, and she knew more or less how the calendar worked. So we decided upon a specific date on the calendar to stage our "Bye-bye, Bottles" ceremony. We told her about five days in advance of this upcoming Big Event and Celebration, and we planned a party around it. Every day, we counted another day off the calendar. By the time the date rolled around, she was actually excited and looking forward to the festivities.

The appointed morning arrived. We brought her down to the kitchen. We poured her a ceremonial Last Bottle. We screwed on the nipple and the ring and handed it to her with a flourish. We took a Polaroid picture (for her to keep) of her last sucks from a rubber nipple.

When at last she was done, we let her gather up all the bottles in the house and throw them all into a big, green, plastic trashbag. She helped tie up the bag with a twist tie and she carried it by herself out to the garbage can at the side of the house. We had picked the day of garbage pickup to do the deed, so that she would see the truck arrive to take away the trash; that way, if she later changed her mind and demanded to have her bottles back, we could say, "But you saw the trashmen take all the trash away. The bottles are gone and there's no way to get them back!" (Those intent on frugality may not wish to actually throw out several dollars' worth of plastic bottles, nipples, caps, and rings, and in that case you might want to sneak out and retrieve the garbage bag.)

When our bottle paraphernalia was all gone, we brought out a cake, blew horns and unraveled streamers, and all drank from matching cups, parents and child together. Our child was enjoying all this attention and feeling very proud of herself, drinking from her new grown-up cup all day.

I can already imagine that you, as the parent of a confirmed bottle addict, are saying to yourself, "Sure, that worked during the *daytime*. But what about at *night?*"

And yes, right before she went to sleep, she did say, "But I neeeeed my bottle nowwwwww!"

And we answered, with false cheerfulness, "Here's your special grown-up cup—you can have your bedtime drink of water from that" and then had to listen to twenty minutes of pleading and sobs as it suddenly dawned on her that all that hoopla wasn't enough to have traded for having given up her precious bottle *for life*.

And it wasn't just the first night either. After she cried herself to sleep that night, the next night was only slightly less miserable. But each subsequent night was a noticeable improvement over the one before. The days were all fine, as she had already come to under-stand that being seen by other children drinking from a bottle at age three was embarrassing. She had learned to do her bottle drink-ing at home—in the closet, so to speak. By the end of four or five days she had stopped asking for her bedtime drink in a bottle. For the next couple of months, especially when she was stressed or un-happy over something, she would tell us that she really, *really* missed her bottles. And we would murmur (with a mask of sympa-thy covering our real relief at being rid of those darned bottles for-ever), "Yes, sweetie, I know!"

Of course, the ceremonial ending won't work for everyone. The most common stumbling block is the presence of a younger sibling. How can you get rid of all the bottles in the house when you've got an eight-month-old who still needs them? Furthermore, any appeal to your child to act like a big kid will probably only incite sibling ri-valry. As hard as it is to give up something you love, imagine how much worse it is to watch your younger brother or sister continue to enjoy your now-forbidden fruit, in your parents' loving arms, with all their warmth and approval. It's practically a prescription for the child to refuse to give in.

That's not to say it's impossible. We have some ideas that you may want to consider. First, what we'll call the "delayed-dual" ap-proach. That's our fancy way of saying, delay the whole process until you can do both your kids at once. Start introducing your eight-month-old to the sippy cup right now. Let your older child know that the time is fast approaching when both children will go to cup drinking only, at the same time. The final date you choose will be more determined by your younger child's readiness than by your older child's. But when that time comes (say, when the younger child reaches the first birthday, or maybe a month or two later), hold your bottle farewell event, and switch both of them over to cups, or one to sippy-topped cups, the other to plain cups) at the same time.

For those who can't (because the younger child is a newborn) or won't (on the grounds that it's too much work to clean up the spills of two novice cup drinkers at once), here's another approach. Let's call it what it is, bluntly: bribery. Find out what the older child most desires in the world. Promise the present for a full weekend of not asking for a bottle. Follow through with the present, even if your child has slipped once or twice and complained.

Well, we finally got our son off the bottle (it was a hell of a struggle, though) and onto a sippy cup, but now it looks like we'll never be able to take off that top! I'm not sure we have the energy left to fight about this. Got any low-stress ideas?

What's wrong with letting him drink from a cup with a lid? (This response comes from Bill, not Peggy.) Adults drink from pop-top soda cans and we drink from water bottles with pull-up tops that are almost the same thing—so why hassle over it? If you're worried about how it looks to have your son still drinking from a sippy cup at five or older, then let him do it only in the privacy of your own home.

However, Peggy adds: Whoever is in charge of the washing up at your house may be tired of washing and putting away separate kiddie cups with lids. If that's the case, that parent has the right to say, the time has come for your child to learn to drink from a regular glass, just like everyone else in the house. Choose a method for getting rid of the sippy cups, either Cold Turkey or in Slow, Incremental Steps.

Also, keep in mind that there are more than two ways to get liquid from a container into a child. Besides regular glasses and sippy cups you can also serve drinks in the following array of vessels:

- Sports bottles and water bottles with pull-up spouts
- Cups with disposable, colorful, bendy straws
- Juice boxes or milk boxes with straws attached
- Lunchbox-style thermoses, decorated with favorite cartoon characters
- Half-pint milk cartons, letting the child drink directly from the spout

We think he'll enjoy learning to drink from each of these different openings. It will increase his confidence in handling liquids in all forms until he's finally able to drink with ease from any type of container opening, just like every other kid. By the time he's six or seven you'll forget completely that he ever took his time getting used to drinking from a plain old glass.

My three-year-old daughter wants to wear the same striped dress every single day. At first I thought it was a harmless whim, and just kept washing the dress and letting her wear it again. But now it's faded and starting to wear out. I've had to resew the hem all around, twice, and even if I could keep on fixing it, it's now two sizes too small for her. Yet whenever I suggest that she put on something else, she just cries "My stripey dress!" until I give in and let her wear it. Oh, and don't try suggesting that I buy her the duplicate dress in a larger size. I tried that, but the colors in her dress have faded so much from repeated washing that the new dress looks completely different and she says she hates the colors.

Yes, you are in a bind, all right, because buying the dress in a larger size was going to be the first of our suggested tricks. For those of you whose children are not yet quite so stuck on a unique piece of clothing, it's probably not too late to stock up on larger sizes.

We do have some other good ideas on how to handle this toughie, however, and they come straight from our six-year-old Claire, a devoted clothes lover. When she was three, she glommed on to her "strawberry dress" with exactly the same passion you describe between your daughter and her stripey dress. It's a long, painful saga, and I'll spare you all the false turns before the ending—but the tale does provide an instructive moral. Claire did get to *keep* her beloved strawberry dress . . . but just not keep on *wearing* it. It's now the garment of choice for her favorite, largest-size teddy bear, Tulip, who's just about toddler sized—and I must say it does look very becoming on Tulip.

We also let her keep another dress as a love object, and sometimes she still sleeps with it in her bed, clutching it like a blankie.

Perhaps the simplest solution is to let your daughter keep on wearing the dress, but only as a nightgown. If you don't mind sewing enough to maintain the seams, she might also be able to wear it as a regular clothing top, with shorts on underneath. This works best with boxy, T-shirt-style dresses.

If you're handy with a needle and thread, and if it's the skirt part of the dress that's the main problem while the top part is basically okay, why not try adding a new skirt and giving it a new life. (Let your daughter see a sketch and understand what's going to happen before you make any irrevocable cuts.)

Another, tougher approach is to wait until the child is out one day, and then make the worn-out item of clothing just happen to disappear. It could end up picked up in a clothing drive for charity, or it could "inadvertently" be included in a bag of hand-me-downs you're sending to a smaller, younger niece (but see the boxed story, "The Coincidental Dress," on page 88 for one mother's cautionary story.)

When an item disappears all of a sudden, the child has got to be very, very focused on it before he or she notices it's missing. That might be days or even weeks, especially if some new item of clothing can quickly become a substitute. It might even be never.

But suppose your child does ask you, "Where's my favorite pair of socks?" Possible answers include:

The deliberately vague: "Well, they were in your drawer yesterday. . . . Why don't you look for them?"

The fantastical: "Do you think maybe the dryer ate them? Or maybe the Sock Fairy came and took them to Fairyland to make sleeping bags for the fairies on their camp outs." (Note: If you're concerned that such tale-telling comes close to lying to your children, see the discussion on lying on page 123 of Chapter Five.)

Cold, hard reality: "They just got so worn out that I had to throw them out."

Which one to go with? We say, consider your child's personality carefully and try to predict how she might react to each approach.

We do caution, however, against the cold, hard reality path, unless you are sure that your child is mature enough—or not so attached to the missing items—to accept the loss with equanimity. Why? Some child psychologists warn darkly that when a parent gets rid of a loved object because it's no longer perfect in the adult's eyes, the child subconsciously begins to fret, "If my parents ever find fault with me, maybe they'll dump me in just the same way." Now, we suspect that there aren't many children who are that insecure, but you might not want to risk the possibility of raising such a fear, not when there are other solutions at hand.

One especially creative suggestion comes from a couple we know whose child developed an intense attachment to a pair of overalls. He kept wearing them until they were finally beyond patching. The parents knew better than to try to make the child give them up, yet they hated to let him go out looking like a victim of parental neglect. Then the mother got the brilliant idea of turning the overalls into a work of fabric art. She pinned them to a canvas and painted on or glued on various other childhood icons around this central subject, framed the collage, and hung it on the wall over the bed in her son's room. He was delighted with this unique tribute to his beloved overalls.

Another family we know saved lots of different scraps of fabric from their kids' favorite clothes over the years and worked pieces of each item into a family quilt. The result was a patchwork masterpiece, an instant heirloom which all three of their children (now teenagers) feel is part of their history. One day the grown kids will fight over which one gets it—but that will be a problem to be solved in some future book to be called *Outwitting Inheritance Rivals*.

THE COINCIDENTAL DRESS

My daughter Megan was so attached to her favorite denim jumper, she refused to acknowledge that she had outgrown it by several inches. It was still in fine shape so I was not about to throw it away. I figured the best thing to do was to wait until the nursery school put on their annual "white elephant" sale, and donate it to a good cause. Once it was no longer hanging in her closet, I figured, Megan would forget all about it.

The giveaway went smoothly, just as I'd expected. Weeks went by before Megan thought to ask what had happened to that dress. I gave a vague shrug and quickly changed the subject. Megan was easily distracted, and didn't get back to the subject, fortunately for me.

What I never expected was that it would turn up again—on somebody else. Megan had finished the nursery school program and had moved on to kindergarten, so why would I think she'd ever run across the toddler for whom the used item was bought? I hadn't considered the day camp scenario. In the summer program our kids have attended, children of different ages are mixed together for certain activities. Six-year-old Megan ended up in the same music class with the four-year-old who was wearing *her* favorite denim dress! I spotted the familiarly clad stranger on the playground the first day, even before the classes were assigned. What will I say to Megan when she asks me how that other child ended up with *her* dress? All day long I agonized over what was going to happen.

At three o'clock pickup time I was waiting by the door for the campers to be dismissed, wondering what would Megan think. And then she appeared . . . skipping out of the building hand-in-hand with the girl in the denim dress!

"Look, Mommy!" she yelled. "I made a new friend! Her name is Tara."

"That's nice," I said nervously.

"See," Megan pointed out. "She's got a dress *exactly* like that one I lost! She's going to ask her mommy if I can borrow it one day. We're going to be best friends!"

"Whew," I thought to myself, that was a lucky break. And I also thought—and I pass along this advice to any of you who are contemplating giving away a similarly loved piece of clothing—choose an overseas relief drive when you do!

—Laura M.
McLean, VA

*O̶ur daughter, at three, is a total TV addict. When this habit got
started, at around age one to one-and-a-half, we weren't worried.
TV and videos seemed so benign, a good way for her to spend
time quietly, without needing a lot of attention from us. But
now—all she wants to do when given the chance is watch TV.
She's hooked on that big purple dinosaur! (How I've come to hate
that irritating voice!) And then there's Blue's Clues. She's seen
every show so many times she's memorized all the clues before
they appear. It's so bad that, when we're on vacation, we can't
take her outside the hotel room, because it might interfere with her
TV-watching schedule. All she wants to do is sit in front of the box
and stare. Please don't tell us just to turn it off. We've tried that,
and we're sick of listening to her scream.*

Have you tried lying to her? (In Chapter Five, page 123, you'll
find an extended discussion about the good uses to which a little
parental dishonesty may be put—and why some parents refuse to
outwit their children by this means.) Seriously, it seems to us the
best way out of the box (is that a pun?) that you've gotten yourself
into.

On the first day of your anti-TV campaign, plan an all-day activity you know she will like. Say that you will be visiting a petting
zoo, or an amusement park, or heading off to the beach. When she
tells you that she would prefer to stay home and watch her show,
you tell her the show isn't on that day. You say that Barney has
gone on vacation, too.

This will make perfect sense to your child, because she has no
idea that Barney is a middle-aged man in a very hot, heavy suit, and
that he isn't performing his routines while she's watching. She'll accompany you on your planned outing, and have a good time, too.

Next time you want to go somewhere and she'd rather watch
TV, try it again. Steve, the detective on *Blue's Clues,* is "taking a
break" today. The *Sesame Street* gang are out to lunch just now. It
so happens (you tell her) that every time you have something
planned, the players on this or that show have something that's
keeping them busy, too.

Now, the day *will* come that your child wakes up to the truth that Daddy invented that business about Barney being away. Will that teach her that she can no longer trust Daddy to tell her the truth? Not at all! By the time she is old enough to realize that a talking, purple dinosaur isn't real, she'll also be old enough to appreciate the cleverness and sensitivity behind her father's ruse. Daddy didn't want his child whiling away the whole vacation because of some silly TV show. Only when she's a little older can she understand that there's more to life than watching TV. Rather than try to argue the point with a toddler, Daddy simply let her believe there was nothing on TV to miss. That belief enabled her to experience the no-Barney week with an open mind—and have a good time as a result. Now, having had a good time, she's found out for herself that watching Barney every day isn't a necessity of life after all.

BRIBERY, THE RIGHT WAY

Giving children rewards for doing what they are supposed to do in the natural course of events is, to put it mildly, a controversial parenting technique. We know lots of parents who are dead set against giving their children anything that smacks of bribery. If it's immoral in public life, they reason, it's bad for families, too. Besides which, it can quickly get out of hand, becoming an escalating spiral. The first time the child gets a reward for doing something he ought to have learned to do in the normal course of events, the next time he expects an even better reward for a similar feat, and the time after that he holds out for something better still. It's not too long before he's so spoiled that he won't agree to take on even the simplest task except for a bigger and better payoff. The child quickly becomes a master negotiator, setting the rates, controlling the agenda. And the parents end up manipulated—and poor.

You know this criticism has merit if you've ever seen a two-year-old tyrant ordering his parents around. The parents alternatively plead and cajole to get him to do something simple, and get rudely rebuffed until they begin to put forth offers of tribute: candy for this action, a special something else for that. They fawn like hapless supplicants before some medieval potentate, hoping to find something his majesty will find appealing enough to prevent the unleashing of his furious, destructive will.

The only sure way, say antibribery parents, to be sure not to end up in the same situation is to avoid taking the first step down that path. That is to say, never under any circumstances offer a child a bribe.

We admire this stance in principle, but we still offer bribes to our kids from time to time. Why? Because it works! But you do have to be *very* careful about choosing the right time to do it. And be warned, your child can and will try to raise the stakes on you, if he thinks he can squeeze just a little something extra out of you that way. It's true that the technique can rapidly become overused. You can expect your child to request a payoff at times when you have no intention of doing so. But all these risks and disadvantages can be managed, or even avoided entirely, if you stick strictly to the guidelines that we propose:

Each and every time you offer your child a bribe (or to use a more palatable term, a "material incentive for a desired action") you should:

• Define your terms well. Propose one specific thing in exchange for one specific act you want your child to perform.

• Set a time limit during which the deal is good. When you promise your child a dollar for cleaning up his room on Monday, he can't come back to you on Friday and say he's done it and expect to claim his prize.

• Use rewards *very* sparingly. Parents who dole out presents too frequently end up with children who have few wants left unfulfilled—and so it's harder to find something to serve as the spur to action.

• Reserve the use of rewards for those tasks that present

your child with a real challenge, not something he can learn to do in a snap. The reward tells him "thanks for putting in the extra effort to do this thing right."

• Rewards should never be given out for ordinary good behavior—which should be expected as a matter of course.

• Reward only positive behavior, not cessation of negative behavior. That is, the desired toy truck can be presented after your son has spent a week visiting his younger cousin and playing nicely with him, without any shoving, hitting, or other roughness. You don't give him anything for stopping a fight that he's already started.

• Be certain that your child knows that a reward is an *extra* benefit for behaving well and should never be the *only* reason for the desired action. In other words, tell your child you want to make sure he isn't just doing what you want for the bribe. You would want him to do what you say anyway, just because it's the right thing to do. If it becomes clear to you that the child cares a lot more about getting the reward than he does about earning your approval, it's time to find another parenting technique.

• Keep the reward small-scale. Disregard this rule and you will quickly end up spending ridiculous amounts of money on bigger and better toys.

• Try whenever possible to tailor the reward to the behavior sought. For example, when your child has successfully made the transition from bottle to cup, a good reward might be to let him choose a special Winnie the Pooh cup from the Disney catalog, or give him a cup with his name and picture on it.

• Avoid rewards that reinforce unwanted behavior. That is to say, don't give your child candy as a reward for eating all his vegetables, because that just underscores the idea that candy is the yummiest thing around, and vegetables are the complete opposite.

• Talk bluntly with your child about your use of rewards, keeping your language and explanations simple, geared to your child's level of comprehension. With a bright three- or four-year-old, you might even explain what the word "bribery" means, and why some parents think it's a bad idea. Tell your child that there are some times when you may be willing to offer a reward, but many more times when you expect him to cooperate just because you say he must. For example, you might offer him something for learning the names of all his relations who will be at the upcoming family reunion, but you would never, ever bribe him to sit in his car seat.

Follow these rules consistently, and you can expect your judiciously applied bribes to reap big payoffs in terms of toddler cooperation—but anytime you doubt that you're getting your money's worth, remember, there are plenty of other ways to outwit a toddler.

5

Why Can't You Behave?

The basic premise behind all of our *Outwitting Toddlers* techniques is that parents are generally smarter, faster, and more ingenious than their kids. But you need to believe this in order to apply our techniques effectively, and with conviction. You must accept yourself as an authority figure—which can be difficult for some of us ex-hippies, whose cars bear the bumper sticker QUESTION AUTHORITY. It's important to be in a clear, unconfused state of mind about your parental role, or else you will hesitate, stumble, and falter. If you doubt the importance of a self-confident mind-set, just pick up any military history to learn more about the necessity of strong leadership and high morale. You will find that whenever one side comes to perceive the enemy to be better-equipped, more cunning, and stronger-willed, that enemy has triumphed in the end.

"But parenting isn't a battle!" we know some of you will leap to point out. Yes—but it will soon become one if you allow the child to see himself or herself as the one in charge.

We seriously doubt there are any parents, anywhere, who *want* to let the child think he or she runs the house. The problem in many families is a far more insidious philosophy that sounds rather reasonable on paper; you'll find it set forth in the books and articles written by some notable parenting experts, Penelope Leach and T. Berry Brazelton among them. That philosophy is—if you will permit a two-sentence summary (which, of course, unfairly oversimplifies the argument)—as follows: Children are by nature very perceptive, intelligent creatures, who learn best when given maximum freedom to discover for themselves how to govern their own behavior. So parents should not be authoritarian, emphasizing rules and obedience, but instead, let them explore, let them express themselves, and find out on their own what works and what doesn't work best for them.

Following such expert advice, parents learn that they should intervene as little as possible in conflicts between siblings or sandbox rivals. Instead of issuing commands, they should always stop to explain why the child should do as the parent requests. Children are told they are due the same respect as adults, and that like adults, they should be able to make their own decisions and live with the consequences of their own mistakes.

We first encountered this childrearing theory in action when we went to pick up our daughter and her little friend from kindergarten. The not-quite-five-year-old girl saw the booster seat in the backseat of our minivan and promptly announced: "I don't have to ride in a booster." "But you do," Bill insisted (naively believing that all she needed was to hear a firm, adult voice to prod her to obey). But that got him nowhere. Apparently, no one had ever told her before that she had to do as an adult said, just because he was in charge. Bill started to argue with her, to give a logical explanation why it was unsafe for her to ride in a car using just the seatbelt designed for an adult—but that was time-consuming. She showed no deference to the grown-ups, instead, acting as if she believed she was the boss. However, behaving like a child, she threw a tantrum. It was clear that her parents had taught her that she could make her own decisions about where she would sit in their car.

After a few minutes of this fruitless negotiation, Bill realized there was no need to waste any more time. "Either you get into that booster," he told her, "or we don't go anywhere." He held the key to gaining her cooperation, he realized . . . that is to say, the car key. In a second, she yielded—crisis over. (At least as far as our encounter with her "independent spirit" was concerned. Who knows what things are like on a daily basis in that little girl's house?)

We've seen such dramas acted out in other places, too. At the playground one day we watched two three-year-olds engage in a heated argument. One was on the verge of tears; the other on the verge of hitting or throwing dirt. One of the moms was about to intervene—to talk with the kids, find out what the problem was, and perhaps mediate a solution. But the other mom held her back, saying, "Let them work it out." Work it out? Three-year-olds? If you'll excuse our being blunt: Three-year-olds just don't have enough common sense or emotional maturity to "work things out."

Yet another example: One couple we know let their children dictate the family's social life. The parents used to be close friends with another couple who had a child the same age as theirs, but their son said he didn't enjoy playing with the other kid all that much. Now the two families don't get together anymore.

There's something very wrong with this picture, we think.

Here are the places where children spend virtually all of their waking time: at school, with their friends, in front of a TV screen, and with their parents. From each of these sources they learn, they imitate, they shape their thoughts and actions. If parents deliberately downplay their own influence and their own standing as role models in the child's eyes, what are we left with? Who will take up the job of shaping their children's moral and social behavior?

Judith Martin, also known as Miss Manners, summed up the problem of parents disavowing parenthood this way: "All of this contributes to the odd notion that children are the best judges of what is good for them . . . they may well be the best judges in families who succumb to this notion."

For those of us who are still willing to assume the mantle of judgeship and who will set the rules and enforce standards that our children are bound to obey, the question remains: How can we preside wisely, fairly, to the benefit of all? Not everyone is qualified, and no one (except for those who become parents through adoption) has to undergo any sort of screening to have kids. What's surprising, given the circumstances, is the fact that most parents, inexperienced as they are, still manage to do a fairly decent job.

But we can all do better in some way or another. Sometimes all it takes is one little suggestion, one helpful tip from a parent who's been-there-done-that, to help us climb over that one stubborn stumbling block we've hit along the way. Maybe you're doing fine getting your child to eat a balanced diet, but it's that nightly battle over bedtime that has got you feeling wrung out at the end of the day. If you've come this far with us, we're assuming you're not one to surrender and just let the child set his or her own bedtime—that is, you haven't fallen for the notion that your child will naturally gravitate to the schedule that best serves his or her own needs (even if it leaves you half-witted from sleeplessness the next morning). You *do* want to set the schedule: you just don't want to come off as Captain Von Trapp (from *The Sound of Music*) in the process.

We look at *Outwitting Toddlers* the way Maria did—coming up with ideas that will have your kids singing as they straighten up and dancing to your merry tune. Okay, okay . . . that's the fantasy we have of what we'd *like* to accomplish. But we do think if you look for the most creative solutions and consider your child's own personality and skills as you try out the various techniques suggested here, you will not only find yourself becoming a more effective director of your child's development, but you—and your child—will find yourselves having a lot more fun.

And that's something almost every parent, no matter what their underlying philosophy, should believe in.

*M*y two boys are always fighting. Who's getting in the car first? Who gets to sit next to Daddy at dinner? Who has the biggest slice of cake? They start out arguing over trivial things and end up punching each other. How can I get them to make peace with each other?

First, they need to learn to keep the peace with you. It needs to be drummed into both of their little brains that violence is not acceptable *to you*. Anytime you see any hitting going on, regardless of "who started it," the hitter is in bi-i-i-ig trouble.

It's normal for siblings to argue and compete with one another, but it's not normal ("Not in *this* house, anyway!") for children to use force to try to get their way. Punishments should not be delayed, such as "grounding" which forbids some outing planned for the future, or depriving a child of the dessert to a meal that's hours away. Punishments need to be immediate and related directly to the offense, like sending them to separate parts of the house. (Note: Sending them to their separate rooms may not work, if their rooms are fun-filled havens of toys. If that's the case, choose a more austere location that allows the child to reflect without distraction upon the offensive nature of his actions. Better to make him sit still in a time-out chair in your own bedroom for five or ten minutes, where you can keep an eye on him and also be sure he's not making an early break for it.)

But before you dole out that sentence, the first and most important action to be taken in any instance of aggression is to make anyone who punched or hit (regardless of who punched first) apologize for doing so. If the apology is snide or insincere-sounding, ask the offender to think about his actions some more in isolation, and then apologize again with a better tone of voice.

Note: The universal kid's response to this is to whine, "I'm *not* using a tone of voice!" It's up to you to get the kid to understand that an apology only counts if those who hear it sense the meaning behind the words. If the child cannot muster any feeling of remorse right away, he needs a period of time alone to be given a chance later on to say he's sorry.

Once you've got your no-fighting policy set in stone, with punishments well known in advance for any infraction, then you can afford to take a long, fairly tolerant view toward arguments that remain on a verbal level. In general, we see it as an unproductive task for parents to get caught up in the *substance* of sibling feuding—especially in the early years when the triggering event may be something ridiculously trivial to an adult. When they're caught up in a hot contest over who gets to sit in one spot that is just a few inches away from an identical spot (as the adult sees it), all you need to do is point out that in the course of human of history, who sat where is not likely to be remembered. Then point to one seat and arbitrarily assign it to one child, and point to the other and order the other child to take it—and no arguing with Mommy or Daddy allowed.

Another approach is to announce flatly, "If the two of you don't end this argument in the next three minutes, *neither* of you gets to sit there"—and you take the disputed seat yourself. This technique works especially well when two children want to play with the same toy at the same time. They either figure out a way to take turns or else the toy vanishes for the next half hour or so.

On no account should a parent play the role of Solomon in these disputes over meaningless details. Do not let each child recount at length his list of grievances against his brother and tell you why his side should prevail. To do so is to legitimize the idea of arguing over trivialities; besides which your decision will always be viewed by the loser as fundamentally unfair. Discourage, as much as possible, any scorekeeping between the boys as to who got to play with the toy first last time, or whose turn it is to get into the car first this time. Otherwise, you will only perpetuate the argument.

Some simple tips that should help to forestall arguments:

• Assign the seats at the dinner table, in the car, in movie theaters, and so on. The parent-dictated seating arrangement should have some logical framework to give it an aura of legitimacy. For example, you assign the younger child the seat on the curb side of the car, on the safety-based rationale that the younger child needs to get out right on the sidewalk, while the older child has the patience to wait and get out of the car according to your instructions—either on the driver's side rear door when you say it's safe to do so, or by scooting over to exit through the rear passenger-side door.

• Seating at restaurants should follow a fixed pattern: for example, Mommy and Daddy at the ends of the table with the children at the sides, or in a booth, Mommy and Daddy together on one side with the children sitting opposite. (That should put an end to the jockeying over which child gets to sit with which parent.) The justifying logic is that the adults who form a couple are meant to sit together.

• "Because I said so" should be all the justification you need—at least until your kids reach thirteen or fourteen* and are seriously into questioning parental authority.

While these suggestions may enable you to solve an on-the-spot conflict, you also need a strategy to alleviate the rivalry between the siblings over the long haul. We advise you to get right to work indoctrinating your two boys in the belief that loyalty and tight bonds between siblings are central to your family's creed. During every squabble, the instant you hear the first insult flung, you remind them, "That's not the way we talk to each other in *this* family!"

Although young children aren't yet equipped to consider the long term, if they hear something repeated often enough, the idea sticks. Then, when they are old enough to comprehend the meaning, the notion is already firmly planted. Any time they treat each other badly, tell your children that it hurts you to see them acting this way. You had children not just for you and your spouse to love, but for them to love each other, and eventually the day will come when they really need each other's help. They'll be glad, then, to know that they can count on each other, because they learned to do so as children.

Come up with a few stories from your own childhood, to show your children what you mean—but only if your family serves as a good example. If you and your siblings used to fight like cats and dogs and never managed to build a warm, supportive relationship, then forget about this one—except possibly to express regret that you never learned to get along and wish you could have that part of childhood back. If you and your siblings had a good relationship but sometimes fought (as we all did), then think back to any conflicts that you solved and tell your children how you learned to settle them.

It's fine if much of your talk goes over their heads, as long as the main ideas sink in—that you don't let bad feelings fester, you don't hold grudges, and you never accept unkind behavior.

---

* Don't worry—by then we expect to have written *Outwitting Teenagers,* and will have advice on how to deal with the demise of "Because I said so" as a working technique.

The idea that children should be free to express themselves without constraint—including their hostile or negative thoughts and feelings—is not one we endorse. Quite the contrary, we would argue that the parent should strive to teach the child to exercise self-control, to learn to know when it's best to hold one's feelings in check. You've got to start young at these lessons, making sure your children understand that their choice of words can leave someone else feeling more wounded than a hammer blow. Yes, the child will feel better for getting his anger out—but there are more than the child's feelings at stake.

We've all met adults who somehow never absorbed this basic fact. As a result, they act like giant two-year-olds, constantly whining and raging over every unfairness they perceive. Someone cuts them off accidentally on the freeway, and next thing you know, they're jumping out of the car, cursing and kicking at the fenders of the other vehicle. You don't want your children to grow up to be like that.

This is not to say that children should never argue or reveal how angry they are. Of course, they'll frequently find something to quarrel over. So along with teaching them that hitting and insult hurling are the wrong ways to express themselves, we need to guide them in the *right* way to disagree over something—even something trivial. Children need the tools to learn to argue fairly, productively, in a way that leads toward a resolution of the conflict.

Set down a few simple rules about arguments—and enforce them. No name calling. No intentionally hurtful outbursts (no "I hate you forever!" or "You're the stupidest thing that ever lived!"). The Golden Rule is simple enough for a two-year-old to understand and respect, if you personalize if for him: "You wouldn't like it if your brother did that to you, so you don't do that to him."

Another important principle that even a very young child can grasp is "Two wrongs don't make a right." You, the parent, make clear that you won't let one child hit or call names just because another child did it first. In fact, you should cut off anyone's attempt to recite a long history of he-did-this-to-me-so-I-had-to-do-that-to-him.

You say, "You know what? That kind of reasoning is why there's been war in the Balkans for six hundred years." (Our own children know a lot more about the history of Southeastern Europe than most kids their age, because for so long we've been using that part of the world as an example—but it has worked, and our daughters seldom have an argument that lasts more than a few minutes anymore.)

You should also put the kibosh on the "Did-not, did-too" routine. That's not persuasion; that's just going around in circles. Tell them, "If you want to keep arguing about [whatever], you have to come up with a new thought, something that you think will help your sister to see things from your point of view."

Teach children as young as three the meaning of the word "compromise." Provide a few concrete examples, so they can see how compromises are reached. Two-year-olds should be starting to get a handle on concepts such as "share" and "take turns." One-year-olds get what you mean when you say, "NO! No hitting your sister!" and "No biting anyone, ever!" Your main goal is to match your words carefully to your child's level of understanding right now, while the underlying concepts themselves—of respect for others, nonviolent ways to resolve conflict, strong bonds between siblings—you are prepared to teach over and over, at every age, at every opportunity, for as long as you are a parent.

A few extra *Outwitting* techniques can help you deal with some specific sibling conflicts:

An age-old method that works to prevent arguments over shared food is to let one child be the one to divide the cookie, while the other child then gets to choose which piece he wants first.

Use random chance to determine who goes first or last. Our kids have often had an easier time accepting the impersonal decision of a coin toss than they have when a parent attempts to play judge. (But DON'T let them start squabbling over who gets to be heads and who's tails!) Coin tossing also teaches your children something about the laws of probability, which will be useful when they get to that topic in eighth or ninth grade math class.

You and your spouse need to model the behavior you want to encourage. Both of you should become conscious of the way you argue with each other in front of the children. Always:

- Keep your tone of voice civil.
- Be respectful of the other's point of view.
- Avoid arguing over something you both know is unimportant.
- Don't keep going around in circles. Move on, after each point is made.
- Seek a compromise solution whenever possible.
- Be ready to apologize if the other person finds your words hurtful (even if you didn't mean them that way).

And may the best talker win!

"WE'RE THE BUNDYS, NOT THE HUXTABLES!"

So you've read the advice about handling sibling fights, and you're thinking: What planet are these people from? In real life . . . that is to say, in your own real family's experience, you know that you always forget these rules the minute you start getting mad at each other. We reply, yes, that's true. No real family will behave all the time in the idealized way we've described. But that doesn't mean you shouldn't put these rules forward as the ideal. You still need to *try*, even as you recognize that all of us fall short of our goals in the heat of the moment.

Accept that fact, and you won't feel let down or discouraged when there's a blowout between your kids. However, you can and should emphasize learning from each episode and striving to act differently next time. Punish them for fighting, of course—but stress reconciliation after the punishment time is up. Reassure them in your strongest terms that you still love them just as much as you did before, and that your love is independent of their behavior. Make clear, when you scold a child, that it's the *behavior* you dislike, never the child. Use words you're sure even the tiniest tot can understand: "I love you all the time, even when you're fighting with your brother. But I do hate to see you two fight."

When children feel absolutely secure in their parents' love, understanding that it's not conditioned on how they behave, they come to accept that as a general principle of family life—and learn to apply it to their siblings as well. So while they may still fight over this or that, they still accept each other and continue to love each other regardless—you can feel perfectly secure about that.

Suspend the First Amendment for Warring Siblings

When we speak to other parents about our views on sibling arguments, we sometimes hear this objection: "My children have freedom of speech in my house. I don't want to order them to apologize or tell them they can't express their true feelings—that just makes me into a dictator."

We think these parents are confused about whether they're running a family or appearing before the Supreme Court. The First Amendment may give a citizen the right to shout on the street corner that some public figure is a pea brain, but that's got nothing to do with the kind of language parents will permit inside their own homes. We can see no reason for allowing one child to insult another by name calling or by belittling words. Even adults are not allowed to slander, threaten, or otherwise verbally harass another with impunity.

Remember, there is no way your children can appeal your decisions to a higher court. You *are* the final judge of what can be said or not said in your presence.

My children fight a lot with each other, but that's not the main problem. It's that they're unequally matched, and I don't know what to do about it. My older son is always picking on my younger one, and when I scold my older one, he thinks I'm always on the younger one's side. But if I try to treat them equally and

*punish them both for fighting, then my younger one really does
end up getting punished more than he deserves.*

Parenting is not a one-size-fits-all process—as parents of very
different children quickly discover. So it's fine to start treating them
differently, with your actions tailored to suit the individuals they
are. The older child may be allowed privileges that the younger one
is not yet mature enough to enjoy. But at the same time the older
one must bear responsibilities that are still too much to expect of
the little one. For example, you expect your older one to know better than to pick on a younger child. And you say so—and back it up
with enforcement measures, if need be.

If your older child cries, "Unfair! You're punishing me more
than him!" then you answer, "No, it's not unfair, because when he
is your age, if he picks on someone younger than he is, I will do exactly the same to him."

There will come times when you have to treat the two unequally,
not because one is misbehaving while the other is being good, but
just because they have unequal needs. Let's say your younger one is
having trouble learning to pronounce his R's. His preschool teacher
may advise you to spend time with him doing speech exercises.
Then your older child complains, "You don't spend any special
time with me!" You could try to count up the hours you spend each
week doing one thing with one child and allocate the same number
of hours a week to compensate the other, but we advise against it.
What's happening in that case is that you've let your older child dictate how you schedule your parenting time. You will be the loser in
any scorekeeping system your child can devise—and the sibling ri-
valry will go on unabated, or even worse than it was before.

It's important for you to be the one to determine the use of your
time and resources. If one child views your attention as being split
unfairly, respond with this all-purpose and philosophically pro-
found response: "LIFE is unfair."

Repeat as often as necessary.

When your children get older, they'll start to question why they
should put up with any instance of unfairness that they believe can

be changed. They'll develop a real zeal for reforming the world. However, during their toddler years, at least, you're safe to use the pronouncement "LIFE is unfair" to put an end to further discussion.

My four-year-old daughter Amy is reasonably well behaved most of the time, but my two-year-old son Jeremy is a real hell-raiser. He's always into one form of mischief or another. Amy frequently notices that he's up to something and tells me about it before I see it myself. I'm not sure how to handle her reports. Sometimes I'm glad that she's warned me when Jeremy is about to hurt himself; on the other hand, most of the time, it seems to me that she's just tattling—and that's something I want to discourage. Any thoughts?

What's bad about tattling is that the child is horning in on the parent's territory. It's not your daughter's job to police your son— that's *your* job. You could propose (in jest, of course) that you punish yourself for failing to catch your son's bad behavior. But that's neither here nor there as far as your daughter is concerned. She does have a duty, however, to look out for and help to protect her brother, and so you can tell her you hope she'll warn you about any *dangerous* activity. That's not being a tattletale; it's being a guardian angel.

Your child should be able to make this distinction, but if she has trouble, you can tell her to ask herself this question: "Will anyone get hurt if I *don't* tell an adult?"

To avoid gratifying the tattler, it's very important not to punish the child who's been told on—even if the reported action was very naughty (as long as it wasn't dangerous). Instead, you scold the tattler. Don't punish her, just tell her firmly, "You're not in charge, and it's not up to you to police your brother's behavior. You watch out for your own behavior—like remembering not to tattle. That should be more than enough for you to worry about."

Some thoughts on scolding (in this and other situations):

- Try not to scold one child in the presence of another.
- Don't let them keep track of who is being yelled at the most. Good behavior is not a contest! (Tell them that bluntly.)

On the other hand, it's okay, even a good idea, for the *parent* to keep track of who's being scolded, how often, and for what. That helps you to keep a sense of what areas of behavior a child needs to work on. It also helps you to realize when your words are being effective—and when they're not.

If you find yourself always yelling at the same child for the same thing, then you can step back and ask yourself, "Why isn't my scolding having any effect?" You may conclude that this child needs a different sort of correction than the other child.

- Be sure to single out a child for praise when he or she does behave well—especially when you can see that your child has been making an effort.
- Ask your child to help you think up ways to do better at whatever problem you're both working on. This will start your child thinking positively about how to alter his or her own behavior.

What *not* to do: Don't let the "good" child gloat or smirk when the "bad" child is being punished. That sort of behavior should be viewed as worse than whatever it was that got the "bad" child in trouble.

THE NUMBER ONE TIP TO HELP YOU TACKLE SIBLING RIVALRY

What follows is the cardinal rule for all parents of siblings, whatever their age, whatever their gender: *Never compare the two. Period.*

You will never say anything along the lines of "Why can't you sit up straight like your brother?"—that is, not unless you really *want* him to resent his straight-backed sibling. Be aware that children tend to assume whatever role they feel they've been assigned within the family, and they also quickly realize when a particular part is taken. If a child sees that his sibling has already assumed the mantle of being "the good child," then he's left thinking the surest way to get his parents' attention is to fulfill the slot that's left over, that of the "bad child."

Sisters fall into this trap just as easily as brothers, but they are even more likely to allow themselves to be labeled according to a more gender-stereotyped division: "the pretty one," who's assumed to be not so smart, versus "the smart one."

Boys are vulnerable to their own gender stereotyping in the labels they may assume, so you should start watching at an early age to see if one or more of your sons is starting to fulfill societal expectations of "the class clown" or "the troublemaker" or "the nerd." Don't even label your kids in a *good* way in the sibling's presence ("You've always been the best athlete"), because your other child will almost certainly complete the sentence for you in his mind (". . . unlike your brother, who's a complete klutz").

Remember, even the most innocent things you say can become grist for siblings to fight over. A large part of your job as the parent of two or more children is to learn how not to be a producer of grist!

"BECAUSE I SAID SO!" (AN IMPORTANT "OUTWITTING" TECHNIQUE)

Your mother said it to you. Your grandmother said it to her. You've probably already said it to your toddler, and then caught yourself and wondered, "Is this really a good enough reason for a child to do what I say?" As with a lot of parenting questions there are, at a minimum, two schools of thought. Some parents refuse to use the phrase, thinking it calls for blind obedience. They want their children to think for themselves, even about the things they think are important. On the other hand, there are those who say obedience is a virtue, and that parents should not have to justify their demands to children—the kids should just do as they're told.

Where do we come down on this issue? We have staked out a firm and decisive position . . . right in the middle of the fence. We say it's fine to say "Because I say so" and then again, it's not so fine that you want to do it very often.

In other words, we think there are a few times and places where you will end up saying it, and will probably need to say it. But don't make it a habit. You don't want to give your children the expectation that you will always explain everything to them, and answer each "Why, Mommy?" or "How come, Daddy?" with patience and forbearance. If you do, you're going to end up spending a lot of time talking that could have been spent going somewhere, or getting something useful accomplished.

Toddlers quickly discover that endless questioning is a great way to delay and perhaps avoid altogether anything they don't want to do. "Because I said so" is a conversation stopper, and there will be times when conversation isn't what you need. So, when you reach that point, pull out the line and use it.

At some point afterward, when you're not so pressed for time, you can (if you wish) discuss with your children why you so abruptly demanded obedience on some occasion. Try telling them this: "Whenever you hear me say, 'Because I said so,' the way I did in the car this morning, it's either because I have run out of time or patience to explain something to you, or because the explanation is something that only a grown-up would understand. But no matter why I'm saying it, whenever you hear those words 'Because I said so,' you should know it's useless to keep on pestering me, because I'm not going to give in—you just have to do what I say."

Here's a case in which Bill used a "because I said so" to avoid having to talk about something too horrible for young children to dwell on. He had turned the TV on and was flipping through the channels, looking for a special on pandas, when he came across a news bulletin about a high school massacre. As fast as he could, Bill changed the channel, but not before our then-four-year-old daughter caught a glimpse of children's dead bodies wrapped in sheets being removed from the school.

"What's that? I want to watch that show," Karen demanded.

"No," Bill said, hoping to find the panda show quickly.

"Why?" she persisted. "What's going on, why are all these people crying?"

"Here's the panda show!" Bill said. "Let's watch."

"No, tell me what that crying show was about," she repeated.

"I don't want to," Bill told her. "It's too hard to explain."

"But I want you to! Go back to that channel!"

Bill declined, but she continued to whine and beg, "Why can't I see that show? I can understand. Just explain it to me."

After one more round of no's and why-nots, Bill finally weighed in with the big, all-purpose, conversation-stopping, "Because I SAID SO!" and that was that. (We're only sorry that we can't use it anymore to defer answering the same sort of questions from our now nine-year-old. When she was watching TV and her show was interrupted by a bulletin about the shooting of children at the nearby National Zoo, we couldn't change the channel on her, and we knew we had to answer all her questions—or else let her rely on whatever she heard the next day from her classmates at school.)

My daughter bites! She's thirteen months old and has teeth, so it's not a gentle little baby nip. She really clamps her teeth down when she's mad, and it hurts! How do I get her to stop? My grandmother suggested that I bite her back—should I?

With all due respect to your grandmother's wisdom—that would be nuts! It would simply give her the message that biting is something that adults do, too. We don't recommend a lot of yelling and screaming in pain either. The drama and attention, and the feeling of power coming from her own actions, would probably be very exciting to her. Our best advice is, pull away at once, making it clear that you don't want to hold her or even get close to her if she does something so dangerous and harmful to you.

If she starts to cry or call for you, say some or all of the following, "You *bit* me. That hurt me. I didn't like that. Children don't bite. No biting, ever!" Keep your words simple and she should get the message, even if she's not talking yet. Keep your voice low and serious—don't yell or scream at her. Your goal is not to scare her but to get her to comprehend that there is a serious problem with what she's done. She's still a baby, so further punishment will not reinforce the lesson but will simply upset her.

However, if the biting victim is a sibling or another toddler, your actions must be a little different. You must protect the other child from further biting, so if you're the visitor, apologize to the other parent and separate the children at once (taking yours home if you can't make use of a separate room in the friend's house). Try to get your child to understand that the visit was cut short because of her behavior. If you're at home, you can put her in her crib for a short time, or if you have a playpen, park her there while you tend to the other child. Do this even if you suspect that the other child provoked the biting by grabbing a favorite toy away from your child. Toddlers can't be expected to be unselfish and share toys at this age, but they can and should be expected to learn that biting is never the right response.

By the way, a child's bite can lead to serious medical problems. If the skin is broken, be sure you wash the wound immediately and follow up with an antibacterial disinfectant ointment.

I've tried lots of tactics to discipline Elizabeth when she's throwing one of her all too frequent tantrums. I've put her in a time-out chair. I've sent her to her room. I canceled playdates. I've scolded, and I've taken away toys. I've withdrawn offers of dessert—you name it, I've done it. But none of it ever seems to make much of an impression on her. She keeps on screaming till she's finished, and then she generally goes to sleep. After she wakes up, she's calm, but puzzled as to why she's not allowed dessert, or can't play with a certain toy. Puzzled . . . but not especially bothered. Am I doing something wrong?

Not wrong . . . but not effective either. But before we launch into a long discussion of what makes a disciplinary measure effective for a child in a particular situation, let's talk about something that may be better for you than a new and improved form of punishment. When it comes to tantrum-y toddlers, prevention is your first line of defense. Try to find out what's setting Elizabeth off, and remove the cause before the blowup occurs. That way, you don't have to worry so much about what form of punishment will work after the fact.

So first, ask yourself, are the tantrums occurring mainly late in the afternoon? If so, your daughter could simply be worn out, needing sleep to restore her to a calmer frame of mind. In that case an adjustment of her nap schedule to allow for more or longer periods of "downtime" may be your best way to help her break the tantrum cycle.

Or maybe they're mainly a morning phenomenon, or happen right around dinnertime. Has she had a good breakfast before setting out on the day's first round of activities? Or could it be that her dinner comes too late in the evening for her? Hunger can all too easily affect a small child's mood, though the child herself may not tell you that's the problem. She just knows that she's feeling something bad, and she starts to get crankier and crankier, until finally she loses control, probably over some seemingly unimportant thing that never would have bothered her on a full stomach.

If her tantrums don't occur at predictable times, you might still look for consistent warning signs. Does she start out getting contrary, objecting to things she ordinarily likes? Does she become silent and look downcast for a while before the thing that sets her off? Once you discern a pattern, you may be able to take steps to calm the building storm, rather than let it reach the breaking point.

Take her someplace quiet, give her a chance to talk out what's bothering her, provide some reassuring hugs—whatever you think is called for. Keep in mind, once the tantrum is started, it's too late to do any of these things, and you're going to have to follow up with some disciplinary consequences, to boot.

Clearly, the ones you've tried so far haven't made much of an impression on Elizabeth. That's not to say that they couldn't be modified to make them work, though. Take a look at our suggestions about discipline to see what might work with Elizabeth.

THE SIX PILLARS OF TODDLER DISCIPLINE

For a disciplinary method to work on a child aged four or younger, it ought to meet six crucial criteria. It must be:

1. Immediate—that is to say, following quickly on the heels of the behavior you want to discourage. You never, ever say, "Wait 'til your father gets home!" because by then, the toddler has forgotten all about her wrongdoing.
2. Of short duration, meaning that the punishment doesn't go on and on, past the time when the toddler has lost track of the reason she's being punished.
3. Related to the offense—so that, for example, you're not banning her favorite TV show because she shoved a playmate on the slide. Far better to make her miss out on sliding for the next ten minutes.
4. Proportionate, so that you're not putting a child in a time-out chair for a onetime forgetting to say "thank you"—just as you do not respond to a child who intentionally hits or bites a sibling by a simple scolding.
5. Realistically enforceable, not an empty threat. If your child isn't ready to leave the park when you say it's time, don't say that you'll go home without him. You can, however, say, "If you're not ready to go in the next five minutes, then we can't see the movie today."
6. Something the child doesn't care to have happen

again, anytime soon. It's no good to send a child to her room, with all her toys, if that's her favorite place. Either take out some of those toys for the time being, or move the time-out chair to the kitchen or some other less interesting corner of the house.

The trouble with all the measures you've tried so far is that they've failed one or more of these tests. Your child obviously doesn't mind a little downtime on a chair in a pleasant room (see No. 6). She can do quite well for the moment without a toy or a dessert (they're unrelated to the cause of her tantrum—see No. 3). And a playdate at some point in the future is just too remote for her to worry about (see No. 1).

As a result, she doesn't find it's a big deal at all to be punished, but it's clear to her that it *is* a big deal to you. It sounds, in that case, as if she's showing you, "Look, I can play this game as well as you. If it's a test of wills you want, I'm more than up for the challenge."

And you know what? Your child is right. The toy or the withheld dessert just isn't all that important, compared to the emotional gratification of beating a parent at her own game. Still, it won't do you any good to try to make the punishments more rigorous. If you try that, by increasing the length of the time-outs or by taking away more toys or treats, you'll violate one of the other important principles of toddler disciplinary actions, the proportionality rule (No. 4).

So what *can* you do? First, recognize that by the time the tantrum has erupted, she's no longer responsive to anything you say. She's screaming and flailing around, completely out of control and unable to stop herself, even if she wanted to. It's useless to yell at her to stop. Anyway, why would she want to? She's letting off steam and getting your full attention at the same time. Generally speaking, negative attention beats no attention, in a small child's mind. Besides which, she probably doesn't know any other way to express herself (yet).

Your best move in this case is to deny her the attention

she's come to expect. If you're at home, make sure she's on a soft carpet and can't injure herself while she's kicking and flinging herself about, but otherwise completely ignore her. You may say—loud enough for her to hear but not in a shout, "I don't like this behavior, so I'm going into the other room." Walk out, adding as you go, "Come and talk to me when you can speak in a regular voice." Or say simply, "I can't understand you when you're screaming like that. Calm down and I will listen." Or even more simply, "No tantrums. You can't get what you want that way." Then stay out of the room until the tantrum is over.

We suggest no other punishment right now than the withdrawal of your attention. However, once the tantrum has passed, sit her down to talk about what happened. Tell her why you think her behavior is a problem. Help to equip her emotionally to express herself in some other way in the future. Tell her you can see it's no fun for her to be acting like a baby, unable to say what she wants in words. Add that if she could just learn to tell you what she wants in words, and not by yelling and screaming, you would do your best to take care of whatever is bothering her.

That shouldn't be an empty promise either. If she's building up to a tantrum because you've said she can't have cookies so close to dinnertime, but she manages to express herself well enough with words (but no whining, or repeated begging!), you should reward her by compromising, if you can. Maybe she could have just one cookie now, though not the three that she'd like to have. Maybe you can write her an IOU for the cookies, to be redeemed after dinner.

Of course, if what she wants is something unsafe (to avoid being strapped into her car seat) or impossible (to wear a pair of red boots, when her boots are blue) then you just have to get her to live with the situation. At some point (it varies with the patience of the parent) you stop discussing, and intone, as Walter Cronkite used to do: "And that's the way it is."

The exception to the above concerns tantrums in public

places. Obviously you cannot walk away from your screaming child in the grocery store or the library or at the mall.
Tell her you will take her straight home—then do it.

If that's not possible, because you really must finish your
errands, go and sit in the car, or in the ladies' lounge, or
some other less public spot, until your child regains control
of herself. Once she's calmed down, be sure to tell her that it
will be a good, long time before she gets to go on a similar
outing with Mommy again.

WHY TODDLERS SHOULDN'T BE "GROUNDED"

Alicia described herself to us as a strict disciplinarian—not
the type to put up with any nonsense from her two-and-a-
half-year-old daughter Lucy. Yet despite many stiff penal-
ties, Lucy continued to defy her wishes. Alicia couldn't
understand why. Then one day we happened to observe an
incident that we think typifies what Alicia was doing
wrong. Here's what happened:

Alicia had come to pick Lucy up at our house after a
playdate with our daughter Claire. "Time to go," Alicia
called, but Lucy refused to budge.

"That playdate was too short!" she whined.

"Stop delaying and come with me!" Alicia said more
sternly.

No response.

"Lucy, if you don't put on your coat right now and get in
your carseat, you'll be grounded. That means you won't be
allowed to go on your playdate to Rachel's house tomorrow," Alicia told her.

But still there was no movement.

Alicia added, "If you don't start cooperating, you'll be
grounded the day after tomorrow, too."

On hearing that, Lucy stuck her lip out and said, "I don't
care!"

Alicia added another day of no play—to no result—and

then another and another. Altogether Lucy racked up two weeks of house arrest because she never did respond to her mother's threats.

Too bad Alicia didn't appreciate a toddler's limited understanding of time. At thirty months, Lucy had absolutely no conception of what two weeks of "grounding" meant, being barely able to think ahead more than a few minutes into the future (much less hours, days, or weeks). She couldn't even have told her mother how many days are in a week.

Alicia needed to be able to anticipate Lucy's reaction to the announced punishment, and to do that she needed to be able to see the situation through her daughter's eyes. When the first threatened day of grounding didn't move her child, it should have been clear a second day wouldn't work either—but Alicia missed the clue. It would not have helped at that point to switch to a different type of threat, because by then the battle lines were drawn. It was a contest of wills, and Lucy had a good shot at winning.

What might have worked in this case? Some way to give Lucy the illusion that she'd scored a big point, but accomplish what her mother wanted—to get her to leave the house. The "timer game" might be just the thing for this situation. Here's how it works. You bring out a kitchen timer and say, "Here's the game. You *can* stay longer—just as long as this timer is ticking. I'm turning it to the five." Point to the five-minute mark on the timer. "The bell will go off, and at that point the game is over. Then we're going home."

The rules seem fair and clear. Lucy gets to stay (for a short time, anyway) and Alicia gets to be the one to say when the time has come to depart. And no one ends up being held against their will—not the parent, not the child.

I've just had a confidence-shattering experience. Some parents of children that my son plays with regularly at our neighborhood playground came over to me and told me they don't want my son in the sandbox when their kids are there. They say he grabs all the toys. He's barely more than a year old!

Actually, what they probably mean is not that they don't want him . . . they just want more of *you*. No one expects a less-than-two-year-old to know about sharing. They expect *you* to, however, and they are saying, in effect, get involved, intervene—so we don't have to. They're saying you've got to take action before your child does any hitting, grabbing, or sand-kicking, because once he's started, it's too late to tell him "No." The other kids are already intimidated, and your child is already getting the message that he's free to do what he wants.

You don't want to start punishing him harshly for aggressive behavior, because punishment after the fact is usually lost on a child that young. Prevention, on the other hand, makes a real impression.

That means that you've got to be close at hand to watch what's going on, so that you can anticipate when your child may be tempted to grab or hit. You can't sit on the park bench at a remove of several yards. You've got to be within arm's length, positioned to pull your child back as soon as you see him move into an aggressive mode.

This goes equally for a caregiver as for a parent. Babysitting a one-year-old is a misnomer, because there isn't much sitting involved. "Baby running" is more like it. Toddlers and playgrounds are just accidents waiting to happen. That's not to say you don't take your toddler out to play. You do, but you (or your caregiver) ought to be one step behind him all the time, so that he won't run in front or in back of children swinging in swings, or climb to the top of the monkey bars and then decide to try flying, or (as your son has already demonstrated) try to grab every toy he sees.

Far too many parents these days have the idea that children don't need to be taught how to play nicely with other children; that they'll just learn by doing, and when other children object to having their toys taken, they'll figure out that it's wrong. Nothing could be farther from the truth. Without parental intervention early and often, some children develop into bullies, others into perpetual victims. The law of the jungle prevails—or didn't you read *Lord of the Flies?*

Besides being both vigilant and quick to step in, you can do one simple thing to improve matters, and that is to make sure your son comes heavily equipped with good toys of his own. That way he will feel less temptation to take what doesn't belong to him. Also, if he's got good stuff, when other kids try to grab his stuff (as they inevitably will), he will learn what that feels like.

When that happens, be sure those parents who used to complain about *your* child see that you are understanding, and not the type to point out to the other child's parents that the shoe (doing the kicking) is now on the other child's foot.

Now for the opposite case scenario:

My little girl always seems to be the victim in playground disputes. Bigger, tougher kids—and we're talking three- and four-year-olds here—take away her toys and she just cries and runs for me. I'm never sure what I should be doing: teaching her to stand up for herself, or going to speak to the children directly and ask them not to bully her, or going to the parents, who sit by idly and don't even seem to notice what their kids are up to? Maybe I shouldn't do anything, but just wait for her to learn to deal with it on her own.

We say a strong no to the last idea. We believe parents should parent while they have the chance. Toddlerhood is the ideal time for parents to teach children how to behave, before they come to the conclusion that you aren't the all-knowing, all-wise, all-providing being you seem to be. (This omnipotence is one of our favorite, though transitory, aspects of parenthood. When your kids are very small, no matter how short an adult you are, you can feel ten feet tall in your child's eyes. Neither of us can carry a tune, but when our children were very young, they both thought we were the best singers in the world. It's great to have such an appreciative audience . . . but we digress.)

When it comes to standing up for your child, your first goal is to protect her from physical harm. Intervene swiftly and directly whenever another child is hitting, biting, throwing sand, or otherwise threatening your child's safety. Never hit the child back. Usually it's enough to go over and stand between the child and your child and say firmly (and loudly): "NO HITTING!"

We can't guarantee, in one hundred percent of cases, that the child will stop. If he or she is out of control, you may need to remove your child by picking her up and carrying her to safety. We do not recommend picking up the other child, especially a child who's aggressive.

We know it's tempting to try to advise the parent or caregiver of the aggressor on the spot, but such advice is seldom well taken. We've heard from parents who have done it, and we present the sampling of experiences to show how ineffective it usually is:

Parent A takes Parent B to task for her child's aggressiveness: Parent B replies, "Well, you see, my son has been diagnosed with a mild form of autism. We're doing the best we can to try to teach him to control himself, but it's been very, very hard. . . ." Parent A mumbles apologies and slinks away thinking to herself, "Thank God my child doesn't have that problem."

Or Parent B replies, "What do you mean, my child is hitting *your* child? I saw what happened quite clearly. Your child was the one who started it! She's been teasing my child nonstop since he arrived, and he finally couldn't put up with it anymore. She's the one who needs to learn manners!" You argue in defense of your own child, and next thing you know you and the other parent are fighting worse than the kids.

Parent B runs over to her child and yells, "Don't you ever, *ever* hit that girl again!" *Whap!* Parent B whacks her kid. "You learn to behave, you hear me!"

Or Parent B turns out to be the nanny, who speaks not one word of English, and stares at you blankly. When it gets back to the parents that you tried to reprimand their nanny, they call you to chew you out for not minding your own business.

Since none of these scenarios is what you're after, and you have no way of knowing how a strange parent is going to react, we think the best thing to do is to focus on your own child's behavior. Teach her that not all children know how to share and behave, but if there's any hitting or biting or kicking, you'll be there to protect her (and make clear to your child's babysitter that this is part of her responsibility, too). Sometimes avoiding ill-mannered children is the safest course. That means that your child may have to be the one to leave the sandbox, rather than the bully. Just make sure your child doesn't feel *she's* the one being punished by having to go; take her someplace else that's even more fun.

When all the playground parents agree that one child is the problem, there's safety in numbers. Their group approach to the parents of that child should be delicate, based on the assumption that the parent is either unaware of the extent of the problem, or else knows there's a problem but is already struggling valiantly to find a solution. You make clear you're not ganging up on either the child or the parents, but are there to help. You offer extra pairs of eyes and ears to monitor the child's behavior. Obtain the parents' permission to intervene and use disciplinary techniques that the child's parents and all the other parents agree are effective.

Hint: Try to get the parents of the problem child to agree that the best technique in any case of hitting or biting is to remove the child at once from the situation—a limited time-out the first time (maybe five minutes of having to sit on the bench)—but after the second offense, the child must be taken home—end of playtime.

*M*y child delights in pulling the cat's tail. What should I do?

Your child should not get away with doing this even once. Cruelty to animals is never cute, never to be dismissed as a childish prank or "just a phase." Respond with an immediate display of shock and horror: Say, "That hurts the kitty!" and follow up by asking, "How do you think you would feel if someone pulled hard on a part of your body?" Even a two-year-old should be able to appreciate the wrongness of the action.

What *not* to do: Don't try pulling your child's arm or her hair to demonstrate; that teaches that there are times when it's allowable to do that to others. However, if your child is under two and may not understand all your words, try using your own body as a live model. Pull on your own hair and say, "Ow! Ow! See how that hurts! Kitty feels just like that, too!"

Make sure your demonstration sinks in. You want to be sure your child "gets" it. Anytime a child appears unable to understand that others feel pain, you should be on the alert. Apparent inability to feel empathy can be a warning sign of a serious developmental problem. Watch carefully and consult your pediatrician if your worries are not soon allayed by improvement in your child's behavior.

LYING VS. CREATIVE OUTWITTING

Many of the solutions that we've found most effective involve getting your child to believe something other than the literal truth. For example, your child demands a candy bar for breakfast.

The standard advice you've probably seen in other parenting books is to offer your child a choice of acceptable alternatives. "You can have Cheerios or Fruit Loops or a banana and yogurt for breakfast," you say, hoping your child will accept the task of deciding among these healthful selections. But you know as well as we do that your average-to-smart child can defeat that strategy without a second's hesitation, by sweeping aside all the choices you put forth to insist, even more vehemently: "I WANT A CANDY BAR! I DON'T WANT ANY OF THAT OTHER STUFF!"

We say, try this approach. "But sweetie, there *are* no candy bars here. Now this is what we have . . ." And you name the same three foods that you offered before.

Most children can accept the fact that no candy bars in the house means no chance to have one for breakfast.

However, we know some parents who would object, "But I *do* have candy bars in the house, and if I say there are none, I'm lying. I don't want to teach my child that lying is ever okay."

Of course, lying isn't okay. However, trickery and the politicians' habit of monkeying about with the meaning of words *is* okay. In fact, it's an extremely useful and clever part of your outwitting arsenal. As an adult, you know that words have many meanings, so put your superior sophistication to work for you. You're like the lawyer who has drafted a contract full of fine print and confusing legalisms. It's not up to *you* to make the other party aware of all the pitfalls in what you present. If the other party lacks the experience or insight to look beneath the surface, then that's something that will be learned in due course—but for now, you've got the advantage. Use it while you still can.

So, if by the phrase "There are no candy bars here" you happen to mean "Here, in this spot right in front of me," then that's what you're saying, and it's not your fault if your child assumes your meaning to be "here, in the house." For this stratagem to work, those candy bars had better not be in plain sight, or hidden in some overly obvious spot, or else your kids will come back with "But I know where they are"—and then show you.

You can do this kind of linguistic sleight of hand in almost any situation. Let's say your child wants to play with the neighbor's child when you want him to take a nap. You say, "We can't go over there to play now. It's Sammy's nap time, too. In fact, I think he's already asleep." Well, at least you're assuming he is . . . and in the absence of any evidence to the contrary, there's no reason to tell your child otherwise. You aren't in the fact-checking business for a timetable of your neighbor's schedules, so it's no big deal if you turn out to be wrong in this particular instance. Besides which, it is not unreasonable of you to assume that all children in the neighborhood take naps around the same time of day. Your child's resistance to napping fades as he accepts the idea that nap time is a universal phenomenon.

Parenting is not for people who can deal only in absolutes and black and white—you may agree with that in principle, but what about the practical side of these questions: What do you do when your children happen to catch you in a lie? Won't they learn to distrust you? Or worse, start to think it's okay for them to bend the truth, too?

Yes, these *are* problems, but you can and should be prepared to deal with them. Here's your warning, right now: Do *not* adopt this technique unless you're fast at thinking on your feet. You need to feel sure you're up to talking your way out of a sticky situation when it arises (as sooner or later it's bound to).

Let's say you've been caught telling your four-year-old that the ice cream store is closed after sundown—forgetting that just last week her grandparents took her there after dinner. You could brazen it out by coming up with a second whopper on top of your first one: "Oh, but that was on a Saturday and now it's Wednesday. Yes, I remember now . . . they do close later on weekends." Or you can change your tune and try to work with the corrected version of reality: "Yes, that's right. Thank you for reminding me. But anyway, it's too late for us to go out for ice cream now, so we'll have to do it another day." Or you can confess, and let your child enjoy the "gotcha!" moment. Then clue your child in on the fact that from time to time you'll try to fool her in unimportant little ways, like what times stores are open or closed, or whether you are able to meet a request to have a treat or a special outing.

We'd advise you try the last suggestion only with a child older than four. Before that age, children are usually so literal-minded they can't take in the concept that words can mean different things to different people, or have several levels of meaning at the same time. (In fact, we've met plenty of adults who have trouble with the latter concept.)

But children of even a very young age can see that people aren't always serious about what they say. Anytime you use your imagination and pretend to be a horsey or flap your arms and say you're flying, or when you utter a magic word and pull a quarter out of a child's ear, you're using words to your own ends—to have fun, to make life a little bit lighter, to escape for a time from the constraints of adult reality. Yet purists for the truth-telling to children at all times ought to object to these activities, too.

But fortunately, only a few parents are so rigidly wedded to the idea of truth. Once you stop looking at the question ideologically and start looking at your own child and his or her needs, you quickly grasp the folly of the absolutist approach. If you never allow yourself to depart from the literal truth with children, then you deny them a world with the Tooth Fairy in it, and Santa and the Easter bunny, too.

Just as you wish to prolong your children's sense of wonder and awe, you also want to shield them—at least during their tender years—from some of the harsher realities that the world has in store for them (something many adults apparently wish someone would continue to do for them. Just listen to the way most adults substitute euphemisms for the words "death" and "dying."). Feel free to judiciously employ some techniques that help make the world appear rosier than it is: whimsy, feeling-sparing excuses, and kidding, to name just a few tricks in the imaginative parent's repertoire.

Sometimes we're not so much covering up the hard reality as we are presenting another version of it—recognizing that every story can be told from multiple points of view: *Rashomon,* for toddlers.

"Yes, but those cases are different," our critics respond. "That's fantasy, make-believe, which enriches a child's world." We say the same about parents' clever word-play and creative storytelling. We think it matters in what spirit and to what end you spin your tale—and how often. We think you need to limit your storytelling to those times when it serves your child's interests as well as your own. For example, when you know your child is terrified of monsters that he imagines in his closet at night, you don't try to persuade him that the monsters don't exist; instead, you get out your "antimonster spray" bottle (actually, a plant mister) and spray those monsters to death. Now, your formerly nervous and sleepless child can get a secure night's rest.

All around the world, in every culture and in every age, storytellers have enchanted young listeners with tales in which people or animals use all kinds of magic tricks and cunning tactics to gain cooperation or avoid a fight. From the African-American folk tales of Br'er Rabbit and Br'er Fox to the Irish tales of blarney-talking leprechauns, the fast thinker is the hero, the one to be admired.

To your child, you ought to appear at least as smart as any of these fabled characters of old!

Zoë's normal tone of voice is a whine. How can I encourage her to speak in a nicer tone of voice?

This is an easy one. You're older now, and your hearing is starting to go, isn't it? You don't budge when she whines for something. Instead, you say, "I'm sorry, I couldn't quite get what you're saying. Could you repeat it, please?"

If she repeats her original whine more loudly than before, then you gently correct her by saying, "Use your inside voice, please."

She'll eventually get the message that there's a right way and a wrong way to be heard, and that the right way leads to a faster and more productive parental response.

But if that doesn't bring about some vocal reform, try this: Answer her whine in an even more exaggerated whine yourself. Suppose she says, "I don't wanna go to the store with you. I'm too tired!"—then you reply in the most irritating tone you can muster, "I don't wanna go eeeei-ther, but we gotta get these errands done to-daaaay." Now, you need to be careful when you try this technique not to let your mimicry cross the line into mockery. That will make her feel belittled, and she'll be less willing in the future to come to you with a request to help her meet any of her needs (in any tone of voice). Try to give your whiny response a funny twist to it, to make her laugh at herself.

If she complains that you're making fun of her, quickly backpedal, saying that wasn't what you meant—it just came out that way. Let her understand that we all sound whiny sometimes without realizing we're doing it, and it just struck you as funny when she did it, so you reacted by copying her.

With that explanation she won't be able to get mad at you—but we think she won't want to give you the chance to do it again soon, either.

Brianna, my two-year-old, is just beginning to talk in complete sentences, and she says whatever is on her mind. We could be on a bus and see a man with crutches and she'll ask, "What the matter with that man's legs?" Or she'll point at someone and announce, "Look at that ugly fat lady!" My question is, can a two-year-old learn to be discreet?

Yes, and if you don't start teaching her now, it'll just get harder for her to learn it later on. But don't worry about whether she grasps the concept of "discretion." Stick with something simpler, something you've already started to teach (we hope): that other people have feelings that need to be respected.

Tell her nobody likes to be stared at, or pointed at—no matter what they look like, or what their health is like. Try to get her to imagine what it might be like to have something that made her look so different that other people stared at her. Would she like answering questions all day or hearing other children point her out?

That's a good exercise, because it gets her to practice empathy. It also helps her to start distinguishing between public and private. Some things—and how someone got an injury is one of them—people usually like to keep to themselves. Tell her it can be annoying for a person to have to explain over and over why he uses a wheelchair, or what's that rash on her skin.

Don't expect a two-year-old or even a three-year-old to remember this lesson every time. The next time you encounter someone with a condition you suspect will provoke her curiosity, you'd be wise to make a preemptive move. Before she can blurt out some unfortunate remark, draw her aside and say in a whisper: "You remember that we talked about how it's not polite to point out people who look different? You probably want to say something about that lady with the green hair and the rings going through her eyebrows, but I just want to be sure you didn't say something out loud. As soon as we get home, I'll try to answer your questions about why she looks like that." (That also gives you the time you need to think about what answers you want to give.)

There's a little boy at my son's daycare center who knows, and uses, all the four-letter words. Now my son is copying him! The daycare center teacher told us not to make a big deal of it when he does it—ignore it and he'll stop using them. But that was months ago, and he's still at it. What should we do next? Confront the parents of the foul-mouthed child?

You could, but they'd probably just tell you to f*** off. Rather than try to police their language, it's time to let your child know the rules in your house, and in the rest of civilized society.

Just as you've taught him not to call other people names, or say rude things, you should teach him not to use these words. You are going to have to tell him explicitly which ones you're talking about.

You don't need to define them. Just say that they're nasty and mean, and they make people feel bad.

The one you'll probably find the most troublesome is sh**, because it seems to be on everyone's lips from old ladies to young tots these days, popping up thoughtlessly in reaction to almost any frustration or minor mishap. You can tell your child it means "poop" or a "number two" or whatever term you use for feces—but make clear that it's a bathroom word, and in your family you only use bathroom words in the bathroom.

He'll understand this restriction far better than he would a total ban on the word. Give him some appropriate alternatives. "Shoot!" works well. "Fudge" and "fooey" are good childish stand-ins for the F-word. Since you won't allow him to insult his playmates, he doesn't need a substitute term for a**h***—though that won't keep him from inventing some colorful terms of his own! (There comes a time in every two-year-old's life when he discovers the power of names to taunt and tease, and he will naturally come up with his own toddler version of a**h***, like "poop head" or "doo-doo face." To which you respond, "No name-calling," and move on.

DIRTY WORDS (RICHARD'S STORY)

I was born a few years after the end of the Second World War. My father, a combat veteran, had come home from the European theater with a typical soldier's vocabulary of curse words—a habit for rough language that persisted well into the 1950s and coincided with my prime language learning years.

When I was three, we moved from an apartment in Manhattan out to Great Neck, a Long Island suburb. Soon after the moving van had departed, a neighbor, dressed in white gloves and a frilly hat, arrived to welcome us to the neighborhood. My mother invited her in, and she immediately started to talk about how wonderful Great Neck was—how "exclusive" it was and how it was always good to have more of the "right" kind of people. She was glad that Great Neck wasn't getting the sort of "riffraff" who were moving into some of the other suburbs.

My mother loathed this sort of talk and would have been glad to have her visitor leave quickly, but the lady kept chattering on. All this time I had been sitting silently by the window, keeping my eye on a huge bumblebee flying around a flower blooming on the other side of the pane.

The lady cast her eye on me and remarked, "What a well-behaved little boy you have! Not like so many fidgety little children these days—he's so quiet, so *mannerly.*"

I chose that moment to announce to everyone what was on my mind, and absorbing all my interest. Using an expression I'd picked up from my dad, I turned to my mother and her guest and said, "Would'ja look at this f***ing big bee!"

At that moment my mother realized it was time to ask my father to watch his language around the house—but she also was grateful that I'd chosen that moment to horrify her visitor, who immediately found an excuse for a hasty departure. Thanks to me (my mother said every time she recounted this story—and it was one of her favorites), she never had to worry that the snob would come to call again.

—Richard R.
Washington, D.C.

My toddler simply laughs at me when I give her a time-out. Then I increase the time she has to sit in the time-out chair from five to ten minutes, but she runs away before I get her to sit in it. Then, when I finally march her over to the chair, I've increased the sitting time to twenty minutes—though I know I can't watch her the whole time. So before the time is up, she's out of the chair. Something's not working. How do I get things back on track?

Have you considered that you might be on the wrong track altogether? This time-out chair sentence isn't scary enough for your child. She knows you won't enforce it, so she doesn't take it seriously. That's why she laughs when you bring it up.

You need to think up some new way to put a healthy dose of fear in her. Is there some privilege that she would really hate to give up? Away it goes. Toys can disappear for a short time. But if you choose that method, don't increase the punishment by lengthening the time. Toddlers have too poor a sense of minutes and hours, and are clueless about longer-term events. If fifteen minutes without a favorite toy doesn't have desired effect, then add a new and different restriction instead of making the deprivation last an hour.

To stop her from running away when you want to discipline her, you've got to show her that you are bigger, stronger, and faster, and that it's pointless to try to evade you. You will only have this sort of physical superiority over her for perhaps another decade, so use it while you can! We don't advocate spanking under any circumstances, but we do think you can pick up a child and put her where you want her. You can grip her tightly while you scold her for even thinking of taking off when you told her to stay put.

Here's what Peggy once did when two-year-old Karen refused to stay in her bed after she'd been told twice that it was nap time. Peggy saw Karen darting down the hallway. "Get back in that bed!" Peggy commanded, but Karen kept on going. Peggy ran after her, caught up with her in a few short strides, and swept her up and carried her, kicking and screaming, back to her toddler bed. Karen tried to get up and run off yet again, and so to make sure that this time she would stay put, Peggy sat on her! (She was very careful not to put her full weight on her—but she used just enough force to bring home the idea that she could keep her where she wanted her.) It worked, and not just that one time. The tactic must have made such a strong impression (on her mind, we mean, not on her back) that she's never tried to bolt on either one of us since then.

One simple but effective tactic parents sometimes overlook is the use of a sharp tone of voice. Toddlers don't like being yelled at. Usually they'd rather be left alone in a chair than scolded for a long time. To achieve maximum impact, you should bend over slightly, so that you are peering down at them from just a short distance above. Maintain eye contact—don't let them look away—and deliver the talking-to for as long as you think justified by the severity of the misdeed. You can start with the classic introductory line: "Now you are going to listen, and listen well!" Keep it up for as long as it takes for your child to get the message.

Do stop sooner if your child seems sincerely sorry for what she's done.

Children should always be given an opportunity to make up for any harm they've caused from naughtiness. If she was playing near the dining table when you told her not to and she knocks over a glass of water, she must help you clean up the mess.

Remember, too, a certain level of mischievousness is intrinsic to being a toddler. They can't easily anticipate how their actions can affect others. Usually the first time they do something bad, they have no idea their parents will find anything wrong with their action. And the second time, it's because they have limited memories and forgot all about what happened the first time. So before you rush to punish, consider that the first two "strikes" may not have been purposefully naughty . . . but definitely by the third strike, the toddler should be called out.

CHAPTER

6

Errands and Outings

Here's what it was like before we had children. We'd go out to a restaurant, nothing fancy, just someplace you'd expect to have a reasonably enjoyable meal, and there'd be this screaming little boy or girl in a high chair, flinging food, banging the silverware, and generally making life miserable for all the surrounding patrons. And we'd think smugly to ourselves: "Boy, when *we* have children, we won't let them get away with that sort of behavior. *Ours* will be taught how to behave in restaurants."

Then, a few years later, when we had a toddler of our own, there we were, in that same supposedly family-friendly restaurant, suddenly aware that there was an inordinately long wait (from an eighteen-month-old's point of view) for the food to arrive, and that when it came at last, it was served on plates too hot for a child to touch. All during the long wait for food, our daughter had been growing crankier and crankier. Having her dinner on hand but untouchable was the final straw, and she erupted in a sudden screech of pent-up hunger and frustration that was so loud and so spectacular that every other patron in the restaurant had to turn and stare.

Our smugness instantly departed, never to return—even though our children are now old enough to know how to behave in restaurants. Soon after that incident we learned to choose restaurants that don't test our kids' patience and how, in case of an unexpected delay, to keep them distracted and prevent restlessness and frustration from building up.

In addition to wisdom gained through our own trials and errors, we have benefited from the many tips and techniques suggested by helpful parents of toddlers from all over, gathered through in-person interviews and e-mail exchanges. We think you will find these useful.

As we've said before, you may not find every tip suited to your own child's personality, so before trying out any of the recommendations that follow, consider well which strategy you think would yield the best results in your particular case.

My husband and I used to love dining out at all kinds of good food places—that is, before we had a baby. Now we dread it. My son Jack, otherwise a fairly well-behaved two-year-old, is (truth be told) a terror in restaurants. I have regretfully come to the conclusion that we ought to stay home to eat. Am I giving up too soon?

Yes, because you haven't yet made yourselves persona non grata in every restaurant in town, have you? You just need to keep looking for the right kind of restaurant. You do have to change your criteria, however. No longer can the quality of the cuisine be your primary consideration. Now good food will be, at best, number five or six on your list.

Here are the four most important factors influencing your choice of a restaurant for any family with young children:

1. *Speed of service.* Toddlers have notoriously short attention spans. They simply cannot sit and wait the way adults can for a meal to arrive. A speedy restaurant with mediocre food should win hands down over a slow restaurant with a more talented chef.

2. *Kid-friendly features.* The restaurant you choose should be the sort that actively encourages parents to bring the kids with all of the following features:

- Safe, comfortable high chairs for babies and younger toddlers
- Booster seats for older toddlers
- Crayons and a paper placemat (or a kids' menu that doubles as an activity book)
- Menu items with child appeal—especially chicken fingers, plain pasta, pizza, macaroni and cheese, peanut butter and jelly sandwiches, milk, apple juice, and/or similar fare

3. *Wait staff trained to deal with families with young children.* That means that your waiter knows better than to put a very hot plate down in front of your toddler without a warning to the parents. You can get the children's food brought out first if you wish, or at least be warned when an adult entrée will require extra time to prepare, so that you can make a different, swifter-arriving choice.
4. *A kitchen that can accommodate special requests.* For example: "Cut the crust off my son's turkey sandwich, please!" or "Leave the marinara sauce off my daughter's pasta." You should also be able to get something simple, even if it's not specifically listed on the menu, such as a couple of slices of well-toasted white bread, or a bowl of carrot shavings.

If you seek out places that fit these criteria, does that mean you will be limited to the same boring old chain restaurants and fast-food places for the next decade? Not necessarily. In almost any sized city or town we've visited, we've discovered interesting places that serve delicious food and that were also fine for kids. However, we did need to do some advance scout-work to find them.

Here's what we advise: Call ahead, if at all possible. Ask if the restaurant has high chairs. Ask if there is a special menu for kids. Or if you're already on foot when mealtime is at hand, stop outside the restaurant door and carefully review the posted menu. Once you see that there are at least a few items that you think your toddler will eat, don't just waltz on in; send an adult in first to survey the scene. Here's what you want to find: Widely spaced tables or booths, with room to walk around between courses. Other families with young children, looking happy and well-fed. Cheerful waiters, moving at a good clip (but not seeming harried by the pace). If that's how the interior appears, then ask to be shown to a table.

Here's what you *don't* want to see: Most of the patrons attired in business suits or other "nice" clothing. Waiters in tuxedoes, moving at a stately pace. Dim, romantic lighting and a hushed atmosphere. Fine linen tablecloths. Not a single other child in the place. In such a setting do not hesitate to decline the maitre d's offer to seat your party, but rejoin the rest of your family waiting on the sidewalk, with a wave to the maitre d' and the line: "Another time, perhaps."

Once you have been seated at a restaurant that looks to be well set up for kids, that doesn't mean you're home free. A dinner at even the most kid-friendly of places can still turn into a disaster if you're not well prepared. You need to put some thought into the arrangements you make for the time you're there. Here's what other experienced parent diners suggest:

1. *Eat early—the earlier the better.* At five-thirty you will have the place to yourself and the waiters will be unstressed and attentive. By six in most places you are still okay; by six-thirty the place may be starting to fill up, and by seven it could well be too crowded, noisy, and slow for the little ones to make it successfully through the meal.

2. *Bring your own appetizers.* Unless you're sure that your children will love the basket of bread the restaurant provides, come well stocked with some things you know will hold them until their main course arrives. A zippered baggie of Cheerios or crackers or a small box of raisins may be all you need to keep your toddler's appetite in check while you wait.

3. *Bring some table amusements.* The restaurant-supplied pack of crayons and the coloring book menu are all very well, but just in case your little one is not in an artistic mood, it's handy to have a

small puzzle, or a pop-up book, or perhaps a favorite stuffed animal to keep your child occupied. Some children with shorter attention spans might need five or six such diversions to get them
through the average-length restaurant meal. But keep them hidden
till you're sure you need them, and then dole them out one at a
time, spaced to last through the payment of the check. If things go
well, you can save a few for next time.

4. *Take a walk when necessary.* When you sense your toddler's
patience is wearing thin, get him out of the high chair and let him
stretch his legs. One adult should be the designated walker during
the first part of the meal; another for the latter part (meaning, don't
let Mommy end up with the duty the whole time). With the use of a
set of palm-sized walkie-talkies, the adult child-walker can even
leave the restaurant to window-shop at nearby stores, until notified
that the next course has been served.

5. *Adjust the adults' ordering to suit the toddler's schedule.* In
crowded restaurants where it's already taken a long time to be
seated or served drinks, the adults should be prepared to modify
their orders as necessary. Avoid any menu item that appears elabo-
rate or is likely to need extra preparation time—and ask the waiter
if you're not sure. Omit appetizers, if necessary—or else request
that your child's main course be served at the same time as the
adult's first course. Then order your child's dessert while the adults
are having their main course. The adults in that case should forgo
dessert and coffee, or else buy a dessert to go and enjoy it with their
coffee at home.

When you've finally had a good experience at a restaurant, you
know your child can be taken out to eat at least at that one place.
So back you go for your next dining-out occasion, and you keep
going back there until you have established yourselves as regulars.
The waiters will learn your family's likes and dislikes, cutting down
on mistakes and shortening the time needed to serve you, and the
owners will come to recognize you, welcome you, and treat you as
old friends.

With each subsequent visit, your child becomes more familiar with the setting and the special rules (Use your "quiet voice" only; no running around; no spoon-banging on the high chair tray) that must be observed during meals away from home.

Pretty soon your "terror" is an old hand at restaurant dining and ready to branch out, to start exploring new places, with different styles of food. When that day comes, we say, don't forget those ethnic restaurants: Chinese restaurants with colorful fish in big tanks; Afghan restaurants with beaded curtains and embroidered pillows on the benches; Mexican restaurants with tortilla-making machines that let you watch a ball of dough go in one end and come out the other flat as a pancake. At all of these your child will find something new to try that he may well come to love, and if not, he'll still enjoy familiar choices like rice or cubed chicken bits without any sauce (which any restaurant should be able to prepare).

Everywhere you go, if you choose the place wisely, your child will find something to delight the senses, and as your child grows familiar with the ritual of restaurant dining, you'll find, too, that your child himself has turned from being a terror to being a perfectly fine fellow restaurant patron.

Grocery shopping with Alec is such a chore! Whenever I bring him along, the trip takes twice as long and ends up costing me a lot more, because I end up giving in to his demands for this or that food I really would rather not buy. Please don't say "Leave him at home," because I'm a single mom and I don't have a sitter on weekends.

Here's where it really helps to be able to outthink your little shopping trip foiler, to keep a step ahead of him and so keep him to the straight-and-narrow path . . . or rather, aisle.

• First, your most obvious strategy: Never let him inside a food store on an empty stomach. A well-fed toddler will be far less likely to whine for goodies if he isn't hungry to begin with. So your best time to run this errand is right after he's had a full meal. For most toddlers, though, that still won't put an end to impulse urges to snack in a place surrounded by shelf after shelf of enticingly packaged junk food choices.

• Second (and equally important), give him something to snack on while he's sitting in the basket of your cart. Once he's enjoying one treat, he'll be far less likely to demand another.

• Third, go with a list. Before you head out, let your son see you writing down the items you need. Tell him, firmly, that you're going to get only those things you put on the list. When you're in the store and he starts pointing to the cupcakes and saying, "I want that!" you simply nod regretfully and say, "I'm sorry, sweetie, but it's not on the list."

• Fourth (because a list won't stop a determined child from repeating his demand), allow a limited compromise. Agree in advance of the trip that once you're in the store, he can choose one special treat that's not on your list. That should be enough to make him think he's getting something good out of being brought along on your errand. You might want to steer him toward a choice he can consume right on the spot, like a doughnut from the bakery counter. When you get to the checkout register, you present the empty bag with its bar-code pricing, and be sure your son knows that you always pay for anything taken from the store.

• Fifth, give your child a mission. A child who has a purpose on the shopping trip is less likely to distract you with demands. Teach him to recognize the boxes of the breakfast cereals you buy. Send him down the aisle to find the right ones. If they're up on a high shelf, he can simply point them out to you. Let him help identify bananas that are not too green but not brown-speckled either. Let him help you with the lighter items, like paper towels and toilet tissue. Challenge him to carry two or three rolls at once. That should allow you time to grab a few more items in that area, as he struggles with his load on his way back to the cart.

• Sixth, cut down on the number of items you buy per trip. Do as much of your shopping for bulk items as possible when you can leave your child at home. You may save money that way too, because you can scout around for the lowest prices in your area on certain products.

• Seventh—and save this one for when you really need it—go to the lobster tank. Let your little boy stand and stare as long as he wants to, while you grab whatever items you need within sight of the tank. Let him give the lobsters names and let him believe people are taking them home as pets (but don't give in to his demand to do the same!).

Nora, my three-year-old, is more or less fine on a shopping trip for groceries or anything else that she understands that our family needs. Where she's really a pain, however, is on a trip to buy something just for me. Yet frequently I have no choice but to take her along when I need a new pair or shoes or some item of clothing. Any suggestions?

Yes—is there a shopping mall in your area that has an indoor playground for kids? If so, you'll usually find trained babysitters available for an additional charge per hour. You must first pay an admission fee to the playground, which makes the hourly rate higher than that charged by an in-home sitter, but then you don't have to round up a sitter in advance or have her working during the time it takes to drive to the mall and back. If you're a speedy shopper and can find what you want quickly most of the time, you may be able to get away with just an hour's babysitting time. And since outlet and discount malls tend to be the ones to have these staffed indoor playgrounds, you may find you're saving enough on your clothing purchases to be able to afford the sitter's fee.

An alternative, especially if there is no such mall within easy driving distance, is to take along a trustworthy teenaged assistant. You can pay her for her time and her help looking after your child while you all shop together, or let her take your child for a walk while you shop alone.

If either of these suggestions is too much for your budget, try shopping with a friend who has a toddler about the same age. The children can keep each other amused, and one parent can take turns looking after both of them while the other gets a little time to try things on. (We know how impossible it is to judge whether an item looks good on you when you have a pint-sized constant critic sitting at your heels.)

However, we think the best, simplest solution is to give up altogether on the idea of trying to shop for clothing with a small child in tow. On-line shopping is the answer we think you're seeking. Get yourself wired to the Internet (if you're not there already) and browse to your heart's content in as many stores as you care to visit. You're not limited by geography as long as there's a parcel delivery service that can reach your house. Use a "shop-bot" to help you find the brands you want at the best prices anywhere. (A shop-bot, short for "shopping robot," is a program that searches the Internet for an item that fits your specified requirements for price and features. A popular and easy-to-use shop-bot is Mysimon. com.) Many clothing e-tailers these days let you plug your measurements into their program to create a virtual model that will "try on" the items of interest in a dressing room in cyberspace. All while your little one is tucked safely in bed!

Tracy, my three-and-a-half-year-old, won't walk along with me when I take my six-month-old baby out in the stroller. After only a few blocks she starts whining that she is tired and wants to be carried. I'd buy a double stroller, but she'd only outgrow it in a few months. Any suggestions?

The first thing to try is asking Tracy to help you push the stroller. Having a job to do will make her feel important and bring her some positive attention for her contribution to the stroll (which, she should quickly discover, is far better than the type of attention she can get for whining and obstructing the effort to get where you're going). The key words here are "*help* push." Don't let her take over the pushing entirely or you will be worse off than you were before. Putting a three-year-old in complete charge of a stroller will result in a walk that is painfully slow or convoluted or hazardous—or all three. If she discovers that you are steadying the stroller or giving it some forward momentum, and she starts crying that she wants to push all by herself, be firm: For safety's sake, a grown-up should always keep a guiding hand on the stroller.

Now let's say you try the "help push" strategy and it works—for all of three or four blocks. What do you do when the thrill of being the stroller pusher has worn off, and you've still got ten blocks to go? Try making your child the navigator. If you think she knows the way home (or the way to the supermarket or the playground or whatever your destination may be), let her tell you how to go. If she's about to turn left when she should turn right, gently offer a course correction: "Try going the other direction . . . yes, that way."

It also may help to involve her in the question of distance. Before she has a chance to start whining about how long the walk has been or how tired she's become, have her guess how many more blocks there are to go. Instead of telling her the answer (assuming you know, that is), have her count off each block as you pass it. Or have her look out for certain landmarks that you know you will see along the way. Animal sightings are particularly good for keeping up a three-year-old's interest: She can keep an eye out for a neighbor's cat that can usually be found sunning itself in a certain spot, or look for the tree that has a squirrel's nest inside a hollowed-out part of the trunk, or when passing a yard with a flower garden, stop to look for butterflies or check whether the flowers have fragrance. Your walk may take longer than if you had not allowed these ministops and explorations along the way, but then again, maybe not, since it is also time-consuming to have a child stopping every few steps, whining to be picked up.

On the other hand, some walks are simply too long for some children's little legs. If, after everything you can think of to make the walk enjoyable, your three-year-old is still giving out and balking midway through one of your longer excursions, then it's time to find another means of getting there. Figure out how far you can usually go before your child starts complaining. Then drive, or take the bus, subway, or taxi, for all distances beyond your child's usual level of endurance.

Last (and maybe best) suggestion: Go ahead and buy that double stroller. You may be able to get a cheap one at a yard sale, which, while it may be outgrown within six months, may still make those six months much easier on all of you. Or you may want to buy a double stroller specifically designed to carry an older child—up to age five or six—and a baby. The "Sit'n'Stand" stroller features a platform in the back for the older child to stand on, making it no wider than a single stroller, and only slightly longer. If you can't find one of those in a baby products store, you can order one through a catalogue or over the Internet. (See the Resource Guide at the back of this book for toll-free numbers.)

WALK THIS WAY, PLEASE!

Can't get your toddler to walk with you in a straight line? Here are some quick tricks to help move 'em along.

Pennies in a line. Toss a penny out a few feet ahead of where you want to go. Your toddler will run to pick it up. Then toss out another, and another.

Under the bridge. Stand with your legs spread apart just ahead of your toddler. Tell her to run "under the bridge." After she emerges, reposition yourself ahead of her again, and let her run under. Repeat as often as she's willing to play this game.

Flashlight chase. Use a flashlight to cast a beam on an evening walk. Shine the beam where you want your toddler to go, and let him chase it.

Mother, may I? Play a sidewalk version of this popular kids' game—except instead of standing at the front of a room, you walk alongside your child, giving instructions: "Take three giant steps. Now take six baby steps. Now take one long running jump. Take five twirling steps." Try to be creative with new and different steps. Demonstrate each step, of course, and get your toddler to copy you.

> Go *"one, two, three, u-u-upppp!"* This one will work for a long time, until your arms give out. You and your spouse (or any other adult) should position yourselves on either side of your toddler, each holding his hand. After three steps, you each lift up and "fly" him the next several paces forward. He definitely won't want this game to end!

My best friend and her husband are not planning to have any kids. They live in a beautifully decorated house, full of expensive antiques and delicate knickknacks—and of course, no child-proofing. The last time I went to visit, with my not-quite-two-year-old son in tow, he just couldn't stay out of trouble. He spilled juice on the Persian rug, he knocked over a porcelain vase (which miraculously, my friend caught before it hit the floor!), and he ran his metal-bumpered matchbox car up and down her carved oak door. In short, the visit was a disaster! I love my friend as much as ever, but I need to know how to handle any future invitations to her place. Should I decline unless I can get a sitter? Or just wait until my son is, say, twelve?

Don't kid yourself—twelve-year-old boys can do as much damage as toddlers (maybe more!). The thing to do is to enlist your friend's help in arranging a visit that will be as much fun for your toddler as it is for the adults—not to mention gentler on the furniture. There are several ways to achieve this:

The first is to move the location of the visit a short distance away—just a few more feet to the backyard. We're assuming your friend would like this idea better than your suggestion that she spend a half hour or so putting her delicate things away, throwing a blanket over her antiques, and otherwise childproofing her house. Of course, you need decent weather for a garden-only visit—and you should also inquire whether she has any thorny rosebushes or other areas that must be declared off-limits. With some green grass as his play mat and a few well-chosen outdoor toys, your toddler should pass the time happily while you and your best friend enjoy your time together. Or:

Meet somewhere else entirely. Go to a kid-friendly restaurant or a park or a playground. Try a large bookstore that has a kids' reading and play area as well as comfortable adult-size chairs, and perhaps an on-site café. If you can stand to eat at a fast-food restaurant, choose one with an indoor climbing structure. Or:

Invite her to your house. If she says, "Oh, but we always go to your place; I need to reciprocate," tell her that you really don't mind being the hostess all the time—in fact, you prefer it. But if she feels strongly that she owes you a lunch, say you wouldn't mind if she brought a dish to your house, and helped you with the cleanup.

Yet another strategy is to accept her offer of an indoor visit, but ask her bluntly for her help in making her home more kid-friendly. Maybe she can childproof just one room of her house so that your son can play safely. A good choice would be a bedroom or den that has a VCR; that way you could bring along a new video or an old favorite, park your kid in front of it, and let him zone out. Or:

Go around nap time, bringing your child's familiar nap pad, along with any sleep object he needs. Rock with him in a rocking chair if that's what it takes to get him to dreamland in an unfamiliar place, but as soon as he's out, transfer him to the nap mat in the darkened room, and leave him alone. You can leave the door ajar to listen for sounds of his awakening, or bring along a baby monitor and keep the receiver handy. Bring soft toys that can't hurt the furniture.

No matter what strategy you adopt, it's important to be flexible. Postpone your visit if your child seems unusually out-of-sorts just beforehand. With the three-and-under set, you can never be wedded to a schedule or force your child to be sociable when he's not feeling up to it. He's too young to understand the concept of being on his "best behavior."

Still, it's never too early to start teaching when the opportunity arises. Even as you keep a tight rein on him in your friend's house, you also explain why you're pulling him back. You say: "No, no, you can't climb on the table at someone else's house." And: "Don't touch! That's could break!" (Important: Until he's at least four, never assume that these verbal commands are enough. You still have to be right at his elbow.)

Watch for signs that he's growing restless, and cut the visit short if need be. Promise to get together again, perhaps just the two of you next time. Arrange for your spouse to stay home with your son, with the promise that you will stay home one night so that he can have some adult conversation with one of his friends, when he needs it most.

That's a solution that probably would do you both a lot of good.

Lori, my two-and-a-half-year-old, is a champion dawdler. It never seems to make a difference to her where we're going or why—she just takes forever to get ready. It drives me crazy! Why can't my daughter learn the meaning of the word "hurry"?

Because she's a toddler. Her brain is hard-wired for exploration, which causes her to stop and wonder at every little thing that you, as an adult, take for granted. "Why do I have ten toes?" "What would happen if I put my socks on my ears?" "What's that cracker crumb doing on the floor . . . and is it yummy? [Yes, absolutely!]" Between the spot where she is and your front door there are dozens and dozens of such mysteries to be investigated; there are adventures in every step she takes—so the more steps it takes to go anywhere, the better.

Each time you're in a rush, you can try to explain that there's no time for diversions. You can raise your voice. You can point to the clock and talk about your need to be out the door in five minutes, or ten minutes, or whatever—but don't expect any of these efforts to work this year. Or next year either. Or the year after that. Maybe in three or four years' time your notions about time (and the need to use it wisely) will begin to make sense to her. Right now, there's just no way for her to get it.

This is a surprisingly hard concept for most parents to grasp. Why? Because for the first full year of parenthood, the baby is, essentially, a carry-on item. You pick it up and take it where you want to go. It's up to you to pack it up correctly, but once you've learned to do that efficiently, you're off without further ado.

With toddlerhood comes a big change. Suddenly, you have another person on hand *with an opinion,* and very likely, a contrary one. Toddlers *don't* do what you say. In fact, it's fascinating to them to find out what might happen if they do just the opposite of what you ask. So when you point to the door and say, "We're going NOW"—you've thrown down a challenge that's impossible to resist.

But if you will just recognize that your toddler is designed to delay, explore, and challenge, you can use these behaviors to your advantage.

For the curious toddler who is rather like a cat following a rolling ball of yarn, try this: Attach a small stuffed animal to a string. Stand by the door and slowly pull the string toward you; your toddler will be sure to follow. Unchanged, this trick works two or three times. It should work a few more times if you vary what's at the end of the string.

Here's a different, simpler approach: Plan for the extra time you know (from experience) you will need. If it normally takes you ten minutes to get where you're going without kids, then to arrive with a toddler, double it. Or triple it if you think you've got a super-dawdler on your hands. There's hardly any downside to being early, and lots of hassle and stress in the prospect of being late, so it doesn't matter if you've been overly generous in your estimate of the time needed. With this strategy you will find yourself doing almost no yelling or screaming, no hustling, tugging, or dragging by the arm. Your toddler won't feel she's being punished for showing curiosity, asking questions, being herself—and you'll still get to wherever you need to be on time.

Here's a way to deal with at least some of those occasions when the rush is unavoidable. Ask yourself, "Is there any alternative to taking my toddler along?" If the answer is yes, then go with it. For example, your whole family needn't rush to the airport to pick up your aunt and uncle—let one spouse handle the job. Or you might have a neighbor who's willing to trade off babysitting with you on an as-needed basis. Or it could be that your errand is better put off until another time. Does your toddler really *need* to have that haircut today? If the appointments are on a walk-in basis, there's no harm in the postponement.

Since we know toddlers like to stretch the limits of what they can do, give them the challenge they seek. Say: "Betcha can't get your coat on and be ready to go out the door before I count to twenty." Slow down your counting as necessary to make the goal an attainable one (or pick a higher number to start out with).

If your toddler is the competitive sort, offer a race. "Who can make it to the door first? You, me, or Daddy?" Slow yourselves down to make sure your toddler can be the winner. You can repeat this trick as often as you think it stands a chance of working: race to the corner, race to the preschool classroom, race home from the playground. (Caution: Never set up a race between siblings—unless you *want* more sibling rivalry.)

For added incentive, or anytime you need a show of speed, offer a prize. "If we can make it to the dry cleaners before they close, we'll have time to stop at the ice cream place next door and you can have a cone." Just be careful not to overuse this strategy, or else your child will quickly discover her ability to make every act of promptness pay.

Yet another technique for speeding your child along is to remove all the distractions that could possibly slow her down. Get her out of her room, which is probably filled with toys, out of the kitchen (filled with food), out of the living room (filled with breakable objects) and into the front hall. Gate off the other exits. Have everything on hand that you need to get her ready to go: her coat, her shoes, a lunch box. Sometimes houses and apartments have a special room just to make exit and entry more convenient; if it's in the front, it's called the "foyer," and if it's in the back, the "mud room." In either case, if you've got it, we say, put it to your advantage in your quick-getaway strategy.

Although we warned at the beginning of this section that you can't expect a toddler to care what a clock says, she might become interested in the workings of a timer. Get a brightly colored one with large numbers on it, one that dings loudly when it goes off.

Give her a few practice runs so she can become familiar with the time it takes for a five-minute interval to end. We don't recommend trying longer periods until at least age three. Then set out what needs to be done before the timer goes off for the first time ("I'll need to get you dressed"), and then the second time ("We'll have your teeth and hair brushed"), and finally the third time ("We'll get your shoes and your coat on and we'll be ready to go out to the car"). Just remember to plan that final timer ding for at least five minutes before you *really* need to be out the door, in case your toddler finds a way to slow you down.

Our final hint for faster exits: Forget about perfection. A neat and proper appearance will probably take too long—and why would a toddler need to look proper anyway? Think of your child as looking "casual," not "sloppy." (If you're the sort of person who finds it hard to stop caring about appearances, then ignore this strategy—but be sure to factor in an extra half hour to get ready to go anywhere.)

For those who have been counting, you just finished "Ten Ways to Deal with Your Dawdling Darling." We hope some or all of them will work for you.

TIPS FOR GREATER EFFICIENCY IN YOUR EXITS

If, despite your best efforts, and the abovementioned strategies, you're still having a hard time getting your little slowpoke to get a move on, you might want to refocus your efforts in a more productive direction—on yourself. Organize things so that you have what you need on hand, sparing yourself the delay, for example, of having one toddler shoe in hand while the other is God-knows-where. The following tips should help:

Shoe box by the door. Toddler shoes seem to end up under furniture when you need them most. But when you know they always get returned to the bin by the kitchen door, you'll be far less likely to be conducting a search when you're already ten minutes late for preschool. (For those who don't like to leave out a bin full of scuffed-up shoes, try a hanging shoe organizer on the inside of a closet door.)

Kids' coat tree. The sooner your toddler can put on her own coat, the better. But how can she do that when she can't reach the hangers in the front hall closet? The answer is to get a child-sized coat tree, available at any kids' furniture store, or from a catalog like Pottery Barn Kids, or online from an e-tailer like Babesandkids.com or anythingjoes.com. (For information on contacting these companies, see the Resource Guide at the back of the book). As an added advantage you'll have an easier time finding your own coat when you have fewer of them hung in the same space.

For those who have a multilevel house, *get good use from your first-floor bathroom.* It's more than just the guest powder room; use it as the main place for kids to brush their teeth and wash their hands in the morning. That way there's no whining about having to go back upstairs.

For toddlers still in diapers, put an additional *changing table on the first floor,* and for toddlers in the midst of toilet training, have *a potty in each bathroom.* They're cheap (about ten bucks for the basic plastic bowl-with-a-seat type) and more than worth it when you're almost out the door but have just heard the voice of delay calling, "Mommy, I neeeeeed to goooo!"

While we're on the subject of clothing changes, remember, the more complicated the clothing, the longer it will take to get your little one dressed. So for efficiency-minded parents, we recommend you *stick with simple clothes:* one-piece cotton pullover playdresses for girls, and for toddlers of both sexes, T-shirts and elastic-waist pants.

This next speed measure we can say in just two words: *velcro shoes.*

And this one in just four: *Keep hair cut short.*

7

The Trouble With Travel

Why do toddlers need vacations? Every day is play for them and everything they do is an adventure. Yet we still insist on packing them up and making them leave home once or twice a year—all in the name of fun. We're surprised when they hate it, and whine and cry and say they just want to be back home.

The parents get upset, because they imagined, when they planned the trip, that the time would be relaxing and pleasant— only to find that travel with toddlers is *really hard work!*

But does it have to be that way? Our answer is a qualified no. You can have a good trip with toddlers, but you *will* have to work at it. However, we think what really makes a difference is *when* your work needs to be done. On the trip, or mostly ahead of time? Our vote is squarely with the latter choice, because if you wait until you're on the road to start dealing with your toddler's travel re-quirements, you will end up desperately running around trying to get this or that item you hope will do the trick to keep your toddler comfortable, to assuage his boredom, and compensate for losses of things that had to be left at home—and you may never find what you need. You'll be so exhausted that, by the time you're back home, you will wish you could take a vacation to rest up from your vacation!

But do your work ahead of time, in the form of advance planning, and your trip will be smooth sailing. (Okay, with a toddler nothing's ever smooth all the time, but at least it won't be a constant storm.) In the months or weeks leading up to the vacation time, carefully consider your toddler's temperament, routine, comfort needs, and other factors, and then work out the best way to maintain his or her normal schedule, prevent boredom, deal with toilet issues, and minimize the strangeness and scariness of being away from home.

Gone are the days when you and your spouse could just take off on a whim any weekend you chose, tossing an overnight bag into the car and driving until you discovered some wonderful little hideaway inn. (Confess: You never actually did that, did you?) But take heart, because children grow up so fast and time just whizzes by. Before you know it, you'll be free to travel on your own once more.

Our two-year-old Ben is normally a very contented and playful child. But he's very set on his routine, and if there's any sort of disruption to it, it's hell on the rest of the family. Usually, this isn't a problem because we just make sure that he gets his nap when he expects it, and we only take him to familiar places to eat or play whenever we go out. That is, except for two weeks when we go on our summer vacation. We might as well book two weeks in hell as far as he's concerned. He just can't stand it, and the instant he sees me start to pack, he cries. He can't sleep in any bed but his own toddler bed at home, with his own blankets and all his stuffed animals (he has about fifty of them). He needs his night-light and all the other lights set just so. He won't eat any food except what I serve him in his chair in my kitchen or those few restaurants we've succeeded in getting him used to (and no, they're not part of any national chain). He doesn't like long car trips, he doesn't like strangers—in fact, there isn't a single thing about the trip that he likes. So I end up staying cooped up in the hotel room with him, trying to jolly him up, endlessly replaying the same two or three videos we bring along (they're all Blue's Clues) *and the vacation is hell for me, too. Our third year of this trip is approaching ... all too soon. Is there anything I can do?*

P.S. Please don't suggest that we stay home. I would love to, but it's a longstanding tradition in my husband's family that we get together every summer at the family-run lodge in Maine.

Things are not irredeemably hopeless ... but close. The trouble is, the family tradition you've established over the past three years is a bad one. We're not talking about taking a trip to Maine—that sounds great!—we're talking about the tradition that you confine yourself to a hotel room rather than ask your toddler to adjust. That tells him *he's* in charge. So he's not the one who's trapped at all—just you. He's holding the keys. It's up to you to come up with an escape plan, but as with any jailbreak, you must expect that it will be a harrowing trek.

Well, we can see no way to avoid the struggle that's ahead this year, so grit your teeth and prepare to fight. Tell your son in advance of the trip that the family vacation is going to be just that: something for the whole family—and he's part of it. That means he will have to do all the things the other family members do. If you go on an outing, he's going along ... and he has to behave while he's on it, too.

You'll need to make heavy-handed use of carrots and sticks to bring about a radical change at this point. You'll need rewards on hand for every instance of cooperation, but be prepared with appropriate deterrent words and actions in mind for any contrary behavior on his part.

If he won't get in the stroller when you want him to, grab him and carry him along, any way you can. When that gets tiring, make your spouse or some other relative carry him. There's no need to be especially gentle with him either. If he complains, tell him he can get back in the stroller.

The minute he starts crying and whining in a restaurant or at some special event, he should be taken outside. You might try getting other members of the family to take turns guarding him during his brief terms of outdoor exile, since he may think it's fine to be alone with his own parent, away from the crowd indoors. Make sure he understands that he can come back inside as soon as he calms down.

Under no circumstances should you agree to take him back to the hotel room—that's just what he's aiming for. If you can just hold firm, he really will see that it does no good to fuss—though it may take three or four such spoiled outings for the lesson to sink in.

Coupled with your new firm and consistent policy, you should make all reasonable efforts to see to it that conditions are as close to home as can be arranged. Obviously, he can't take all fifty stuffed animals with him, but five or six would be okay. Let him choose the ones to ride in the suitcase, assuming he's not crying too hard to complete this task. If that's the case, then you should go ahead and pick the ones you think he'd miss the most.

As to the lighting problem in his room at night—of course, you can't expect to reproduce the exact dimness/brightness level of home, but you can at least bring along his old familiar night-light.

We're going to assume you're not willing to disassemble his toddler bed and strap it to the top of your car (although other parents have done so—see Judy's story), but it may be a good idea to get him used to an alternate bed at home, well before the trip begins. Try putting him down for his nap on a mat with some familiar blankets, or use a kid-sized sleeping bag on the floor in his room. Once you've got him liking something different on occasion in his own familiar house, you should be able to bring the alternate bed with you and so in large measure ease the trauma (as he sees it) of having to go to sleep in an unfamiliar setting.

But despite these and any other accommodations you make on his behalf, you should be prepared for him to react badly at first, just as he's done in times past. It may seem like half the trip is gone before he's finally able to sleep through the night. And to make matters worse, he may refuse to nap at all the first several days. Of course, that will make you and your spouse lose sleep, and so you will undoubtedly end up more exhausted on this vacation than you were in past years, but at least you're on the road to change now, and you can have confidence that things *will* improve. Day by day, in small, almost imperceptible ways, you will be less miserable, because (that is, if you don't cave in before he does) your son *will* adapt. You may not see the progress because you're too close to the situation to be objective, but here is what's actually happening inside your son's stubborn little head: He is gradually, grudgingly, opening up to the possibility that there's nothing so terrible about being away from home. Though he can't use words to describe how he's feeling, he's becoming more confident and secure—because ultimately his sense of security is derived not from the presence of this or that familiar object, but from the love and caring of his family around him.

HAVE BED, WILL TRAVEL
(JUDY'S STORY)

As a baby, Liza always found it difficult to sleep in strange places. She was *so* attached to her crib, she'd just cry whenever we tried to put her down anywhere else. She wouldn't even nap in a moving car. After the first few miserable attempts, I stopped trying to get her to sleep at friends' or relatives' houses, since she simply refused. So the first time we went on a family vacation, I didn't bother to take along a port-a-crib. I just pulled out her old familiar, intensely loved crib mattress, strapped it to the top of the car's roof rack, and drove off. Now, I'm not proposing this as a solution for other families, but rather as a warning of what you'll end up having to do if you don't make your baby learn to sleep in a strange crib from the start. Liza is now ten, and while all her friends enjoy slumber parties and sleepovers at each other's houses, she doesn't go because she still hates to be in an unfamiliar bed!

—Judy S.
Sherman Oaks, CA

My one-and-a half-year-old is now too old for her infant car seat. We just bought her a toddler seat, but are having the worst time getting her to sit in it. She cries and fights whenever we try to put her in the new seat. Please don't tell us to shop for a different model seat—this one was so expensive, we can't afford not to keep using it.

Too bad there isn't a trial period for toddler car seats so that you can find out, before you blow a hundred bucks or more, whether your child finds the seat comfortable. Still, it could be that comfort's not the issue; she's just upset that the old familiar seat is gone and she wouldn't like *anything* new that you offered.

We wish we could come up with some guaranteed way to make her fall in love with her new seat, but before we offer any suggestions, we'd like to emphasize one point: This is one of those questions with no room for compromise. We might have a few ideas that might help make her think of riding in a car seat as fun, but even if she keeps on hating it, you must keep strapping her in each time. Don't even think about giving in and letting her ride out of the seat, even if it's just for a trip down the driveway. There are absolutely no exceptions to this rule—not for sickness and not for any other reason (real or imagined) that her creative mind can think up.

Use your superior strength to pin her down if she kicks and squirms. Make it absolutely clear that no amount of struggle will get you to ease up. And you've got to make clear to her that you aren't going to fight about it time after time, either. When it comes to her safety, it's "Do as I say . . . and NOW!"

Having told her that, you should, of course, do whatever you can to make the car seat more attractive and more comfortable for her. Maybe it's the tight edges of the straps against her shoulders that bother her. You can get Velcro padding to cover the straps where they cross her neck and chest.*

Because infant seats usually have the baby reclining more than toddler seats, you might want to adjust the angle of recline of the new seat (if possible) to make it feel more like her old one. Or maybe it's already too reclined for her to see out the window. Readjusting it to a more upright position may improve her view enough to make her see some benefit in the change.

* You can find this product, called Prop-O's Head Support, in The Right Start Catalog.

You may also encourage her acceptance of the new seat by means of a small but highly desirable, material incentive (you know, a bribe). M&M's or other small candies may be just the thing.* Tell her she can have some at the start of every car trip for the next few outings—but only if she climbs in quickly and cooperates completely while you click the belts in place. Do make clear from the first, however, that this offer will not go on forever, so that she won't expect a treat for every car ride for the rest of her life. Do withhold the reward at the least bit of protest or complaining.

For more suggestions on ways to make car rides more comfortable and enjoyable, we turned to other parents, who told us about some products and attachments that had improved their lives on the road.**

• Attach a toy "busy bar" across the front of the toddler seat. Give your child a wheel to turn, a horn to honk, a teether to chew on, and other distractions.

• Hang a canvas multipocketed pouch from one of the armrests of the toddler seat, holding crayons, an activity book, a favorite stuffed animal, any other amusements you think she'd like. (The treats she finds in the pockets should become unavailable whenever she gives you a hard time about getting into her seat.)

• Use your backseat cup holders for bottles, juice boxes, or sippy cups, to make sure she's got something to quench her thirst within her reach, without having to ask you to stop while you're driving.

• Use Ziploc baggies to make up snack packs that she can eat neatly and safely while strapped in her car seat. Goldfish crackers, bite-sized carrot bits, halved seedless grapes, and dried fruit-and-nut mixes are all good choices because they pose little danger of choking.

• Install a child-view mirror (one that allows you to see your child without turning around) so that you can safely keep an eye on her as you drive. That way you'll become aware if she's growing

---

* But not lollipops! Any candy on a stick is dangerous to consume in a moving car, because it could get lodged in the throat during an accident.

** Most of the products mentioned can be found in infant/toddler products stores, online shopping sites, or catalogs such as The Right Start and One Step Ahead.

uncomfortable, or has dropped her drink, or in some other way could use your attention. (Always pull over and park safely before you tend to your fussing child in the backseat.)

• Try a headrest or car seat pillow specially designed to make it easier for a child to fall asleep while buckled in. You may find a set of cushions that go on either side of the head, or a single pillow that you can attach with Velcro to the back of the car seat, or a U-shaped chin-and-neck rest that allows your child to nod off with her head falling forward. Fleece or lambs' wool makes a soft outer covering on some of the products you can buy. Others may come in animal shapes, turning the car pillow into your child's special friend.

• Use a car seat cover to prevent the metal buckles from becoming too hot. You can buy a specially shaped one that has a reflective coating, or just toss an old blanket in the back to throw over the seat whenever you can't park in the shade.

• Use car window shades to keep the whole car cooler in hot weather. You can get custom or standard windshield covers or just use those cardboard accordion shades that you can buy in a drugstore. There are also pull-down shades for your back passenger windows, decorated with teddy bears and ducklings and other designs your toddler will approve of.

• Get a variety of toys that you can keep in the car for fun on the go. An Etch-a-Sketch or a Magna-Doodle will allow your child to create pictures without any mess. Pop-up books and picture books without words can be enjoyed anywhere without an adult to do the reading. Sticker boards and felt boards allow her to create designs and then remove the figures and start all over again. A pair of simple sock puppets may provide the inspiration for a whole three-act play that your toddler can put on while you drive.

FOR CAR SEAT INSTALLATION, GET EXPERT HELP

The most comfortable and best equipped car seat is actually worthless if it's improperly installed—as is the case with perhaps 80 percent or more of those sold (according to the National Safe Kids Coalition). To make sure yours will pro-

tect your child fully in a crash, take advantage of free in-
spections and installation advice available at over eighty
auto dealerships around the United States. To find one near
you, call 1-877-348-4254 or log on to www.fitforakid.org
or www.safekids.org.

*Our whole family is going to spend the summer in a small
California coastal town. I won a research grant to study marine
life and I'm just thrilled about it. We've sublet a beautiful cottage
within walking distance of the beach, which I think will be wonderful for my almost-four-year-old boy and my one-year-old girl.
The only trouble is how to get there. We live in New Jersey, and
we need to bring along so much stuff that it seems the only workable option is to rent a U-Haul and drive. We're a close family, but
truth be told, I think 3,000 miles of closeness is too much for any
of us to stand. Do you think we'll make it—and if so, how?*

Slowly, that's how. Don't try to shorten the trip by driving
straight through. You might be able to make it in six days or fewer
. . . but you'll hate yourselves if you do. Instead, go for the long and
leisurely approach, driving a few hours, then stopping a few hours.
See the sights; stretch your legs. Don't try to set any speed records.
You will get there eventually, say, in eight to ten days. Or longer, if
you've got the time to spare. (We think you'll be glad you did.)

Plan your route and think about good stopping points well in
advance of the trip. Bring along several detailed family-oriented
guidebooks, one for each region you'll pass through along the way,
and a cell phone linked to the most comprehensive service network
you can find. That way, you'll have the tools you need to change
your plans "on the fly." If you're driving along happily, with your
kids napping peacefully in the back, you can pass by that motel
you'd noted with a dog-eared page in the guidebook, and keep
making tracks until they wake up. Then, if you think they could use
a half-day's break in a state park with a waterfall you've read
about—just a ten-minute detour off the highway—flip to that page

in the guidebook and use your cell phone to call for information about the park's food facilities, hours of operation, or other useful details that you need to find out before you make the detour.

Your cell phone will save you valuable time that you might otherwise spend driving around looking for vacancy signs. If you don't already have a cell phone, we think you'll find it worthwhile to make arrangements to rent one for the three-month period that you'll be away from home. These days a cell phone is more than just a convenience; it's a valuable safety feature of highway driving, as it provides a direct link to emergency services, saving you from having to wait for the aid of a passing motorist (who may not be a good Samaritan). Be sure to program in your pediatrician's number, too!

Even with lots of planned stops and activities along the way, there will inevitably be long, long, boring stretches of empty highway along this journey, so stock your car well before you go. Consult your four-year-old about what activities and amusements he might like best.

Let him choose his favorite *tapes and/or CDs*. So that you don't have to listen to endless replays of "Baby Beluga," we suggest you equip him with his own personal CD player or Walkman. Look in an electronics store or a large toystore for a version especially designed for small kids, with big, color-coded control buttons, and earphones designed to fit comfortably over smaller heads.

It will also help build his enthusiasm for the trip if you give him his own *atlas* with the roads you'll take highlighted in yellow marker. Perhaps he can follow along with an orange marker, coloring over each stretch of the trip along the way.

Of course, you'll want to have *coloring books and crayons and backseat activities* to help him pass the time. We recommend Rand McNally's *The Best Travel Activity Book Ever* and the Klutz Press's *Kids Travel: A Backseat Survival Guide,* which comes wtih a pad and a pouch of game pieces (for children age three and up only). *Car bingo* is a great game that can be played by almost anyone over the age of two. (You get a card with various roadside sights on it—a barn, a speed limit sign, a pond, a tanker truck, etc.—and the first person to spot five sights in a row has bingo.) A padded *lap desk* (available at many bookstores) makes it easier for your backseat artist to draw, color, or play games.

Teach him *the license plate game.* He may not be able to read the names of the states yet, but he can recognize the different symbols, and you can read off each state's tag line.

Teach him some long, funny *car songs.* Let him sing all the verses of "99 Bottles of Beer on the Wall"—but don't let him sing it all over again from 0 to 99!

For long, uninterrupted stretches of driving, you may find it worthwhile to have a *VCR* installed to allow your kids to watch videos while you drive. Go to any automotive sound shop and explore your options. The screen can be positioned so that it drops down from the inside roof of the car, or it can be fitted into the frame of one of the front seats. In SUVs and minivans, the unit is generally mounted on the floor between the two front seats, facing the rear seats. This will be quite an expensive modification, whichever way it's done, but some veterans of long trips with children say it's well worth the price.

A cheaper, but for some children equally absorbing, form of entertainment on a long trip is a *handheld electronic game,* such as a Nintendo Gameboy or a similar brand. Before buying your son a Nintendo set, you should consider that if he uses it daily on a cross-country drive, he'll arrive in California a true Nintendo addict, and you'll have to wean him off of it afterward. (Expect that part to be rough going.)

We have not forgotten your one-year-old. She won't be able to work a child-size CD player, nor will Nintendo hold any fascination for her. *Rattles and busy boards* will only hold her interest for so long, so you'll just have to acquire brand-new things along the way. Roadside souvenir shops usually have a good selection of cheap board books. Look for ones that have a little something special—a squeaker inside the fuzzy chick on the last page, or pop-up surprises, or a lift-the-flap peekaboo game. There are also some toy sets that seem perfect for toddler play while buckled in a seat: look for cardboard and metal "paper" dolls with magnetized clothing you can take on and off; "magic color" slates that start off all black but turn rainbow colors as you move the stylus across the board;

and a favorite of our kids at that age—the set of connected blocks with animal parts, allowing you to create a strange hybrid creature by turning the head block (start with a parrot head, for example) and then the body block (try a dinosaur's middle) and then the tail part (finish off with a braided, ribboned horse tail).

What *not* to bring along on the trip: anything requiring the use of glue or scissors; any game with tiny parts (because it's a certainty that some essential piece will fall to the floor and roll under the seat or into some opening too small for you to retrieve it); anything that makes an annoying noise.

Even with all of the above recommendations, we think that a cross-country drive with kids your age will still be trying on all your souls, so we'd like to toss out two alternatives to consider.

The first is the *fly-drive option*. You (or your spouse, whichever one would be the best at handling a solo long-distance drive) should take the car and the U-Haul and hit the road. The other spouse flies with the kids. This can be economical if you can find a good deal on airfare. Try a big-volume, big-discount travel agency, or check out on-line travel services and price-bidding brokers such as Priceline.com. After you consider that the solo adult can stay in cheaper motel rooms for fewer days total, you may actually save money from the deal. There's no question that this option's a sanity saver.

The other course is to *rent a huge RV* and make it your hotel on wheels. Load your own car up with your stuff, hitch it to the back of the RV, and tow it along. Now your kids don't have to be confined all the time, and the whole trip will become a fun adventure. Plus, you save on hotel rooms. (But not quite as much as you might think, after you figure in those exorbitant trailer park hook-up fees!) You'll also need to plan your trip ahead to reserve spaces at trailer campgrounds along the way, and be sure to give yourself some extra time up front to recover from the shock of finding out the cost of a two-week RV rental.

THE COST OF CUTTING OUT THE QUESTION "ARE WE THERE YET?"

How much would you give never to hear that annoying whine: "Are we there yet?" Would you spend two or three bucks? If that amount doesn't strike you as extortionate, then try this game. Give each child a stack of dimes at the start of the day's drive. Twenty dimes per child should be enough. Announce the rules of the game: Anytime a child asks, "Are we there yet?" or "Are we *almost* there?" or "When are we gonna *be* there?"—or any variation on that theme—the child must pay you a dime. You also have a collection of dimes, and you tell them they can earn a dime every so-many miles traveled without a destination query. (You need to set the rate based on the total number of miles before a stop.) Make clear that there will be no payment if there is any whining, fighting, or other banned behavior during that interval.

For children who are too young to care about money, you can substitute little candies.

—Suggested by many parents

We're going to be taking a nine-hour flight overseas with our toddler, Sonia, who is about to turn two. Tell us we're not crazy, and that it can be done. I mean, it can . . . can't it?

Absolutely. We've done it ourselves, and we know lots of other people here in this highly international city (Washington, D.C.) who have turned their toddlers and babies into frequent flyers. It won't be pretty, it won't be fun, but it can be done.

Our first and most important tip is not about any actual product or physical adjustment that will help. It's about attitude: Keep your expectations reasonably low, so that you stand a chance of being pleasantly surprised by how well Sonia does overall.

What is "doing well" under these circumstances? It's getting through the flight without causing the other passengers in your row to demand that the flight attendants move you to some other part of the plane (like the baggage compartment). You can certainly hope to achieve that much . . . if you come prepared.

The most crucial preparations concern the booking of the route, the choice of airline, and reservation of particular seats.

You should always try to get the most direct flight, without a layover or change of planes, if at all possible.

The departure time of the flight is very important. With a long flight, it's usually an advantage to go overnight. Small kids will sleep most—and if you're lucky, almost all—of the time. You'll need far fewer trip amusements to pass the hours (making your carry-on bag a little lighter), and you won't have to worry about how your child's nap schedule will be maintained.

If several air carriers serve your destination, find out how they handle families with young children. Is there a changing table on board? Individual TV screens in each seat back, with a kids' channel? (You'll never be so glad to see Barney and Baby Bop or the Teletubbies as when they appear like magic in front of your fussy toddler and cajole her into joining in their singalong fun.) Are there special meals or treats available for kids? Will you be allowed to preboard? Ask all these questions of the reservations agent before you put down your nonrefundable 21-day-with-a-Saturday-night-stay advance fare!

Reserve your seats at the earliest possible opportunity to do so. Make sure you have a seating chart of the airplane in front of you to help you consider your choices. You should find this on your airline's web site (if you book directly) or you can ask your travel agent to show you the seating chart if you're booking through an agency. Most parents tell us they prefer the bulkhead seats for the extra leg room. You'll certainly need an aisle seat, since you will be getting up to walk around fairly frequently on such a long flight.

We strongly urge you *not* to book a single seat for yourself and the baby. Even though she's under two and you are not required to pay for a separate seat, at the end of the nine hours, you will be *so* glad you did. Skimp on something else—like desserts for a year, if need be—but get her off your lap. This expenditure not only makes good sense for your own sake, but for safety's sake, as well. All safety experts agree that an adult seat belt gives little protection to a baby on an adult's lap when there's bad air turbulence. Lap babies have been known to be flung upward to the ceiling. You can prevent this only by bringing along an FAA-approved car seat, which you buckle in place using the adult seat belt. Whenever the seat belt sign is lit, your toddler should be in that car seat with all straps secured.

Here's a step all too many parents leave out—to their regret: At least a week before a long-distance flight, *call to confirm,* including the seat assignments. Then, the day before the flight, call to confirm *again.* (Oh, the stories we've heard from parents who neglected this simple step!)

The secret weapon in the parents' war against fussiness on airplanes, we've learned, is the well-stocked carry-on bag. There are three factors to consider in this regard:

1. The bag itself (size, shape, number and location of pockets)
2. Edible contents (that is, what you've got for your child to eat and drink)
3. Nonedible contents (that is, books, games, puzzles, and other amusements)

Under the first category comes this principle: Bigger is better. Your bag should fill every allowable cubic inch of the space under the seat in front of you, for maximum stuffing with goodies. Be careful, however, not to make it so big that it will fit only in the overhead compartment. You want this bag to be right at your feet, accessible at all times—even when you must have your seat belt fastened.

As for shape: Tote bags, we think, offer the most interior room with the fastest, easiest access. An exterior pocket on each side and a couple of interior pockets are useful to help you remember where certain items are kept. For example, keep all art supplies together in the outer pocket. Any other items you want to keep grouped together can be packaged in gallon-size zip-top freezer bags.

A general note about the contents, both edible and nonedible:

Make your choices based on the time of flight and consideration of your child's usual schedule. That is, if the flight is during the day-time, does it cover three meals and two snack times, plus one nap time? Or three meals, one snack time, and two nap times? Pack ac-cordingly (and don't forget the nap blankie!)—but always strive to err on the side of too much rather than too little.

When it comes to the matter of food on board, there are two dif-ferent philosophies. Pack light, because toddlers love the special foods on airlines—all those things in little packets, served on little trays—because you can always ask the flight attendant for extras of this or that snack pack. Or pack heavy, because you never know if there's going to be anything at all that your picky child will like. Know your own toddler, and let her past dietary history guide your carry-on choices.

A few items, however, we recommend universally—for example, something spill-proof for your toddler to drink from. Even if she can normally drink well from a regular cup without a sippy top, you'll be wise not to let the flight attendant serve her a milk or a juice in one of those flimsy plastic airline cups. On anything but the smoothest flight that's a sure way to end up with soaked clothing (yours as well as hers!). Either bring along your own disposable juice boxes or milk boxes, or else transfer the drink—carefully—to a sippy cup and then screw that lid on tight!

Other items that take up little room in the carry-on bag and don't need refrigeration include: breakfast bars and toaster Pop-Tarts (they're fine at room temperature); saltines; Goldfish (put them in individual-sized snack baggies); dried fruit-and-nut mix; bananas; rice crackers; or any other special food you know your toddler can't go long without.

We generally try to limit junk food in our kids' diet, but on a special occasion—and a nine-hour flight certainly qualifies as that—we think it's fine to offer some otherwise forbidden treats. So if you know Sonia would really love a bag of potato chips or a candy bar or any other high-fat, high-sugar treat, go ahead . . . make her day.

Don't forget to bring paper napkins! (We've noticed that airlines have become very stingy with their paper products lately.)

When it comes to trip amusements, be creative. Your carry-on becomes your magic bag of tricks. Consider what kinds of things would delight your child's senses. Here are a few we especially recommend:

- Wooden Jacob's ladder—blocks that are connected by a string.
- Twisting puzzles, which are like a toddler version of Rubik's cube.
- Magic picture books—your toddler uses the special pen to color in the blank pages and pictures magically appear.
- "Woolly Willy"—a bald face inside a plastic shield surrounded by metal shavings, plus a magnet pen to drag the "hair" to cover Willy's face with various styles of beards and haircuts.
- Read-aloud books. If you think Sonia would be able to follow the story line of a simple chapter book, then get started on it the day before the flight. You can space out the chapter reading as needed to last the whole flight. Or stick to picture books, depending on what you think she would prefer. Remember, paperbacks are lighter and easier to pack.
- Paper and markers and/or crayons for free drawing.
- Coloring and activity books.
- Sticker books. Look for the type that have removable, reusable stickers, so that your child can create a scene, then clear the board and start over.
- Cards. Even a two-year-old can play "Slap Jack." The only rule is, when you see a jack, slap it. The first hand down on it wins the pile. Your toddler will enjoy this game a lot more if you move your hand ve-r-r-ry slo-o-o-wly, whenever a jack appears.
- Check out the airplane's music system to find the kids' channel. Set the volume control at a good level and fit the earphones on her head. Or if the airline allows it, bring along your own personal CD players and the CDs you know she loves best.

Don't be limited to the above list by any means. Go to a toy store or novelty store a few days ahead of the trip and scout out the possibilities. Buy as much as you think you can fit into your carry-on, leaving room for the food items we discussed earlier, and for the diaper supplies that we will detail below.

But first, a few words about your overall diaper-changing strategy. Since you probably are already aware that a crowded airplane is a bad place to change a toddler, you want to do whatever you can do to take care of matters on the ground.

That means you should change her diaper (unless it's perfectly dry) as close as possible to boarding time. Once you're on the plane, don't bother with wet diapers, unless they're so soaked, heavy, and dragging down her bottom that you're starting to worry about leaks. But do change her very promptly after a poop.

If your flight plan involves a stop or a change of planes, see if you can wait till that point to do the change in a normal-sized bathroom.

When you can't wait any longer and you know you must change a diaper on board the plane, find out whether one of the bathrooms comes equipped with a fold-down table. On some planes parents of diaper-wearing children are directed to use a flat surface not in the bathroom but in the rear of the plane. It's good to have this information ahead of time.

You'll have an easier time dealing with diapers if you bring along a separate diaper bag containing all the supplies you need, stowed in different, easy-to-access compartments. The bag should contain:

- A sufficient number of diapers for a normal day, plus three or four extras
- Disposable gloves (you may not be able to find a sink to wash up when you need it) and/or sealed packets of hand-sanitizing towelettes
- A vinyl changing pad and alcohol wipes to clean it afterward, or a disposable changing table liner
- A travel-size package of wipes
- A packet of tissues for drying
- A plastic trash disposal bag—with handle ties or drawstrings to seal it
- A small tube of diaper rash cream

However difficult it is to deal with diapers on the plane, it's still much easier than dealing with a child who's in the middle of toilet training. That is the worst time in any child's life to be put through a long flight! Imagine you're two and you're just starting to feel able to cope with the demands of knowing when you have to pee or poop. Maybe you have certain times of the day when you think it's right to visit the potty. All of a sudden, you're taken away from your familiar routine—time gets all jumbled up—and you have no idea where to find a potty when you need one. Finally, when you get up the courage to ask Mommy to find one for you, she drags you off to this tiny, dark cubicle, with this strange-looking type of toilet with no water in it, and she expects you to sit on it. No way!

Perhaps this helps you to understand why your otherwise reliable toddler *will* have an accident.

So what's a parent to do with a child in this in-between state? Not fly? Well, if it's at all possible to postpone the trip, we say that's a fine thing to do. Realistically, however, we realize that few parents can be so flexible about their travel plans. If that's the case, see how your child feels about the idea of going back to Pull-Ups "just for this one night on the airplane." Explain that you know she's a big girl and is good about going to the potty, but that sometimes there are lines of people waiting to use the bathroom on the plane, and you don't want her to have to wait too long. If she resists the idea, despite such persuasive reasoning, then go ahead and let her wear underwear—but bring along the supplies you need. These are: a few changes of underwear and a complete change of outer clothes (don't forget the socks!). Another thing that might help is to bring along a familiar, thick bath towel that you know she likes. Explain that you're putting it on her seat to make the seat feel softer and more comfortable. That way you can always whisk away the wet towel if you need to, and she'll have a fresh, dry seat for the rest of the flight.

If you can handle their bathroom needs, their food and drink needs, and if your seating is adequate for *your* needs (well, coach seats never are, but we mean you've done the best you can) and you can manage to keep them busy for most of the flight (except when they're sleeping), then you're clearly ahead of the game.

Now for those few extra tips that can make the difference between "doing okay" and "doing fine."

• Take measures to combat ear pressure pain. Try to get your child to yawn with her mouth stretched as wide as possible during both takeoff and landing. (Don't offer chewing gum to toddlers, because it's too easy for them to choke on it.)

• Keep her well hydrated. The air is extremely dry in the plane and your child will need extra fluids to stay comfortable, so offer drinks frequently (and be sure she's wearing a "nighttime absorbency" diaper to deal with the consequences).

• Avoid flying if your child has a cold. If that's not possible, call your pediatrician to find out the strongest measures you can give to help keep your toddler's ear tubes and nasal passages cleared.

• Pique her interest in flying ahead of time. Read her a book about an airplane flight. Make her a paper airplane and attempt to explain how the plane's curved wings create "lift," which keeps the plane up, even though it's heavy (though don't expect her to understand much of your talk).

• Ask the flight attendant if your child can have a lapel pin with the airline's logo or some other little souvenir of the flight. She will probably be delighted with any little gift she gets from the cabin crew.

• Take advantage of times when the flying is smooth and there's no food service cart blocking the aisle to get up and walk around the plane. Your child will undoubtedly be restless during some of the flight and will need to stretch her legs. Let her ask questions about everything she sees on the plane, and do your best to make your answers fit her level of comprehension. Give her complete reassurance if she expresses any fear about crashing. Don't let a hint of doubt cloud your talk (regardless of what you think privately).

Take advantage of the scenic beauty of air travel. Point out landscapes, city skylines, clouds, ocean waves—whatever there is to see out the window. (Of course, if she's sleeping, don't wake her up for any reason!)

The above parenthetical remark holds true for any sort of travel with toddlers: Let sleeping toddlers lie!

My Trip on Air Torment

My ordeal began the moment I arrived at the check-in desk for the cross-country flight that I had booked for myself and my three kids. Only it didn't exist anymore!

The check-in clerk shrugged as she told me the news. The flight had been rescheduled to depart an hour earlier. I was supposed to have received a phone call about the new time—only I hadn't! Now the plane was gone, and what were we to do?

The desk clerk shrugged again and started checking other flights on her computer. At last she said, "I've put you on another flight that departs at noon" (two hours later). "You'll connect in Dallas–Fort Worth."

Although I'd chosen that airline and that flight specifically to avoid having a change of planes, now I had no choice but to accept the new flight plan. But that connection would be tight—barely a half hour to get from one side of that huge airport to the other.

But that wasn't the worst of it, by any means. The clerk found us four seats on the first leg of the trip, but they weren't together. Each was in a different row.

"Don't worry," the agent assured me. "Once you get on the plane the flight attendants can sort the situation out. People will move around for you, so you can all sit together."

But that's not how it went at all! Instead, the business travelers hunkered down in their seats and refused to budge. The flight attendant made a few weak appeals to them to cooperate, until one of them snapped, "I paid full fare for this aisle seat. I booked it weeks ahead of time. If your airline can't guarantee me a seat under these circumstances, I can always take my company's business elsewhere."

It appeared clear that a mother traveling on a once-a-year trip on four highly discounted tickets could not win a seat war against a business flyer paying in full, so there was nothing to do but surrender. So I seated my children and buckled them into their separate seats between strangers, and then moved to my own middle seat, several aisles away. I ended up having to spend the whole three hours (except for the few minutes after takeoff and before landing) running back and forth between my kids' separate seats, tending to their needs.

I did have my little revenge, however: The man who complained the most about my request to switch seats got my youngest child—my eighteen-month-old—as his seatmate. And as expected, she screamed at top volume throughout the entire flight.

Afterward, I wrote the airline a letter of complaint. I did receive an apology and a free ticket good for a round trip anywhere in the continental United States—but it's only for one person, so it's not likely to do a single mom like me much good!

—Jeanne B.
Rockville, MD

Authors' note: The story above, while indicative of how insensitive the airlines can be toward traveling families, is also instructive for parents about the necessity to confirm all flight arrangements involving children. If Jeanne had done that, she would have learned of the flight rescheduling in time to avoid the ordeal that followed. She's learned her lesson, however, and now calls at least *twice* before every flight.

We're starting to wonder if we should give up on the idea of taking a family vacation at all. Our son, Kevin, was so miserable on the flight last year, when he was three. His ears hurt, despite the decongestants I gave him, and he threw up all over me during the bumpy part of the flight. But the year before, when we drove over a thousand miles, things were even worse. He just hated the long,

long stretches of being confined in his car seat. He was too young to enjoy any car games. But this year he'll be four. My husband says we should try a car trip again. I say, the plane trip was awful—but at least it was over in a few hours. What do you say?

We say neither. Take the train!

It's absolutely perfect for your needs. Your child won't be confined in a seat but will be able to get up, visit different cars, get food when he's hungry, sit down at a real table to eat with his family, or maybe just play a game. The bathrooms are bigger and not quite so scary. It's so much more comfortable than being confined to a car—and it's cheaper than flying.

If the distance is far, then book a little cabin on an overnight train; your child will love the bunk beds and will be gently rocked to sleep by the rhythm of the rails.

In the daytime he'll enjoy the passing of scenery, as you will, too. Motion sickness won't be an issue, because it's rare on trains or in any situation allowing the person to move about independently in relationship to passing scenery.

You can make the train time part and parcel of your vacation by buying the type of tickets that allow you unlimited travel during a certain time period. That way you're not on the train the whole time, uninterrupted. You can decide to visit a particular place of interest en route, stay overnight, and then take the train out the next day. Check with Amtrak about rail passes and special vacation packages for travel within the United States, or log on to Cyberspace World Rail Road (www.cwrr.com) for information about good family rail vacations on both U.S. and Canadian railways.

From time to time I find myself in a public place with my one-year-old baby in need of a diaper change, and there's no good place to do it. I take her to the bathroom at a restaurant, for example, but it's so tiny, with just an adult stall and a freestanding sink, there's no surface to lay her down. But if I try to change her discreetly on the booth in the restaurant, I get nasty looks from

*the other patrons. It seems there's no right thing to do in this case
... or is there?*

True, once you're already there, you're in a bit of a bind. The
best thing would have been prevention, calling ahead to make sure
the restaurant is set up to deal with babies and diaper-clad toddlers.
By not having changing tables in the bathrooms, the restaurant
sends the clear signal that it prefers to be a baby-free establishment.
In other words, it doesn't really want your business.

Nevertheless, once you're there, and the diaper is dirty, you have
to find someplace to go to change it. We offer two other ways of
handling this issue.

One: Learn the "stand-up method" of diaper changing. This
works for any child who can stand on her own two feet and follow
simple instructions. Take her into the toilet stall, or if it's too small
in there to fit the two of you, then use the hallway that leads to the
bathroom.

Raise her dress or lower her pants just enough to allow you to
release the diaper tapes and whisk away the dirty diaper. You
should always have a plastic disposal bag with you, so you don't
need to be in reach of a trash can. Stuff the old diaper in, and while
she's standing with her legs apart, give her bottom a quick cleaning
with a few wipes from the disposable packet you carry in your diaper bag. Pat her dry with a couple of tissues and then fit the new,
clean diaper on and tape it in place.

You might want to practice this routine at home first. You'll
want to get your timing down to under a minute. Once you've become good at the stand-up quick-change method, you can take
your diapered toddler virtually anywhere without fear of nasty
looks.

Another place that can serve as your anytime, almost-anywhere
changing table is your own car. As long as it's not parked too far
away, put it to work for you. In minivans, station wagons, and
SUVs the cargo area in the back is the perfect changing surface. Lay
down a protective pad and go to work. For standard sedans, you
can take your choice: front passenger seat or across the backseats.
In the former case, you stand with the passenger door open and

work from that position; in the latter, you have to get in the car and do the job squeezed into the space between the back of the driver's seat and the backseat, but at least your child will have room to lie down flat on her back. In any of these locations, it's a good idea first to lay down a beach towel, under the changing pad, to protect your car upholstery.

INVENTED HERE: THE SINGLE-USE DIAPER KIT

If there ever was an inconvenient place in which to change diapers, we've been there. I think we've probably changed a diaper at every rest stop along I-95 between New York City and Washington, D.C.

But even in the best of circumstances—lovely changing rooms, spacious tables, little bowls of potpourri on the counter to give off a counteracting fragrance—you still would rather not have to. You yearn for the days when your toddler will finally be free of that saggy, soggy bulk around her bottom.

Until the diaper-free day arrives, you resign yourself to never being able to travel light. Wherever you go with your baby or un-toilet-trained child, it will be accompanied by your trusty diaper bag—which weighs about the same as your toddler, loaded down with all its necessities.

We aim to help you lighten the load—yet still be assured that you have every possible thing you need to cope with the full range of your little one's excretory possibilities. We'll pass along an organizing tip that Bill invented and that we used to great advantage. It's called The Diaper Kit. The principle is essentially this: You package all the supplies together that you need for each diaper change inside a plastic gallon-sized zip-top bag. Then you figure out how many diaper changes you can expect (erring on the side of frequency, just to be safe) and pack that number of kits in your diaper bag.

Here's what we suggest to pack up in each diaper kit:

- One diaper
- One 3-foot sheet of wax paper, folded to a smaller size
- Several sheets of paper towels
- One travel-size packet of wipes
- One travel-size packet of tissues
- One pair of disposable latex gloves
- A couple of packets of individually wrapped hand sanitizer towelettes
- A couple of individually wrapped packets of diaper rash cream

Now you have a diaper kit. The wax paper serves as your changing table liner. The paper towels can be used for a variety of purposes, including creating extra layers if you need to put your child's bottom back down on something clean, and drying the bottom. The purpose of the diaper and wipes are self-explanatory. Latex gloves keep your hands clean, and the towelettes mean you don't need a source of running water and soap to clean up afterward. When you're finished changing your child's diaper, you can put all the old, dirty material back into the same zip-top bag, which now becomes your garbage bag. Any individually wrapped packets that you haven't used, just slip into your pocket, and save them for the next diaper kit you make up.

The beauty of the diaper kit is that you don't have to carry around a separate box of wipes, assorted diapers, and other stuff. You don't need to fish in your huge, multipocket diaper bag for each of these separate supplies. When you need to change your child's diaper, you just grab one of the kits you've brought along, and you have everything you need. If you have a one-hour outing, just take a single diaper kit; for longer excursions you can take several. Your diaper bag gets lighter and lighter as the journey goes along.

CHAPTER
8
Getting Them Out of Diapers

While compiling this book we collected e-mail messages from parents of toddlers from all over the country. As we began separating their questions, tips, and remarks into categories, we quickly became aware of what problems were the most troublesome for which parents. For parents of children over two, there was no question about it: "(The envelope, please . . .) And the winner is, 'Toilet Training!' "*

Now, if you've ever read up on this subject before—and we suspect you have—you will probably be familiar with the general advice that most experts give these days, which is to wait until your toddler is really ready before you start to train. We looked at the toilet training advice found in books by Dr. Spock, T. Berry Brazelton (who is also a spokesman for Pull-Ups brand disposable training pants), Penelope Leach, Burton White, the *What to Expect* authors Arlene Eisenberg, Heidi Murkoff, and Sandee E. Hathaway, plus a few other notable childrearing experts, and were not surprised to see that they all agreed on more or less the same course, which we will gladly summarize for you (saving you from having to go out and buy their books):

* In case you're wondering what won in the category of "Most troublesome for parents of toddlers age two and under," the answer is: "Sleep" (see Chapter Ten).

Wait until your child is at least two years old and shows all of the following signs:

- Can understand and say words for urine and feces (pee-pee or wee-wee or number one; poop or number two or B.M.).
- Can follow simple directions.
- Can pull pants up and down.
- Knows when diaper is wet or poopy, and asks to be changed.
- Can stay dry for about two hours at a time.
- Has regular bowel movements.
- Has a sense of pride about learning a new skill.
- Wants to imitate you or others who use the toilet.

Your toddler must be the one to express his or her interest first. Never attempt to train a child who is not yet asking questions or otherwise exhibiting curiosity about the potty and its use.

For purposes of simplicity, we'll call this overall point of view the "child-led approach to toilet training." The underlying philosophy is that children grow and develop according to their own internal timetables. The time will come when your toddler will notice that big people don't wear diapers, that they use the toilet. He or she will want to be a big person, too, and wear underwear like Mommy and Daddy. By that time the child will have the physical awareness to recognize when it's time to go, and will be able to handle her own clothing, and so will quickly become trained—almost entirely on his or her own, and without a struggle. So you, the parent, should not become anxious if your child is still happily in diapers, uninterested in the potty at two, or three, or even three-and-a-half.

But if you get impatient waiting for that day to come and you try to force the issue, you will end up putting her on the potty before she's emotionally, physically, and intellectually ready; as a consequence, she will feel awkward and incompetent and have many accidents, which will make her feel like a failure, which in turn will get the notion stuck in her head that the whole business is just too much for her to handle. So she'll resist the idea of learning, turning the potty into a battleground, a contest of wills—and since you can't control your child's bowels or urinary tract, this is one battle your child *can* win.

This philosophy sounds right and reasonable on paper, which is why it's so prevalent. It works well, for many children, too. Possibly for most. But not all.

We've heard from plenty of parents who tried it, and found their children didn't quite progress along the course that the experts predicted. Here's some of what they've told us:

"My child is well over three and still hasn't expressed a bit of interest yet in learning to use the potty."

"My child started out interested, and then for some reason (a bad experience with the toilet, perhaps, or just growing boredom with the no-longer-new thing) stopped using the potty."

"My son says he doesn't *want* to be a 'big boy.' He says he loves his diapers and never wants to give them up!"

"My daughter doesn't mind being wet or poopy, and it seems to us that she likes having servants (her parents) at her beck and call to change her."

Parents tell us they've waited and waited, ever patient, but somewhere around age three-and-a-half, they begin to wonder, "Is my child *ever* going to want to train?" There's a growing phenomenon of children past age four who are still not using the potty (as evidenced by the new, super-large-size diapers available that go up to eighty pounds!).

They turn to the same experts for help, and notice that quite a few of the books and articles by these experts contain a reassuring line that goes something like this: "Relax—no child ever went to college wearing diapers!" But *that's* not the fear these parents have—it's the very real possibility that their children won't be toilet trained in time for kindergarten.

Given this trend toward later and later training, it was perhaps to be expected that there would be a backlash. A parenting movement has sprung up led by experts who now advocate the opposite of "child-led" toilet training—firm parental control over the process from start to finish. The most prominent leaders of this new approach are a couple, Gary and Anne Marie Ezzo, who run the

Growing Families International parenting organization (web site: www.gfi.org) and are authors of numerous books on parenting; and John Rosemond, author of *Parent Power: A Common Sense Approach to Parenting in the nineties and Beyond* and *Making the Terrible Two's Terrific*. Pick up any of their books that deal with toilet training to get a fuller understanding of their views, but for a short summary of what we're calling the "parental firmness" school of thought, read on.

The parental firmness school of thought holds that it should never be left up to a child to determine the right time to learn an essential life skill. That, clearly, is the parents' responsibility. Children naturally want and expect parents to make the important decisions, and feel lost and abandoned when such decision-making power is thrust upon them so young. Children can be trained easily enough at very young ages (under age two) if they believe that this is something they must do and *can* do, and are given sufficient opportunity and encouragement along the way.

Parents, however, must take an active role, sitting the child on the potty many times a day, and waiting for as long as it takes for the child to go.

Parents must be consistent about taking the child to the potty, not slipping the child back into diapers for an outing, or just to take a day off from the rigorous training schedule.

Parents should praise success—but be wary of overpraise. Their attitude should be, "Going to the potty is a normal part of life—not a huge accomplishment."

Parents should never punish a child for accidents, but make clear that there are consequences that have to be dealt with. The child should always be asked to help the parent clean up the mess.

The Ezzos and Rosemond point out that this was basically how toilet training was handled a generation or two ago, and it worked perfectly well. Few children reached their third birthdays still wearing diapers.

The child-led toilet training advocates have counterattacked (you knew they would). They say the parental-firmness method all but crushes the child's incipient sense of self-esteem, and in some cases is so traumatizing that the children as adults end up on the therapist's couch having to recount how their parents humiliated them, made them feel ashamed of their private parts, or worse—merely for being slow to train.

The parental firmness side scoffs and says the "child-led" parents are wimps, raising overly indulged little tyrants who won't even go to the bathroom on their own.

Maybe some of these back-and-forth charges are true, and maybe they aren't—we're not going to go any deeper into the debate, because neither side represents our own approach, which is not to take an ideological stand about the issue in the first place.

We say, forget about the philosophical underpinnings—just go with what you think will work best for *you*. *And for your child*. If you think you've got the time and the laid-back sort of personality to wait until your child brings the subject up, then follow that approach. If you think that another two years of changing diapers will drive you around the bend, then buy a potty, and sit your child down on it, and get to work.

In order to help you identify what conditions and characteristics might predispose you toward one approach over the other, we've compiled a list of statements. When you know yourself and your child and when you have confidence that what you're doing makes sense for your family, we think you'll do okay, either way. If you do run into problems (like those in the question-and-answer sets that follow), we think you can solve them with a little creativity. Whichever training method you try, whatever tips you try, the one thing we tell all parents is to remain calm, no matter what, because, as we all know (and if we didn't know, there are crude bumper stickers to remind us):

SH** HAPPENS.

TOILET TRAINING: WHICH SIDE ARE YOU ON?

Read the statements under each column. If you find yourself agreeing with four or more of the sentiments or descriptions on one side, then you will probably be more comfortable and more easily successful using that side's approach to toilet training.

"Child-Led" Approach	"Parent-Led" Approach
My child is generally adventurous, not afraid to try new things.	My child tends to be timid, afraid to try new things. He/she likes to stick with the familiar; hates any change in the regular routine.
My child is fairly good at making his/her wants and needs known to me.	I usually notice when my child needs changing before he or she does.
My child is fairly dextrous for his/her age. He/she likes to figure out how to do things independently.	My child often comes to me to do things for him or her. He/she seldom figures out how to do something new without adult help.
My child doesn't like to be changed on a changing table. He/she is squirmy and impatient with the cleaning-up process. He/she will be likely to think that not having to be changed is a step in the right direction.	My child seems quite content with the usual diaper changing routine. He/she doesn't seem disposed toward using the potty on his/her own.
My child is frequently around other children who already use the potty and/or plays at other homes or attends preschool where potties are available and use is encouraged.	My child's day is spent mostly with adults or younger toddlers and babies in diapers.
My child is a second-born or later child.	My child is an only child, or a first-born with an infant sibling, or a twin without other siblings.

In general, I consider myself a laid-back person. I don't feel that certain things need to be accomplished by a certain age. I don't need to have things tightly scheduled. I like spontaneity.	In general, I would say that I'm an organized person. I like to get things done according to a certain schedule. I prefer things to be well planned and orderly.
I'm definitely not a "neat-freak." I don't mind dealing with diapers and all the attendant mess for a while longer.	I will be really, really glad when the diaper-changing days are done. The sooner we make the transition, the better.
Because of my work schedule it would be difficult for me to devote a long block of time to the potty-training process.	I'm an at-home parent, or my employer gives me the flexibility to devote an uninterrupted block of time to the potty-training process, or I have a caregiver who will reinforce my efforts.
Buying diapers isn't a big deal for us, either in terms of the expense, or getting them home from the store.	Buying diapers is an added expense that my budget-conscious family would be better off without. Besides, it's such a chore lugging those huge bags of diapers home from the store.
I'm not under any external pressure to train quickly (a preschool deadline, for example) and I don't care what anyone else thinks about how long my child's been in diapers already. I just tell them to mind their own business!	I really need my child trained by the start of preschool, and/or I'm sick and tired of hearing stories from other family members about how they trained so-and-so to use the potty at eighteen months.

Help! My three-year-old son is starting nursery school in September. He's supposed to be out of diapers by then. It's the start of summer, and so far he's completely ignored the potty. Time seems to be racing by, and I have no idea what to do. Got any clever ideas?

Yes, our first suggestion is just perfect for your situation: Do your training outdoors. Let him run around naked in the sunshine, with the potty nearby on the patio, or just by the back door. Turn on the sprinklers, and then suggest that he can "sprinkle" in the potty himself, whenever he feels like doing it.

It will be hot out, so be sure that he's drinking lots and lots of water. If he's drinking more, he'll have to pee more, which will provide more opportunities for him to try the potty. Sooner or later his urge to go is bound to coincide with a potty-trying period.

Once you've had your first success, go over the sequence of events with him to let him know what he's done right. Your speech should go something like this:

"Remember how you went in the potty perfectly last time? You had a lot to drink and you knew it was time to go, so you went to the potty and the pee came right out. Well, now it's been a while, and you've had another big drink. So it's probably a good time to try again. Maybe you can do it twice in a row! Come on, I bet you can!" (Note: Throwing in a challenge at the end doesn't work with all children. If you think your child would get a kick out of showing you he can do it, then add that line. But some children would feel a bit intimidated to attempt something a parent has posed as a challenge. Parents of more timid children, avoid this tactic!)

Repeat your invitation to try as often as you think necessary. Repetition and reminders should be kept up steadily throughout the learning period. (Actually, you should probably figure they'll need reminders to go to the bathroom until they're about seven. And some parents still, to this day, ask their fully grown children if they need to use the toilet!) Only with lots of practice will your child develop his own sense of when he needs to "go" and how often to expect it. Frequent reminders are necessary, not only because toddlers have short attention spans and are easily distracted, but also because they have so little experience of life, they need someone else to help them make sense of the experiences they do have.

One of the big advantages of training outdoors is that you can easily deal with accidents. Just hose the child off and say, "Whoops! Next time you'll run to the potty in time!" Indoors, when pants and underwear need to be pulled down and pulled back up, and clothing can get stained and smelly if there's an accident, it's easy for a child to become discouraged, and jump to the conclusion that the whole potty thing is just too complicated to deal with, and want to return to diapers.

In addition to hot weather, outdoor training, you might try a few other tricks to make the process more fun for your three-year-old. How about trying a few of the following:

Potty bull's-eyes. Baby product catalogs like The Right Start and One Step Ahead carry these, as do many baby product stores. You put them in the bottom of the potty and your child tries to hit the bull's eye with his stream of urine.

Toilet boats or fish. These are little tissue paper cutouts in various shapes that your toddler tries to sink by peeing on them. Available from the same sorts of places as the potty bull's-eyes—or you can easily make your own.

The finger-in-warm-water trick. Your toddler may sit on the potty but not pee, even when you're sure he's got a full bladder. When he's been there a minute or two without result and says he wants to get up, ask him to wait just another second. Bring over a cup of warm water and ask him to stick his finger (or his whole hand) in it. For most children, that's enough to get the urine flowing.

Other inducements to use the toilet are: the sound of a faucet dripping or running; a warm bath; drinking a full glass of warm water; eating salty food, which causes thirst, which in turn will lead to increased drinking and the need to pee.

"Big boy" or "big girl" charts. You can buy (or with a little time and effort, create your own) progress charts. Each day of the week is divided into time slots or boxes. For each successful pee in the potty, you place a silver star in the appropriate slot or box on the chart; for poop, use a gold star (or use your child's favorite colors and shapes). After a certain number of stars are posted (let's say for a whole day of perfect potty use), you may give a reward (a longed-for toy perhaps, or a special food treat).

On-the-spot rewards. Many parents use candy. A Hershey's Kiss or a handful of M&Ms (or any other type that comes in small pieces) makes a quick and easy "payment" for a pee in the potty. Some parents find they need to offer a bigger incentive for a poop, and so offer a bigger piece of candy for that. (Parents who don't want to reinforce the idea that candy is the most desirable food may prefer to use stickers, instead.)

A big, deferred reward. Offer a trip to an amusement park or a drive-through safari or a petting zoo. You say: "We would love to take you to [name of special place] but it's not really that good a place if you're in diapers. To enjoy the rides [or whatever the activity is], you really need to wear underwear all day. I know you're ready to do that, so here's what we'll do. We'll try a week of wearing underwear all the time. If you can go the whole week in underwear and remember to use the potty during the day, we'll take you to [the special place] at the end of that week." You should neither ask for nor expect perfection during that week, instead reassuring your child that an accident or two won't wreck his chances. Since he's probably too young to have a good number-sense, don't set a specific limit, but just judge for yourself whether you think by the end of the week he's made enough progress to have earned the reward. If he hasn't, then tell him you think he needs more time to get better at knowing when he needs to go, and give him another week to try. At the end of the second week, if he's made an effort and there's been improvement, he should certainly get the reward (even if he is still far from reliable about his use of the potty).

Desirable underwear. Your child may find it easier to keep his underwear clean and dry if he chooses them himself from the store and they're decorated with pictures of dinosaurs or jungle animals or Winnie the Pooh and friends. ("Nobody wants to pee or poop on good old Tigger!" you can say in your best imitation of Tigger's growly voice.) Your local department store may carry only whites or solids, but for a good selection of toddler-appealing choices, try the Disney Store, the Disney Catalog, or Sears.

Psychological motivation. Don't just assume your child only cares about candy, clothing, or other material incentives. It is undoubtedly very important to your child to earn your approval. But though you should congratulate your child, be careful not to go overboard with the praise and the hoopla—that will come across as just an act. Your child knows quite well that while using the potty is something good, it's not an accomplishment that no other child has ever done before. It's not climbing Mount Everest, so don't treat it as that. Say "Great job"—and be sure to add, "I knew you could do it!" to reassure your child that you had confidence in him from the start.

Psychological motivation II. Your child not only loves you and wants your approval, but he also wants to be like other people he admires. Does he have a favorite story character? Does he want to be like Peter Pan? Well, *he* doesn't wear a diaper! (It would drag him down when he's flying.) Or does he want to be like one of the Power Rangers or some other TV or movie hero? (Just don't choose an animal hero, because it's harder to call up an image of an animal—even a talking animal like Simba, the Lion King—using the potty.) Be sure to add that the admired figure was once an ordinary little boy in diapers, just like him, who learned to use the potty.

One thing *not* to say is that some other *child* he knows has already learned to use the potty. That's counterproductive, because your child could all too easily decide it's too hard to try to live up to some other child's example. Instead, he'll just resent that other child—especially if it's a sibling! You can use real people as motivators, but only if they are already adults (a favorite nursery school teacher, perhaps, or some older relative are good choices).

Do Books and Videos Work?

If you've been to the bookstore, you know there are a number of books you can buy just about teaching your child to use the potty. (Our local bookstore had eight different titles on the shelf.) *Toilet Training in Less than a Day,* by Nathan

A. Azrin and Richard M. Foxx, is perhaps the number one seller of this sort, having been in print for over a quarter of a century with two generations' worth of devoted followers.

But can you really get your toddler to start using the potty based on what you read in a book (not to mention doing it in a single day)? Wouldn't that be rather like trying to learn to ride a bike based on what you read in a book? You can read volumes and volumes written by bicycle designers and other experts, but no matter how much you read, you will certainly learn far more from an hour or so of actual practice than from any amount of time spent reading about it.

On the other hand, we must think written advice is of *some* use, or we wouldn't have put this chapter in our book! But books should not be followed blindly. They tend to treat every child as the same, and teach parents according to a one-method-fits-all philosophy. That was certainly our sense of *Toilet Training in Less than a Day*.

Authors Azrin and Foxx claim that their method, if followed diligently from the first step to the last, will work for every sort of child in every sort of family. The method was designed originally to train mentally retarded children and others with severe developmental delays, and relies heavily on behavioral techniques (repetition, mimicry, and rewards). If your child doesn't seem to be "getting it" by the end of the first morning, the authors insist you must not be following their instructions correctly. They don't admit that some children just aren't amenable to being trained according to their step-by-step system.

How about books that you read to your child? Choices include: *On Your Potty*, by Virginia Miller; *The Princess and the Potty*, by Wendy Cheyette Lewison; *I Want My Potty*, by Tony Ross; *The New Potty*, by Gina Mayer; and many more. If you visit the Huggies Pull-Ups web site, you can even arrange for a personalized book to be printed that addresses your child by name and uses your preferred toddler's terms for urine and feces. (Visit www.pull-ups.com.)

We had quite a selection of read-aloud potty books when

our children were toddlers. They asked us to read them aloud over and over again . . . but we can't say they ever consciously tried to copy the characters in the books.

Videos, however, definitely made some impression. We especially liked *It's Potty Time* (from the Duke Family Series) and *Once Upon a Potty,* which has a companion book by Alona Frankel.

The first one is certainly interesting and entertaining enough to hold a toddler's attention for the hour-long running time. It teaches lots of separate actions, using real children as models: boys peeing standing up, girls pooping sitting down. And it's discreet—you see the boy only from the rear, and the seated girl has her dress around her. It teaches proper wiping—using a teddy bear as a model—and washing hands afterward, all with lively songs. Yes, your child *will* run around the house singing (to the tune of "Row, Row, Row Your Boat"), "Wipe, wipe, wipe yourself/Always front to back/Carefully, carefully, carefully, carefully/Now you've got the knack!" . . . and probably will do so right when you're on speakerphone during an important conference call with your boss—but at least they're happy about learning.

The second video, *Once Upon a Potty,* is also available in an edition packaged with the book of the same name, plus a doll on its own toy potty. You can buy the set in a version aimed at girls, or one for boys. The video is shorter and less detailed than the Duke Family series tape. Our kids found the doll and the potty fun to play with. But the doll has a soft body and can only sit on the potty and pretend to pee; it's not the type that can be filled with water and actually squirt water out a hole in its bottom.

If it's a training model that you want, we think you'd be better off going to a large, well-stocked toy store to find one that actually "wets."

We're pretty confident you can train successfully without any of these aids—but if you think your child would enjoy the process more with them, by all means, buy one or two.

We've been taking the laid-back approach to toilet training. My son Jerry, age two-and-a-half, usually will pee in the potty, but he's too impatient to sit there long enough to try to poop. Any ideas for keeping him sitting long enough to make it worthwhile for him to try?

If he likes to be read to, get him interested in an exciting chapter book with lots of action. Read him one chapter a day if he will sit on the potty for as long as it takes you to read the chapter. Good chapter books to hold attention at this age are *My Father's Dragon,* by Ruth Stiles Gannett; *Rabbit Hill,* by Robert Lawson; and *The Littles,* by John Peterson.

Here's another approach: Instead of trying to make him sit still until he really needs to go, get him involved in some activity that he can do in his room or in the kitchen or playroom, keep his bottom naked, and keep a potty right at hand. He will probably recognize when the poop is actually starting to come out and have just enough time to seat himself on the nearby potty. If you put him back in his underwear and let him go on about his business, he'll figure that by the time the poop is on its way, it's too late to try to make it to the potty, and he'll have an accident. Then he'll claim he "never got the feeling." With every one of these near-accidents (and you can expect several days of them), he will slowly gain the experience he needs to tell a bit sooner when the time has come for him to take a seat.

If you don't like the idea of keeping him confined in one room with the potty (or if he objects to that plan, because he can't play as freely as he used to), then vary the technique this way: Let him go about the house as he wishes, but still with his bottom naked, and simply move the potty from room to room as needed. That way he'll have no excuse for not being able to get to it in time.

HOW I TOILET-TRAINED MY CHILD ON $10 A DAY (FRANK'S STICKER STORY)

I thought I had found the perfect incentive to get my daughter Julia to use the potty. Stickers! She loved so many different kinds: animal stickers, flower stickers, rainbow and clouds stickers, stars, moons, hearts—you name the shape or type, she always seemed to want more stickers.

So I ran to the store and picked out some especially fancy types. They cost a dollar or two per sheet, so I bought about fifteen dollars' worth. If that would get me through toilet training, I thought, it would be a bargain.

Well, the first day went great. I showed Julia one of those one-dollar sheets of stickers, and I told her she could have a sticker after she used the potty, and you know what? She sat right down and peed. So I started to peel off one of the stickers on the sheet, but immediately, she protested. It was clear that she thought I had offered her the entire sheet. Not wanting to be guilty of false advertising, I said fine.

The next time she went to the potty, she did a poop. That seemed to me like a big advance, so I offered her a full sheet of an even higher-priced sort of sticker that cost two dollars. She went for it right away.

The time after that was a pee, and I started to hand her a single sticker, but she waved it away. "Not that kind," she sniffed. "It's *ucky*." So I fished around in my bag of stickers to find something more acceptable. I had to throw away about four or five dollars' worth of stickers before I found a type she liked.

Well, I'd found the right motivator all right, but I was quickly coming to see that toilet training with stickers was going to end up costing me a lot more than fifteen dollars. At about a dollar a pee and two dollars a poop, I'd calculate that by the end of the first week—not counting the "free" times that she had accidents, but counting all the ones I had to throw out because she didn't always like the first choice—toilet training Julia was running about eight dollars per day.

I kept having to go back to the store to buy more. The worst part of it was when Julia discovered the bag where I kept the stickers well hidden (or so I had thought). After that, she always demanded to see what reward was available *before* she went to the potty. When she had to poop, she'd take the bag with her and look over her choices while sitting there, waiting.

I never tried to tone down her demands, because she was doing so well, and having so few accidents, but I have to say, if I had it all to do over again, I would have picked some cheaper incentive, like one M&M per potty trip. But then, at least I didn't make the mistake of one couple I know: They started out giving their daughter a new Beanie Baby every time she used the toilet—and by the time *they* were done with the training process, I think their daughter had a collection worth in the thousands of dollars!

I've made a critical mistake early on in my effort to toilet-train my daughter and now I'm hoping there's some way to fix this situation. Here's what happened: One morning she spontaneously announced that she had to pee-pee. I rushed her to the nearest bathroom, the one in the basement, where we had never placed a potty. No matter, I helped her pull down her underwear and sat her down on the adult seat, and she promptly peed. Success, right? Yes, so far . . . until I made the fatal error of pushing down on the flush lever before she had a chance to get off the toilet. All of a sudden right under her bottom she heard this tremendous WHOOOOShhhh noise and felt a gust of air on her skin as the water was sucked down the drain. (Our basement toilet has got an especially powerful flush!) She started to cry and has not been near a bathroom ever since. I've tried talking to her about it, moving her potty to her own room, getting her dolls that come with their own potties, showing her toilet training videos—but still she silently shakes her head at all these attempts. How can I get her un-scared?

First, by not bothering her over the whole business for a long, long time. What's long enough for a toddler? Two weeks at a minimum with absolutely no pressure to use a potty, no talk about toilets (not even in the form of reassurance)—just time to let her memories have a chance to fade. Then go two more weeks only occasionally mentioning the subject, but not actually asking her to use the potty. Make it four to six weeks, to be on the safe side, if you think you've got a child with an exceptionally strong recall when it comes to frightening events.

Then, when you do get back to the business of toilet training, make sure she knows she doesn't have to use a big toilet anytime soon. That means you make sure you've got a potty for each bathroom in your house (the basic plastic bowl with a seat model is pretty cheap). Let her wear diapers or Pull-Ups when you're not within a few second's distance of a bathroom with a potty, and be laid back about having to change her if she has an accident.

Make clear that toilets are for big people when they go. If the idea doesn't gross you out, let her watch you a few times when you're using the toilet. She'll probably get a lot of reassurance from seeing you do so, safely and easily. Ask her if she'd like to flush for you. You can put the lid down to make it less noisy. If she still seems scared and doesn't want to flush it herself, maybe you can have one of her favorite stuffed animals do the flushing. You may feel like an idiot complying with this next suggestion, but as the pee-pee is going down the drain, say, "Goodbye, pee-pee! Have a nice trip to the water treatment plant!"

Explain in terms that she can understand that what's flushed away isn't gone forever. The toilet has a pipe that goes under the house to another pipe under the street, and that the pipe under the street goes to another pipe that takes the pee-pee and poop (or whatever toddler words you use for urine and feces) to a place where the water gets cleaned and put back into the river or the ocean. You might want to show her the picture board book *Look Around the City,* which has a page showing how underground pipes connect each toilet to the sewer system. This knowledge helps her to understand that once a toilet is flushed, things don't just vanish or get sucked into an endless pit, but they go someplace that's specially set up to deal with them. Your words make the process sound ordinary, everyday, something even a small child can make sense of.

If she's still scared after that talk, you might want to address her fear more directly by some sort of simple demonstration of how harmless a toilet really is.

Go back to Chapter One to the suggestions for dealing with fear of the bathtub. Do essentially the same thing with a large doll and the toilet. Prop the doll, naked, of course, with its legs apart on the toilet seat. The doll needs to be large enough to be able to sit on its own, so that it will be clear that it is not at risk of falling in.

Then say: "Now what do you think would happen if she went into the toilet?" and give her a shove to make her fall in—plop! "Now what do you think would happen if the toilet got flushed while she's in it? Do you think she would go anywhere?" Flush the toilet. Ask these questions in a funny, puppet-show sort of voice, your voice high and squeaky, like you're some mischievous character in the play. Your child should find this sequence of events hysterically funny.

"Wheeee, she's getting a water ride!" you say next. "See, she's just a little wet, having a swim in the bowl. She's wa-a-a-ay too big for the flush to make her go anywhere." Now pull the doll out quickly and take her over to the sink. "All she needs to do is get washed off with a bit of soap and dried with a nice, soft towel. She's not hurt a bit." Give the doll a quick bath, and then dry her off and give her back to your child to play with. Don't worry that doll is now contaminated. Unused toilet water is not especially germy, and once you've washed the doll thoroughly with soap and water, she's probably a lot cleaner than most of the other dolls your child plays with.

We have another couple of ideas for other things that might help you to work around her fear.

Wait till she's out of the bathroom before you flush. Don't try to teach good flushing habits right now, given the situation. Wait on that until you are absolutely sure she's long past her fear of the flushing sound.

Try a toilet seat insert. Baby and toddler product catalogs and stores have these in several different models. You put the insert over the regular seat and it makes the toilet seating area larger and the bowl beneath seem smaller. Some of these inserts are padded, too, to make sitting more comfortable. Other types fold up and can be slipped into a plastic bag and stowed in a diaper bag for travel.

Get a step stool for each toilet in your house. Being able to get on and off independently, rather than being lifted on and off, gives a child a feeling of competence and control, which in turn helps her feel confident about her security. A step stool also addresses any unspoken fear she may have about being stranded on the toilet, while you do something elsewhere.

Get a funny refrigerator magnet in the shape of a toilet, the type that has a sound chip to make a flushing noise when you push it. She's almost guaranteed to enjoy pressing the button and hearing this little toy make its noise.

Give her a doll that comes with its own toy potty, so she can pretend to be the mommy teaching her child. Don't be surprised if you hear her gently reassuring her child in the same words you've used with her, "Don't be scared, Dolly. It's easy to sit on the potty." She can practice pulling the doll's underwear up and down, and familiarizing herself with the whole bathroom ritual from beginning to end, but in miniature—and without any risk to herself. She might especially enjoy the sort of doll that can be filled with tap water and squeezed to make it "pee" in its potty. She can even let it have an "accident" and tell it cheerfully, "That's okay. Even big girls sometimes forget to go! Let's just clean it up and try again later."

You might also try reading her Jan Pienkowski's *The Toilet Book: Don't Forget to Flush*. It's about a line-up of assorted animals that each have a galloping need to go. There's a sound button that makes a loud but funny flushing noise you can activate after each character is done in the bathroom. We recommend this book for any toddler, not just scared ones!

I think I know why I'm not getting anywhere with my son's toilet training. It's because he just doesn't mind being in wet diapers. He doesn't mind the feel of poop on his bottom either. Why should he bother to interrupt his play (he probably thinks) if he's perfectly comfortable being in a wet or dirty diaper? How can I help him on motivation? By the way, he's over three and is coordinated enough to pull up his pants by himself. I'm quite sure he can control his bowels when he wants to, since he has never "gone poop" by accident when I give him a bath or let him play naked in our backyard wading pool.

This is a case for getting rid of the diapers cold turkey. Forget about using Pull-Ups or those highly absorbent training pants. These things just keep him feeling dry, giving him little incentive to learn to use the potty. Tell him the time is coming very soon when he'll start wearing underwear. Let him go to the store with you and pick out a pattern of underwear that he likes.

Then, about a week ahead of time, start marking off the days on the calendar until U-Day (Underwear Day) arrives. Tell him how exciting and wonderful it's going to be once he's a big boy.

When the big day comes, take him out of his last diaper and put him in his new underwear. Let him get it on by himself, with only a tiny bit of guidance, if you can. Tell him he'll need to visit the potty very often at first, to try to figure out when he needs to go pee or go poop. Reassure him that you will remind him when it's time to try, just in case he forgets. Promise that you won't get mad at him if he has accidents sometimes, but you feel confident that he's ready for this, and you know he'll do well. Tell him how proud he's going to feel when he shows that he can keep his underwear dry.

That's the easy part. Now for the harder part: Dealing with that first day in underwear, and that first accident, when he's thinking to himself, "This is harder than I thought. Maybe if I stop trying, she'll give me my diapers back . . ."

And there *will* be accidents. The main thing, which sounds counterintuitive but which works, is to check your natural desire to clean up the mess promptly. You'll need to go slow, to let the feeling of being wet and uncomfortable sink in for a few minutes before you come to your son's rescue. Don't come running when he cries, "I wet my pants!" Or even "I have a poop in my underwear!"

Just answer back, "Yes, I know it's not comfortable. I wish you had gone to the potty in time. But next time, I know you'll remember." Then calmly walk him over to the bathroom before you begin to help him get out of his wet clothes. Do *not* take him to his room or anywhere else for the cleanup. You want it to sink in that pee and poop are bathroom things, and that everything involved in dealing with them must be handled in the bathroom.

Involve him as much as you can in the cleanup effort. Make him wipe himself off with toilet paper, which he should pull off the roll and handle without your help. Bring him new underwear and have him put it on. Have him wash his hands, too, just as you do.

If there's any other cleaning to be done—of the floor or a chair where the accident occurred—he should assist in that effort, too. Pretty soon he will start thinking all three of the following thoughts:

a. If you have an accident, it's a *lot* of work dealing with it afterward.
b. No matter how many accidents I have, my parents are not going to let me go back to my diapers.
c. Having an accident in this new underwear isn't at *all* like having an accident while wearing my old diapers or Pull-Ups. Before, I barely noticed being wet, but in this thin stuff, I feel awful!

After the first day or two of nothing but accidents, either your son will start to get better at remembering to try the potty, or else (and this is the more likely turn of events) he'll start complaining about how much he hates being "a big boy" and whine to wear diapers once more.

You should appear to sympathize, saying things like, "Yes, I know it's hard to remember to go when you need to," but go on to point out: "That's why it's important to go to the bathroom as soon as you get the feeling you need to."

Now your son immediately will protest, "But I didn't get the feeling!" Never argue about that. You know you can't win an argument about what feelings someone has or has not had. Just say, "Well, then you need to go to the bathroom and try when you *don't* have the feeling. A lot of times the feeling will come to you just as you get to the bathroom."

For the first few days the parent (or the child's daytime caregiver) is going to need to be very vigilant about making the child visit the bathroom frequently enough—even if many of the times will be without result. This effort feels like one big drag for both adult and child, but once a child has become strongly resistant to the idea of toilet training, and thinks it's not worth doing, then it's up to the adult to make it clear that it *is* worth doing—and that it *is* going to happen, one way or another.

My daughter Sarah is four and she's been out of diapers for almost a year, but she still has lots of accidents. I try to be patient and understanding as I clean up the mess, but it's difficult when I don't think she's making much of an effort. What should I do?

We'll start out with one thing you definitely should *not* do: Don't threaten to put her back in diapers. She'll think you're bluffing—and she may just want to keep on having accidents to find out whether it's true. Either you'll lose credibility, or if you try to do it, it will send her the message that you have no confidence that she can improve.

What we recommend in this case is some sort of super-motivator. You need to come up with something that you think she would want so badly that she would put forth her very best effort to get it. Something she cares about as much or more than you care about getting her to stop having accidents. When you've found what she most desires in life, you've got the key to gaining her cooperation—so analyze her personality and habits carefully before you announce the prize.

That's just what did the trick for one of our children (though we won't tell you which one). What she desired most in the entire world was to own a sparkly, sequined ballet skirt from the dress-up collection at F.A.O Schwarz. It cost far too much to be an ordinary gift, or even a birthday gift. Besides, (we told her) it was made of such a fine, delicate, beaded fabric, it couldn't be cleaned if she happened to have an accident in it. We would give it to her, we said, only if she could show that she could wear it without ruining it. After she had proven that she could go two full weeks keeping her underwear clean and dry, we bought her the skirt.

That's not to say she never had an accident again, but she did become much, much more conscientious about trying to go to the bathroom in time.

Your special motivator needn't be a piece of clothing—though that does have the added advantage of being something a child would really want to keep clean. All you really need, however, is some rationale for why the gift must be tied to a decline in the number of accidents. Let's say you've offered a new tricycle. You show it off in the store and say, "Look at this fine, smooth vinyl seat. Now we've got to be sure you're done having accidents before you can sit on a nice seat like that!"

Use your creativity and ingenuity both to think of the best motivator for your child and to create a reason why she needs to be accident-free to have it. Any set of lessons requiring a special costume (a leotard for gymnastics or ballet) will work. Anything involving sitting in a special seat (on an amusement park ride or on any type of transportation) is also plausible. And of course, anything involving swimming is more than appropriate for your purposes—there's actually an important public health reason for your insistence on toilet reliability before you take her into the water. (We only wish all the other parents of accident-prone kids followed this policy at public pools!)

During the week- to two-week test period, help your child to meet the challenge by issuing frequent bathroom reminders, and even escorting her to the bathroom at regular intervals.

Also, be as generous as you can be about interpreting what's an accident. A little pebble of poop doesn't count, nor do a few drops of urine that leak out as she's on her way to the toilet. You should also ignore any stains in her underwear. These are probably not accidents at all, but the result of not-terribly-thorough wiping after she's used the toilet. If they're there after every poop, then it's time for some more wiping instruction.

If, after the challenge period is over, your toddler still hasn't earned the prize, then it's time to sit down and try to figure out *why* she's still having accidents. Do they occur at the same time of day? Pee accidents generally mean that she's not going frequently enough. If she's usually at school when the accident occurs, work with her teacher on ways to make her more aware of her need to go. Preschool programs often keep the kids so busy that they don't want to miss a minute of fun. Your daughter probably needs more than just an opportunity to use the bathroom from time to time—she needs to be taken there and told flat out to sit down and try.

At home, you or your caregiver can keep track of how many times a day she goes, or at least tries.

If you don't see improvement after a week of such vigilance, then there may be a physical problem that your pediatrician should investigate.

A Few Toilet Training "Don'ts"

Although we usually tell parents to trust their own instincts and go with whatever they think will work best for them, when it comes to toilet training, we don't think "anything goes." Most of this chapter is devoted to things you can do. Here are four things we strongly urge you *not* to do:

1. Don't threaten or punish. Rewards are fine for using the potty, but punishments for failure to do so are not. In fact, they're counterproductive, because from the child's point of view, peeing and pooping are not something under his control, therefore not his responsibility. If he's punished before he has the confidence to gain control, he'll get discouraged and start to feel the whole business is a losing proposition.

2. Don't point out another child of the same age, or a sibling of any age, who is already using the potty. Instead of

being spurred on by the competition, your child more likely will feel inadequate by comparison.

3. Don't make jokes that your child will misunderstand. When toilet training, you have to watch your mouth. Adults sometimes without thinking say vulgar or joking things in private about their own bathroom activities, which they don't realize their toddlers have heard. For example, if your toddler happened to catch you talking about "dropping a load" or "sh**ing a brick," he could easily become very frightened about what might come out of *him* one day when he is on the potty.

4. Don't start toilet training during a time of great change or stress in your toddler's life. Times *not* to start toilet training include:

- Just before or just after the birth of a sibling
- Just before or after the move to a new house
- During the first few weeks with a new sitter or in a new daycare arrangement
- At the start of a new year of preschool
- During an illness (either the child's or a parent's)
- During a parental breakup or divorce

*M*y son David is closing in on five, *and we're still not getting anywhere!*

Don't you sometimes wish there was a toilet training school you could sign your child up for? Just send him off to learn under the care of competent, experienced professionals? And wouldn't you pay a bundle in tuition for such schooling if you could? (We certainly would have done so, gladly!)

But there isn't—so maybe you should accept any help you can get. You are doubtless so exhausted and frustrated by now that you've lost faith in your son and in your own ability to gain his cooperation. Do you know of anyone not caught up in this battle who could take over, and give you a needed break?

Sometimes grandparents are not only up to the challenge but eager to say, "I told you so." Why not let them? Or if not the grandparents, consider whether an aunt, or an uncle, or a babysitter, or your best friend (your very, *very* best friend) might be able to pull it off.

Send your son off for the weekend to that person's house; shift the scene of the battle, so to speak—and now he no longer enjoys "the home court advantage." He may figure that this is strange territory, and the rules are different here, and accept the change in his toileting procedure without protest. The change of venue provides him with the opportunity, also, to surprise you, to return dressed in underwear, like a triumphant warrior coming home to the adoration of the ones left behind.

One thing we should mention, before you try this or any other strategy: When children reach this age without having become trained, there could well be some medical condition at the root of the problem. Occasionally, a child has developmental delays that go unrecognized, which make it difficult for him to learn the steps involved in controlling his own bodily functions. Other medical issues include digestive or urinary tract abnormalities or infections that could affect frequency of elimination and hinder toilet training progress.

There are also psychological obstacles that can impair his ability to concentrate; for example, if the parents are divorced and one is trying to train by one set of instructions while the other is telling the child to do something different. A consultation with a pediatrician and/or child psychologist should be arranged if these or any similar possibilities need to be investigated.

Constipation is something that all too commonly interrupts a child's progress towards diaper-free living. The child learns to urinate in the potty or toilet without accidents, but continues to prefer releasing stool into a diaper. He dislikes the pressure he feels he's under from parents or other adults to poop in the potty, and starts to think that he should just avoid pooping altogether—that will take care of things—so he successfully holds in his stool for a day or two; then, when he finally can hold it in no longer, he has a really large and painful bowel movement.

That painful experience leaves him even more determined to avoid pooping than before, and so he holds in his stool even longer, leading to an even larger and more painful poop the next time. By then a cycle of constipation followed by painful elimination has set in, with the child ending up in fear of everything having to do with his own feces and its elimination.

This cycle can be very difficult to break and is accomplished usually only with expert medical help. Prevention, however, is something that parents can and should do on their own, the minute they suspect that constipation might be a problem. Measures to help prevent constipation include:

Increasing fiber in your child's diet. Never give your child a laxative without a doctor's advice, but do make sure your child is getting an adequate supply of fruits, vegetables, and grains that contain fiber. Especially good are apples, pears, peaches, plums and prunes, grapes and raisins, peas, corn (including popcorn), and of course, beans and bran cereals.

Increasing fluids. Constipation often starts as a result of too little fluid in the diet. Because you don't want your child to fill up on sugary fruit juices, the best way to increase fluids is to get your child to drink water frequently during the day.

Taking the pressure off your child. Stop all bowel training for the time being and allow your child to poop in Pull-Ups or a diaper, without comment. Wait until bowel regularity is back to what it was before, and the stools are no longer painful to pass . . . and then wait another two to three weeks beyond that, before you bring the subject up again. Now, when you ask him to get back to trying to learn to poop in the potty, be low-key about it and don't make a big deal about accidents.

One final note about accidents in four- and five-year-olds of either sex, but especially boys: Don't expect dryness at night. It's perfectly normal for children of this age to wet the bed. In most cases, they simply grow out of it as their bladders grow big enough to hold eight or nine hours' worth of urine. If you dislike the chore of changing sheets so often, you can place a highly absorbent pad between the fitted bedsheet and your child's bottom. Or you can let him sleep in diapers or Pull-Ups at night for as long as necessary (they come in very large sizes these days). If night wetting is still going on as the sixth birthday nears, then talk with your doctor about the pros and cons of the various treatment options available. These days there are quite a few.

CHAPTER

9

For Health and Safety's Sake

You don't know just how clever your toddler can be until you've walked into the kitchen to discover that the cabinet you thought was toddler-proofed is now open, with the pots, pans, and utensils scattered all over the floor . . . and the lock seems to have vanished without a trace.

How did those tiny hands manage that feat? you wonder, half-admiringly.

Or how does a two-year-old figure out that you've scheduled his checkup with the pediatrician, when all he possibly could have heard when you called to tell your spouse about the appointment was your spelling out the letters "D-O-C-T-O-R"?

It's funny—but it also can be deadly serious as, for example, when your toddler is so clever about surreptitiously spitting out the medicine you thought she'd swallowed that you no longer have any idea how much of her medication she's received. Or what if it wasn't the pots and pans cabinet that got unlocked, but the household cleansers and insecticides?

To make sure that none of the not-so-funny stuff happens in your family, we put forward some ideas, gathered from parents around the country, for some things you can do to deal with common health and safety problems.

I can't get my son to take his medicine, no matter what I do.

Pediatricians are always prescribing things—take this syrup every four hours, put these drops into his eyes twice a day—and never telling you how you're supposed to accomplish these feats. Sometimes you get to watch the nurse giving the dose—and she makes it look deceptively simple. You *think* you're doing the same moves at home, except when you try it, the medicine ends up on the floor . . . or worse, on your new $200 slacks (which leads us to Tip 1, before the chapter even gets going: Wear old clothes, or an apron).

With our first child, we have to admit we were slow learners. In the beginning, we probably had no better than about a 50 percent success rate. Sometimes she'd just balk and clamp her mouth shut, and keep it that way as we tried to find some way to get the gooey liquid past her stubborn little lips. Sometimes she'd run and hide the minute she saw the medicine bottle being opened. Other times, she'd feign defeat, seemingly swallow the dose . . . then spray it all over the floor.

Part of the problem is that small children simply can't see the point of taking medicine. The idea of doing something unpleasant for a few days in order to prevent something even more unpleasant later on is way too abstract for them. Besides which, they have a strong gag reflex and haven't learned about the principle of "acquired taste." You know what I mean: the adult ability to enjoy things like blue cheese, oysters, hot sauce, and haggis. And the problem isn't always their fault either. Those so-called "bubble gum" flavors in children's medicines aren't very tasty. Kids aren't fooled.

But taking medicine—all of it—is important, especially with antibiotics. If your child does not take the complete course of antibiotics, a bacteria-resistant strain could take hold. Your child will end up needing a stronger, longer-term course of a different antibiotic, and you'll be even worse off than you were before.

Now for actually getting the medicine into your child: The first principle is to know your child. Try to discover what he most dislikes about the medicine. Is it the taste? That bubblegum flavor commonly used for ear infection syrup may not be the only thing available. Some pharmacies carry flavorings separately, and you can add them to the base syrup, according to your child's preference. Choices typically include: chocolate, licorice, orange, strawberry, banana, and tutti-frutti. If your local pharmacy doesn't carry flavorings, it might be worth checking around for one that does.

Maybe it's the concentrated, spoon-fed nature of the delivery system that your child finds distressing. Check with your pediatrician and find out if the medicine comes in a capsule that can be opened up and mixed with applesauce or chocolate pudding or some other food that your child will eat up without ever noticing the granules of medicine.

If that solution isn't possible, then ask whether the liquid form can be mixed with a full cup of juice (or a full bottle, if your little one isn't a good cup-drinker yet) without harm to the effectiveness of the medicine. A grape-flavored medicine may be undetectable when "hidden" in eight ounces of grape juice.

If you're sticking to spoon-feeding, be as creative as possible. "Here comes the choo-choo," or "Here comes the airplane," accompanied by train or airplane noises, gets old and tired pretty quickly, even for an eighteen-month-old. How about this one: "Look! It's a spoonful of fairy juice!" Or: "It's Winnie the Pooh's special honey dip!" (That works best with medicine that's amber or golden-colored.) Or how about this: "This is what the astronauts take before they get launched into space." Use whatever line you think would tap into your child's imagination or play off his special relationship with a favorite storybook or movie character.

Another possibility is to forget about liquids and try training your child to swallow a small pill. Pill taking is quick and easy once your child learns how. You can use mini-M&M's to teach the skill, and your child will probably enjoy the lessons. Tell him he can finish off the bag after he has successfully swallowed one whole with a drink of water. If he gags and coughs the pill out on each of several attempts, then give up on the pill-taking lesson—but let him have the mini-M&M's for his effort.

Not all pills need to be swallowed whole. Ask your pediatrician whether the medicine comes in a flavored chewable tablet. (Although we'll warn you right now, our children always spat those right out, making faces that said, "What *is* this stuff, chalk?") There's also a relatively new type of pill you can get that instantly melts on the tongue. It's virtually without taste, and it can easily be broken in half to create a toddler-sized dose. One medicine we know that's available in this form is the prescription allergy drug Claritan.

No luck with any sort of pills? Well, what about suppositories? We know of one couple who tried every trick they could think of to get their daughter to swallow liquid Tylenol—but nothing worked. Yet her fever was so high, the doctor told the parents that if they didn't get some medicine into her fast to bring it down, she'd have to be taken to the emergency room. The girl was so sick and so worn out from all her parents' tries to make her swallow what was on the spoon, she just couldn't try anything anymore, and fell fast asleep. While she was lying in her toddler bed, the mother tried inserting a Tylenol suppository—and was surprised to discover how easy it was to do so without waking her child. Within a half an hour, the temperature was down significantly, and the crisis was over.

If all else fails, you can bring our child back to the pediatrician's office to consider your options. Many antibiotics are now available in a single shot. That's certainly preferable (at least from the parent's point of view) to ten days of struggling four times a day to get a spoonful of something down the throat of a fussy fourteen-month-old.

Whatever you do, don't give up. Medicine taking isn't one of those things where letting the toddler have his way should ever be an option. It's more like the car seat issue: If you can't outwit him into doing it your way, then hold him down and do it by force. You don't *have* to be clever and find ways to make your child like what you do 100 percent of the time—but you do have to protect him and look out for his health 100 percent of the time—even when, in the short term, your child seems to hate you for it.

THREE CAUTIONS ABOUT GIVING MEDICINE

Watch out if you suspect your toddler is becoming *too* enthusiastic over a medicine's taste. Some toddlers actually love that pink bubblegum–flavored amoxicillin syrup, and will clamor for their dose. The parents may be so pleased that it's easy to give medicine, that they don't consider the downside of the situation: The child comes to consider medicine a treat, like candy. He or she may then claim to have a sore throat, a headache, or a tummyache when there's really nothing wrong. The child who is already on a prescription drug may request a dose when it's not time, and the parent might even forget to check and end up giving an extra dose absentmindedly. The latter problem can be averted by following these two rules:

Rule One: Be diligent about following the medicine-taking schedule. Most medicines need to taken at the same time(s) each day to be maximally effective. To be sure you're giving the proper dosage at the proper time, keep a chart with the whole course of medicine laid out day by day, and check off each dose after it's taken. Your pediatrician's office should be able to supply you with one if you ask. If not, it's easy enough to create one yourself with paper and pen.

Rule Two: Don't let a toddler drag out the dose-taking process. Some toddlers, when given medicine on a spoon, will take a teeny-tiny sip and then insist on taking a long drink of water. And then another teeny-tiny sip. And so on and so forth until you realize that it's taking twenty minutes or more for your child to get the complete dose. First of all, it's frustrating for the parent to be holding a spoon steady for so long, and second (and more important), it gives the toddler too much of a sense of being in control of the medicine-taking process. When the child first tries to take the medicine in tiny sips, you need to insist: "You can't do it that way. You have to take one big swallow." If your child won't swallow quickly on her own, you may need to transfer the dose to a small plastic syringe (the type sold in pharmacies to give liquid medicine to infants or cats or dogs) and squirt it into her mouth. Don't let her spit it out!

Ben, my twenty-month-old, hides under the bed when he hears the word "doctor." How can I get him to be less afraid of his checkups and his sick visits?

How well we remember the incident at our pediatrician's office when a three-year-old ran out of the examining room naked and dived under the small space beneath the fish tank in the waiting room. It took both parents and two nurses to half-coax, half-pull the boy out.

Our own daughter, at fourteen months (when she was just barely saying single words), started to writhe in her car seat just as we pulled up to the parking lot in front of our pediatrician's building, and came out with her first two-word sentence: "NO DOCTOR!" When this nice, gentle, caring pediatrician appeared in the examining room, she greeted him this way: "Away, man, away!"

So we know what you're going through. We also know what it took to get our daughter to view the doctor with less terror . . . but you're not going to like the answer: It's about three more years' experience. By about age six, Karen understood the purpose of these doctor visits well enough to know that they were not optional, and had enough memory of past visits to be assured that after the shot would come the reward. (Our pediatrician doesn't give lollipops but lets children pick out a sticker or some other small prize.)

We also explained to Karen, starting when she was only two or three, that shots, while they hurt for a moment, protect her from a far worse hurt later on. Children who don't get their shots can get very, very sick—and even die. But don't try saying that while you're on your way to your son's checkup. The time for this sort of talk is a day or two beforehand, and then repeated a few times the morning of the visit. Tell him that you got shots yourself when you were his age, and you didn't like them either. But tell him you'll be there with him, holding him, and doing what you can to make it better. He may not follow everything you say but he will get some reassurance from your tone, and from your acknowledgment that shots do hurt—that doctor visits are no fun.

Here are a few other things that could help to improve his attitude:

A toy doctor's bag. He'll be less afraid if he's got his own stethoscope and thermometer and blood pressure cuff. Give him a stuffed bunny that you say has an ear infection, and listen to him reassuring his furry patient, "Take your medicine and you will be allll better!"

Read him a book or two about visiting the doctor. A good one is Jan and Stan Berenstain's *Berenstain Bears Go to the Doctor.* Another is the Golden Books title *A Visit to the Doctor,* which comes packaged with a play stethoscope, thermometer, and syringe.

If you have a pet, let your child accompany you and the pet on *a trip to the veterinarian*—but only if the trip is for some standard, nonscary procedure. Let him see the family dog get a shot, or watch the vet gently checking around the cat's ears for mites. Children identify easily with pets, and pets, like young children, need to be reassured about procedures. This visit will also give the child the opportunity to switch roles, and assume the normally "parental" part of the one who offers reassurance and helps to calm the frightened patient.

Once you are in the doctor's office, there are a number of things you should and should not do.

Do's

• Bring along your son's comfort object (a blankie, stuffed animal, or whatever) and let him hold on to it throughout the entire examination.

• Bring a few toys and books to keep him distracted while waiting. The toys you find in most waiting rooms are in banged-up condition and get boring after the first two or three visits.

• Bring something to drink (in a bottle, sippy cup, or disposable drink box) along with some sort of nonmessy snack. Remember that the wait can turn out to be longer than you expect, so stock your bag accordingly.

• Seat your child on your lap as shots are given, holding him in a big, cross-armed hug, tight enough to prevent squirming, which can make shots hurt far worse than they ordinarily do.

• Remind him ahead of time that there is a reward once the visit is over. If your pediatrician doesn't give out stickers, lollipops, or some other token for "bravery" (and most do), then take him to a store on the way home and let him pick out some little trinket for consolation.

• Phone the office before the day of the appointment to find out if the visit is likely to include a shot or any other skin-pricking procedure. Warn your child sometime shortly before the shot is due, so that he won't feel ambushed by needle-wielding strangers. Remind him that you will be there with him, holding him for the few seconds that it takes.

• See if you can have the same nurse as on past visits (that is, if the nurse was friendly and nice), to allow your son to build up a relationship, if not a friendship.

Don'ts

• Don't lie to your child and say something won't hurt, when you know it will. That will almost guarantee that your child will resist any future visit, no matter what reassurances you offer.

• Don't let harried or busy staff members elbow you aside. You know your child better than they do, and if you think he needs your reassuring presence, then stay put. A good pediatrician will have sensitive staff members who are willing to accommodate your reasonable requests about how and who handles your child during a procedure. If that's not usually the case with the people who work for your pediatrician, then it's time to look for a new practice—

even though you may be happy with the doctor who sees your child.

• Don't let your questions go unanswered. If you're not sure why your child has been put on a new medication, for example, or needs another blood test, keep asking questions until you understand the reason. If the doctor or nurse uses medical jargon that you need translated, don't be afraid to say so. You won't sound stupid— you'll come across as thorough and concerned, as any parent should be. Your doctor and his or her staff may be so used to rattling off the same information that they don't always wait to make sure you've got it—so be as persistent as you need to be.

• Don't ever threaten your child with a doctor visit as a consequence for misbehavior. Let's say your child is running out into the snow without a hat and mittens. Don't call out, "You'll catch pneumonia and have to see the doctor!" Aside from the fact that children don't actually catch pneumonia that way (no matter what your parents told you!), you will lead your child to look upon medical treatment as a form of punishment. That's definitely not the attitude you want to foster.

SPECIAL TIP FOR THE TRULY TERRIFIED KID

If just the sound of the word "shot" has your child in hysterics, then talk with your pediatrician in advance of your child's next checkup about the EMLA disk. This is a local anesthetic that your doctor can prescribe. It is applied to the skin about a half hour prior to the shot, and it numbs the area completely and makes the shot pain-free. Your doctor may need persuading, however. They tend to view the patch as an unnecessary extra step, as do health insurance companies (which probably won't reimburse you for the charge). But to parents of terrified toddlers, it's a godsend, and well worth the out-of-pocket expense. For more information, visit the web site www.emla-usa.com, or call 1-800-262-0460.

I'd like to bandage my daughter's "boo-boos," but she won't even let me get near them.

Take her Band-Aid shopping with you sometime soon, when she has no boo-boos to bandage. Choose the largest drugstore with the biggest selection of first-aid items in your area. Let her take her time viewing the selection, and choose the type she finds most appealing. The choices these days are enough to make any toddler long for a scratch, just to sport a cool covering over it.

There are mermaids, and butterflies, and strips of neon-bright colors or glittery holographic patterns, and an amazing roster of cartoon heroes to choose from. There are all kinds of different shapes and sizes, from tiny fingertip covers, to knee-sized squares, from round dots to H-shaped knuckle bandages.

If she doesn't like any of the conventional adhesive strips, let her have the type that look as if they're tattooed right onto the skin. Designs for these bandages include rainbow swirls, roses, various animals, hearts, and much more.

The next time your daughter gets a scrape, remind her that she can wear one of the bandages she picked out herself.

But first, of course, you've got to get the cut cleaned off. You may not have handled this part as gently as you could have in the past, and that could be part of the reason she's so reluctant to accept your nursing now. Don't scrub or coat with stinging mercurochrome (as your mother most likely did with your childhood scrapes). A gentle washing with warm water and liquid soap is the best way to clean off most surface cuts and scrapes. A dab of Neosporin or some other antibiotic ointment will guard against infection and help the skin heal faster. Just follow the directions on the tube.

Now to apply the bandage: How about making it a two-person job? You engage your toddler as your nursing assistant (as well as take her mind somewhat off the hurt) if you will ask her to hold one end of the bandage and help you guide it into place. You retain just enough control to keep the bandage from becoming twisted or going over the wrong bit of skin. Let her determine how tight to make it and which way to lay it down over the cut. Let her play with the bandage scraps, too.

Also, keep in mind that with small, superficial cuts, you may be better off forgetting about the covering. Just wash off the broken skin and apply a thin coating of some antibiotic ointment—that should do fine.

For big boo-boos, the type that need something circling the knee or going all the way around an arm or leg, you'll want to avoid using sticky-backed bandages. Instead, put down a square gauze pad over the wound (best are the type with a nonstick liner) and then use an elasticized wrapping that secures with a metal-pronged clip to hold the pad in place. Or you can use surgical tape, which is backed by such a light adhesive that it can be pulled off a child's skin many times without the child even knowing it.

For some children, it's not the pain of a cut that causes distress—it's the sight of their own blood. If that's the case with your daughter, try to get her to look away while you patch her up. Someone else can be recruited to make funny faces or otherwise amuse her, or you can give her a job to do: Tell her you need her to keep her eyes on the door because you're expecting someone to come, or ask her to count to twenty for you, as if you need to time some part of the bandaging process.

TIPS FOR UN-BANDAGING WITHOUT TEARS

Getting the bandage on is usually the easy part. It's removal that sends 'em running in most families.

Here are a few useful tricks we've heard (and some we've tried with success) to make the job easier:

- Rub the bandage with mineral oil first. Let it soak in for several minutes before you attempt to pull on either end to remove.
- Put the child in a warm bath. A washing first with a slippery sort of soap may help to loosen the adhesive.

Then let her soak for a long time. If you're lucky, the bandage will just fall off by the time the bath is done.
- Use ice to numb the skin under the bandage.
- Pull from the middle first, rather than from an end.
- Do it super-fast!
- Do it while your child is engrossed in a video, or eating something yummy.

Here's our last and perhaps best trick: Call for a visit from the "Band-Aid Fairy" (Bill invented this idea). You tell your child not to worry about having the Band-Aid taken off, because in the middle of the night a special fairy, who collects bandages from children's boo-boos all over the world, will come to take the Band-Aid away. You are that fairy, and you can rip off even the most stubbornly stuck bandage without fear, if you wait until your child is in a deep sleep. Don't forget to leave some little token under the pillow to show you were there! (A shiny penny or dime should do fine.)

My friends use all kinds of baby exercise equipment on their toddlers: walkers, jumpers, and wind-up or battery-operated indoor swings. I think these look like fun things for my one-year-old, but I've heard that pediatricians have safety concerns about them. What's the story? I don't want to put my daughter at risk—but my friends tell me not to worry.

Let's start with baby walkers. It's true that the American Academy of Pediatrics would like to see them banned. Right now you'll have to look high and low for a toystore or baby products store that has the wheeled type for sale; in most stores, walkers have been removed from the shelves because the stores don't want the legal liability. All you'll find instead are those stationary "walkers" or "exer-saucers" that allow your baby to bounce, swivel, or rock in place. They can't scoot anywhere, as they could in the old wheeled type.

The problem was that every year there were many injuries to babies in walkers, and even a few deaths. Virtually all of these accidents occurred when the walker went down a flight of stairs, because the parents did not restrict the walker to a gated-off or otherwise enclosed area. For a few years walkers continued to be sold, but stamped with big, yellow warning tags telling parents that the walker must be kept away from stairs, and that an adult should always be there to supervise while the walker is in use. But still there were some parents who ignored the warnings, and some emergency room admissions (a few serious), and then the American Academy of Pediatrics issued its call for a ban.

And that in our view is a shame, because all those parents who would conscientiously supervise their babies and use the walker safely are now deprived of the pleasure of seeing their babies go "Wheeee" and fly across the floor in matchless delight under the power of their own little legs.

Our daughters loved their walkers more than practically any other piece of equipment during their late infancy/early toddlerhood. And we also loved the times we spent with them on our fully enclosed porch, able to read the Sunday paper or chat with friends, while our not-quite-one-year-old kept herself entertained by whizzing back and forth.

The wide wheel bumpers that completely encircled the bottom part of the walker and the large tray in front and to the sides made it impossible for her to hurt her fingers or toes. The tray also held crackers or other bite-sized foods (nothing she could choke on while moving around) or let her put down her bottle, so that she could eat and drink when she liked. How great for her (especially compared to one of those stationary models, in which the baby wiggles and jiggles, but can't really get anywhere)!

Since you probably won't be able to find that sort of walker in a store anymore, you'll need to cruise the yard sales in order to buy one. If you do, make sure it's in top condition: no rust, no stuck wheels, seat fabric clean and unbroken, and most importantly, wheel bumpers intact and wide enough at the base to protect her feet as she glides around the safe area you've arranged for her to use.

Now as for doorway jumpers: They're still being sold, and with recent safety modifications there's less and less reason to worry when your baby is in one. Follow all the instructions to the letter about how to install it, so that there's no danger at all that it could come down while the baby is in mid-jump.

Before you buy, be sure that you have a doorway that meets the proper specifications for height, door framing, and unobstructed access all around.

A few cautions here: Unlike in a walker, a baby should not be holding anything while jumping—especially not holding a bottle or eating any sort of food. (It's too hard to swallow and jump at the same time, and the baby could all too easily choke.)

Also, you can't really go about other business while your baby is in the jumper; you need to keep an eye on her the whole time, so that you can see immediately when she's ready to get out. You don't ever want your child to feel trapped in a piece of baby equipment— although the jumpers are designed so that it's impossible for her to climb out, tumble out, or bang into anything while jumping. They all now have a wide cross-bar above the baby's head that acts as a guard against bumping the door frame.

Note: There is nothing preventing a baby in a jumper from banging into a piece of furniture that's too close, either in front or behind the doorway—so be absolutely sure there's a clear space of at least three or four feet in each direction.

Also be aware: Neither the doorway jumper nor the walker will help a crawler learn to walk. They're purely for fun—a function they fulfill extremely well.

Now concerning the baby swing: Most babies love to swing, and will happily sit for ten or fifteen minutes or even longer in one, but those indoor swings are really designed for younger babies, between about four months (when they can hold their heads up steadily) and a year old.

Once a child weighs more than about twenty pounds, she's too heavy to be pushed efficiently by the swing's motor (whether powered by D-cell batteries or springs that you crank up), and you won't get very much swinging action before the motor starts to slow down. Instead of having to get up and crank every ten or so minutes, you'll get maybe two or three minutes from each winding that you do; with the D-cell driven motors, the batteries will give out after a half hour or less of total usage time, instead of several hours (and those batteries don't come cheap!).

But toddlers past the twenty-pound mark are the perfect size for those rubber "bucket" type of swings found at many playgrounds. You just fit their legs into the holes, and then be prepared to hear the command "Push! Push! More! More!" until your arms are ready to give out. It's great for parents who otherwise get little upper body exercise.

You can get the same experience at home (that is, if you really want it!) by hanging a home version from a couple of hooks in your porch ceiling or from a tree with the right sort of branch (sturdy and mostly horizontal) coming out from its trunk. Fisher-Price makes a high-backed plastic version with a pull-down T-bar in front to hold your toddler securely in place. (Call 800-747-8697 or go on-line to www.fisher-price.com to order.) Or you may go for an entire swingset, including a choice of activities: toddler swing, double swing, climbing tower with slide, or other options. Just make sure the individual pieces can be easily changed to older-kid versions in the years to come.

However, if your toddler is still quite a bit short of the twenty-pound mark, an indoor swing could still be worthwhile for the next several months. Rather than buy a new one, it would probably make sense to borrow one from a family whose older child has outgrown the swing (give it back when their next child is old enough to use it) or else buy a swing that looks "like new" at a yard sale. It's best to get one that is being sold with the original instructions on assembly and safe usage. Ask the previous owners if they filled out the warranty card, too. That way, if the Consumer Product Safety Commission should ever issue a warning or a recall of that model, the sellers will be notified. Make sure they have your name and address (and your e-mail address, if you have one) so that they can pass along any critical safety information to you.

Be reassured, however, that swings, when used according to the manufacturer's directions, are very safe. As with the two other pieces of equipment considered here, you can never simply leave your child to sit in them unsupervised. Parental vigilance is always an essential ingredient when it comes to these devices.

As the warning sticker on almost every piece of toddler equipment puts it: "Do not leave child unattended!"

SWINGERS!

Jennifer loved her swing, right from the start. We began putting her in it when she was two months old, quickly discovering that the swing was the fastest, surest way to rock her to sleep. We fondly recall those first few weeks when all we needed to do to keep her sleeping peacefully for hours at night was to give the wind-up swing a good, long cranking. Sometimes the noise of the wind-up mechanism set off her startle reflex and she'd come awake for a few seconds with a very funny little jerk—but then she'd promptly put her head down and fall back asleep.

Nine months later, however, the situation was far less wonderful. Jennifer by then was a confirmed swing addict, unable to nap or sleep anywhere else. And by then she weighed almost eighteen pounds, and the swing mechanism wouldn't last long on a cranking, and so one or the other of us was constantly getting up every few minutes to wind it up again, or else she'd start howling.

Around the one-year mark, we knew we were going to have to wean her off the device. It was hard, which is why I'm telling this story. Swings are great—but in moderation—and don't let them get started on the swing too young, or they'll get hooked the way Jennifer did.

—Andrea W.
Silver Spring, MD

Tony (my husband) brought T.J. to the playground one day. They'd been gone a long time, and I was beginning to wonder what they were up too. T.J. was about fifteen months old then and not much of a climber.

I was happy to have some time to myself and started to get really involved in a new mystery novel when the phone rang. It was Tony, using his cell phone to call from the playground. I had to come and help him out, he said. T.J. was in one of the toddler swings, and he loved it so much, he wouldn't let Tony get him out.

"So just lift him out!" I said, wondering why a 160-pound man would have trouble with a 22-pound child. "What's the big deal?"

"I . . . just can't," he insisted. "You have to come here and see for yourself."

So I got into our second car and drove over. It was twilight and all the other children and parents had left long ago. But there was T.J. sitting in the swing, squealing with joy. There was my husband, pushing and pushing, looking glum—but he perked up when he saw me.

"Just stop the swing and take him out!" I said, instead of hello. "Why did I have to come all the way out here for this?"

Then he showed me what happened when the swinging stopped. T.J. started to wail, and he clung on to the safety bar in front of him with an iron grip. To get a child out of that type of toddler swing, first you need to raise the bar. You have to hold it over the child's head with one hand, while simultaneously lifting the child out with your other arm. But if the child puts up any resistance, it's impossible to keep the bar up and remove the child at the same time. Tony was right—it *was* a two-person job.

Tony and I both went to work trying to un-pry T.J.'s tiny but incredibly strong fingers from around the front bar. Then he quickly raised the bar—but T.J. immediately moved his hands to get a solid grip on either side of the swing, and now we had to get to work each prying loose one hand, so that Tony could at long last lift him out and bring him back—kicking and screaming all the way, I might add—to the car.

After that, whenever we went to a playground, we looked to see what type of toddler swings they had. And we avoided those front bar swings if we possibly could.

—Marcy P.
Sarasota, FL

My son Matthew is just an unstoppable explorer. He climbs over stair gates like a mountain goat. He can do bookshelves as easily as going up the steps of a playground slide. And as for child-proof locks—my husband has a harder time opening "locked" cabinet doors than Matthew. I really can't keep up with him—but the alternative seems to be to keep him confined to a playpen much of the time—and I really don't want to do that either. So what else can I do?

He's curious, so give him some safe places to satisfy his curiosity. Take those locks off the cabinets within easy reach, but first move everything out of those cabinets that could possibly be harmful. All cleansers, pharmaceuticals, and other health and beauty products should be stowed in your highest, least-accessible cabinets, secured with a different type of cabinet lock than the type you've used before. Given your child's manual dexterity, we recommend buying a bicycle-type cable and padlock that can only be opened by a combination. Let's see your little Houdini try to crack that one!

What you keep in the lower cabinets, within reach, will be things that present no actual danger—though it's still annoying if he pulls them all out: pots and pans, paper supplies, plastic ware, packaged goods like cereals, and so forth. Let him see what's inside, so these spaces will lose their mystery, their forbidden allure. After he's had the chance to see for himself, he will probably conclude that these spaces hold only the most mundane things, and not keep going back to open them up.

However, if he's the persistent type, it may occur to him that the contents could change, and so he might still try to pull things out from time to time. So unless you don't mind putting things back after these forays into the cabinets, you should get to work on teaching the lesson that not every drawer or cabinet drawer is meant to be opened. To teach him that something is off limits, say something like this:

"*No*, Matthew! You can't play with any of the stuff in there."

If he doesn't obey, you repeat the command. Tell him sternly to shut the cabinet door *at once*. You can use a playpen as a time-out spot if he disregards your second warning.

You may have to teach the lesson quite a few times before he gets the message, but ultimately, your house will become a much safer place once he learns to respect your restrictions (instead of depending on physical barriers to keep him in check).

Coupled with teaching him what places are not play areas, you should give him one or two special places of his own, where he is specifically encouraged to look for treasures. Establish a fun-surprise cabinet just for him and lead him to it. A plastic or wooden play kitchen with a child-sized cupboard is the perfect place to create such a cabinet, but any sort of playroom cabinet would do as well. So would a low dresser drawer. Stock the fun-surprise space with old scarves, pop-beads, empty egg cartons, cardboard boxes with smaller boxes inside them, wooden spoons, rubber bands, paperless toilet rolls, jumbo plastic paper clips, and other child-safe household items. Change what's in that cabinet from time to time, so there's a good chance of something new to discover each time he goes exploring.

Another thing you might want to do is create a totally toddler-safe room in your house. That way, whenever you need to be sure he's not getting into trouble, you won't have to confine him to a playpen, but can feel secure knowing he's got a whole room to run around in. You might have a basement rec room or a finished attic room that would work for these purposes—just be sure that the room can be completely closed off by a door (not a toddler gate).

Now to make it easier for you to supervise from a nearby room, replace the solid door with either a door with a glass window in its top half, or a Dutch door (that is, a door with a separate top and bottom half, either of which can be opened or shut and locked independently). Cap all unused outlets in the room, secure all electrical cords, and remove anything that would be dangerous if climbed on or pulled down. Furnish with foam-block chairs and plastic toddler-sized tables, and line the floor with soft but ultra-stain-resistant carpeting. Toss in lots and lots of toys. Now add a two-way intercom or a two-way baby monitor—or if you want to spend the money, go ahead and install a video monitor. You now have someplace safe to put your toddler while you need to run to answer the door or take a shower or otherwise can't be right nearby to watch him.

The reason for the two-way talk feature (rather than the one-way sound of most baby monitors) is so that you will be able to talk to your toddler from another room, to tell him you'll be there in a minute or two, and take advantage of his increasing ability to understand. He'll have an easier time learning patience if he knows you've heard him and have responded to his call, rather than sitting and crying, not having any idea whether or not you will appear.

Another electronic device that's a big help at this stage in his life is the portable motion detector. Home security stores sell them to customers who want an alarm to protect a limited area—perhaps a detached garage that's not part of their larger home security system. We put motion detectors to great use when our children were between one and five, to let us know right away if they'd entered certain rooms. For example, the living room, which has several fragile items—instead of gating it off entirely, we just turned on the motion detector in the hall leading to the living room. It "beeped" when anyone passed by. If our two-year-old made it beep, we knew she was on her way toward the "forbidden zone" and we could dash over and redirect her before she made it through the doorway.

You could do the same with your stairs. Keep that stair gate in place, but also put a sound-emitting motion detector on a stairstep a few steps past the gate. If and when your toddler climbs over the gate, the sound will alert you, and you can rush to remove him before he gets all the way up the stairs. Pretty soon he will start to associate the sound of the detector beeping with the fact that you appear to stop him from going farther—and of course, you scold him for having made the attempt in the first place—and he will get the idea that it's useless to keep on trying to climb that staircase.

Motion detectors are battery powered and cost in the $30 to $60 range apiece, so use them only in those areas of the house that you most need to protect.

If some or all of the above strike you as beyond your ability to carry out, then we suggest you turn to a professional baby-proofing company. Look in your telephone directory under "Baby Products" or pick up a parenting magazine for your metropolitan area and check the ads in the back for companies that provide this type of service. Someone will come to your home and inspect for household dangers, room by room. That person will then draw up a list of measures that he or she recommends you take, including outlet covers, stove shields, fireplace hearth bumpers, doorknob covers, and of course cabinet locks and stair gates. After you explain that your son has managed to take off your previous cabinet locks and climb over your stair gate, you should be able to count on the baby-proofing company to come up with better locks and gates that your child cannot defeat. That's what you're paying for, after all.

There is one thing about this approach that troubles us, however: You may become tempted to rely exclusively on all these barriers and locks to keep your child from harm, and so may seldom have to say "NO, leave that alone!" Your child never learns that some things in the house are dangerous, and that he needs to listen to his parents to find out what they are. Consequently, he may not have any sense of what he's allowed to touch or not touch when he's in another, less toddler-safe house. Toddler-proofing is supposed to be *extra* assurance, the safety net in case supervision lapses momentarily, not your first line of defense.

CHAPTER

10

Getting Some Sleep

Now we come down to the toughest question of all—the number one problem for parents of babies and young toddlers: how do you get them to sleep? We've saved this one until almost the end of the book, because we didn't want to lead off with a defeatist attitude, but we're ready to admit it here: *You can't.* There is just nothing on earth you can do to force anyone to fall asleep. And the more you try to fight about it, the more the child gets stressed, and the more stressed he or she becomes, the less likely that child will sleep. It's a vicious circle.

We might have ended the chapter here, and saved you a lot of time and bother, but then you might feel cheated out of the price of a book that included a chapter called "Getting Some Sleep." Besides, we do have *some* helpful thoughts on the subject—even if we can't promise you that any of what follows will actually succeed in making your wakeful child drift off to dreamland.

Our best contribution could be indirect. We can help you budget your time so that *you* are able to get some sleep yourself, even if your child is still up more of the night than you'd like. And we think we can point out some simple mistakes that many parents make, that you'd be best off avoiding. In the questions and answers that follow, look for the paragraphs that begin with "What *not* to do" for this important advice.

Even before we get to the first question, let's get started on that time-budgeting tip. If your child is keeping you up too much of the night, grab *any* free time you have during the day to take a nap yourself. Resist the urge, during any of the time that your toddler is napping, to catch up on your correspondence, or return telephone calls, or read that novel that everyone else is recommending these days. People have lower expectations of parents of small children when it comes to the social niceties. They'll understand if their calls and letters go unreturned for a while—and anyway, if you tried to write or call in your present condition of extreme sleep deprivation, you'd probably garble what you meant to say anyway, or else let some random rude thought slip out. And that fine novel you meant to read will still be around a year from now.

DR. FERBER VERSUS DR. SEARS

We said in the introduction to this chapter that we realize there's no way to make a wakeful child sleep and that, to a certain extent, we feel ill-equipped to advise parents how to proceed.

Other childrearing experts don't feel that way, however. There's no shortage of people who are happy to give parents advice on this most difficult of issues. When we were doing the research for this book, we looked at the other parenting books to see what kind of guidance parents are getting to help them with various problems, and when it comes to sleep, this is what we found: There are two major authorities on dealing with childhood sleep problems, each of whom has written a best-selling book describing a particular method he thinks can be made to work if properly applied, and each with a huge following of parents who believe passionately in that method.

The trouble is, these two sleep experts have totally contradictory views of both the nature of the problem and its proper solution. One expert is Dr. Richard Ferber, the Director of the Center for Pediatric Sleep Disorders at Children's Hospital in Boston. His book is called *Solve Your Child's Sleep Problems* and it's been in print since 1985, selling many thousands of copies each year. The other is Dr. William Sears, who's on the advisory board of *Parenting* magazine and is the author of dozens of parenting and pediatric medical guides, including *Nighttime Parenting*. Like Ferber's book, Sears's guide to dealing with a wakeful child has been a constant strong seller ever since its publication.

Read Ferber and follow his program and you will learn that good sleeping habits should be taught early in infancy. Children need to learn how to get themselves to sleep on their own. They shouldn't be rocked to sleep, nursed to sleep, or allowed to sleep in their parents' bed. They should be placed in a crib in their own room, awake, and kissed good night, and the parents should depart. If the child cries for them, the parents wait a certain interval before coming in to say good night again. They do not pick the child up, feed the child, or do anything to attempt to soothe the child back to sleep. Ferber's book lays out the schedule of how long such parental visits should be, and what actions should or should not be allowed during them. He prescribes a similar response to dealing with waking in the middle of the night.

He presents evidence that his methods are effective for virtually all children in all situations if followed conscientiously. Millions of parents swear by the good results they've achieved.

Millions of other parents, who follow Dr. Sears's diametrically opposite philosophy, decry Ferber's views and call him rigid and unfeeling, and wonder how any parents can leave a room with a screaming toddler alone and miserable in his crib. Looking at the e-mail chat groups where sleep is discussed (or rather, screamed about in capital letter messages), we see the most common term of abuse for Dr. Ferber is "the sleep Nazi."

Dr. Sears, the guru of the anti-Ferberites, in his book *Nighttime Parenting* (along with many other works) says that small children belong in bed with their parents. In nature's plan, a breastfeeding mother and baby are meant to sleep together. Of course a baby will fuss and fight to stay awake when separated from its mother, the source of warmth and nurturing and food. When babies are left in separate cribs, Sears writes, they feel abandoned. When their cries go unanswered, they don't "learn" to go to sleep on their own; what they really get from the experience is the sense that no one cares, that they can't depend upon their own parents to respond effectively to their needs. They learn to be suspicious and detached, right from the start.

Of course, Dr. Ferber's defenders have their retort to these charges. They say children who grow up sleeping in "the family bed" get the mindset that it's only their own sleep comfort that counts. The parents are supposed to sacrifice their own good night's sleep to the child, not minding the loss of privacy and opportunity for marital intimacy, or the burden on the mother, who will then need to wake several times a night to nurse. (Dr. Sears is a great advocate of extended nursing, well into the toddler years, weaning only when the child starts to lose interest.) And then there's the problem of how to get the child out of your bed when he's older. If your two- or three- or four-year-old has never learned to sleep through the night anywhere else but with you, when—and how—are you ever going to get that child to move to his own bed in his own room? Or are you still going to have a "family bed" with a twelve-year-old boy in it?

We could print what the Sears believers say in response, but then in the interest of fairness, we ought to print the other side's rebuttal, and so on, and this section would end up like one of those endless Internet forums on children's sleep problems, nearly all of which have devolved into "flame wars" between the two opposing sides.

Besides, as we said in the introduction of this book, we

generally look with disfavor on any one-size-fits-all approach. We can't see how any one solution will serve all different types of children, and all different types of parents. Rather than start from the ideological assumption that children's sleep problems proceed from the same cause (whether it's the need for a nearby warm body all night, or the need to learn how to get to sleep independently), we think each family ought to look at its own unique situation and search for the solution that will best suit the sleep patterns and preferences of its members.

So if you and your spouse are perfectly comfortable with the idea of having your baby and toddler in your bed all night, and you think you'll be able to get enough sleep that way, we say, fine, try the family bed solution. Your baby certainly will find it easier to fall asleep next to you—no question about that.

But for those of you who know you'd be kept awake by having a snuffling, wiggly baby in your bed, or for those who are simply uncomfortable with the idea of a third person in your marital bed, there's no need to feel defensive about using a crib: Multiple generations of Americans have grown to healthy maturity from their start as babies in separate cribs, without turning into detached or suspicious adults.

The real problem, as we see it, is not that there's anything ideologically wrong with putting a baby to sleep in a separate crib. The problem comes from the practical details of the Ferber method. We've talked to plenty of parents who tried to go by the Ferber book, but found they couldn't stick with the program. Here are the three main reasons we've heard from parents who say they've given up on the Ferber approach:

Soft-heartedness. One or both parents just couldn't last out the fourth fifteen-minute interval of the baby's screaming, without intervening and breaking the program.

Child's persistence and stamina. Ferber says by day seven of the program, virtually all children will have learned to go to sleep on their own. We have no scientific data to the contrary, but we've certainly read plenty of e-mail messages posted by parents who claimed that their child was quite capable of staying awake and screaming for hours at a time each night, for longer than seven nights in a row.

Disagreement between the parents. One of the parents has talked the other into trying the Ferber method, but after the first night or two with a screaming child, the dissenting parent asks to discontinue the program.

What, then, can parents do if the Ferber method doesn't seem to work but they're uncomfortable with Dr. Sears's recommendation to let the child sleep in the parents' bed? We see no need for an all-or-nothing approach. It seems to us it's quite possible—and really, unless you've got some philosophical objection against it, quite practical—to try out a combination of the two approaches. Here are some suggestions for how to do just that.

Parent in the child's room. Buy a fold-out futon couch, a comfortable rocker, or an easy chair, and put it facing the child's crib or toddler bed. Do your bedtime ritual in the child's room, but settle down yourself, with the child, and pretend to fall asleep (or actually do so) as the child falls asleep. After the child is actually asleep, creep out and return to your own bed. Of course, if there's a middle-of-the-night wake-up, you won't be there, and will probably end up having to come back in.

Family bed at the start of the night. Put your child in bed with you, let your child fall asleep with you, and then move the child to his or her own crib or toddler bed once deep sleep has set in. Warning: This does *not* work for children who wake up the instant they're picked up. It's not worthwhile if you find yourself having to move the child back to your own bed and start all over again after a wake-up.

Modified Ferber. Put the child to bed in his or her own room, follow the brief bedtime ritual prescribed by Ferber in *Solve Your Child's Sleep Problems,* but don't be so dogmatic about going back in to visit or comfort the child according to the intervals prescribed by Ferber's chart. Phase out the bedtime visits more gradually than Ferber recommends. It's okay to pick up a crying child, or rock her back to sleep. Ferber promises that within a week for most children, and two weeks for hard cases (*if* the parents don't cave in and wreck the program), your child will learn to get to sleep unaided—but what's so special about accomplishing this within Ferber's specified time frame? What's wrong with three weeks, or four, or eight? Just be sure your visits do, in fact, become shorter and less frequent over time, or else you'll continue to be trapped by a lengthy, labor-intensive bedtime job, and may even find the process getting longer, rather than gradually phasing out altogether.

These are not the only possible bedtime variations that might work. We urge you to be creative, be flexible, and consider your *whole* family's needs when crafting the strategy you hope (and pray!) will get your child to sleep through the night.

My son Greg has passed his first birthday, but he's still waking up three times a night. My pediatrician says he doesn't need milk during the night, but giving him a bottle seems to be the only way to get him to go back to sleep. I've tried ignoring his cries . . . but he can go on for more than an hour, which is beyond my endurance limit.

Sure, it's easy for your pediatrician to tell you not to feed Greg. He doesn't have to listen to him at night. And we believe you that he can keep up his protests for more than the forty-five minutes that Dr. Ferber seems to think is any child's maximum scream time.

What has seemed to work for some parents under these circumstances is a lengthy fade-out of night feedings. They say do it like this:

The first few nights, continue to provide a bottle as you've been doing, but reduce the amount in the bottle by one ounce. So if you've been giving a six-ounce bottle at each feeding, bring it down to five ounces the first night—and maybe the next night or two thereafter. Once that change has been accepted, then reduce to a four-ounce bottle, wait a while, and then go down to a three-ounce bottle.

Somewhere between two and three ounces, you institute another change. You start diluting the formula (or expressed breast milk) with water. Begin by adding just a bit—not even an ounce of water—not enough to affect the taste. Almost by imperceptible amounts, increase the water and decrease the amount of formula in the bottle night by night. By the time you're down to a bottle with only two ounces in it, with three-quarters of it water and only one-quarter formula or breastmilk, your child is no longer getting much at all in the way of food value; he's mostly getting the satisfaction of seeing you come in and give him a bottle to suck on.

Now go to work on the frequency of your response and the way you go about giving the bottle. First of all, accomplish the bottle feeding without turning on the light or otherwise disturbing the scene. Try to talk as little as possible, and if you must say anything, keep your voice to a whisper.

You could say, "Just take a sip or two, because I need to go back to sleep." Or:

"It's the middle of the night. Drink quickly, because I'm too sleepy to stay up for more than a minute or two."

You make clear, either with words, or just with your own sleepy movements and draggy, tired attitude, that it's a hardship for you to have to keep getting up. Before you put your son to bed, you start to propagandize him with the idea that, at his age, most children sleep the whole night through, and that you need your sleep. Start working on him to take in the notion that your night visits with a bottle are going to come to an end . . . and sometime soon.

We think (or at least other parents have given us reason to hope) that your son will adjust to these changes, as long as you keep each night's change small. His wake-up feedings should now only take a minute or two each (especially since you've prepared the night bottles in advance and have only to take them out of your refrigerator).

Now you're ready to lower the boom. After the first wake-up of the night, which gets him a two-ounce bottle of virtually all water, you respond to the second wake-up by going in with nothing but a sleepy refusal to bring another bottle. You whisper, "Go back to sleep. I'm too tired to get you anything else." You might give him a quick kiss and say you'll see him in the morning before you leave.

If he's been making progress . . . and if you're lucky . . . he'll cry a short time but be able to go back to sleep on his own.

You'll be helped in your campaign if he makes good use of any special comfort objects in his crib: a favorite blanket, or a stuffed animal, or some other "lovey."

You'll also move him further along if you work simultaneously during the day on eliminating the bottle altogether, in favor of a cup. That would help him to make sense of the changes in his nighttime routine: It's not just that you've decided arbitrarily that he can't have his bottle at this particular time—it's that the time for bottles has passed altogether.

To help strengthen your resolve, when it's in danger of deserting you, do a little research about the effect of nighttime bottles on children's dental development. Although your child is probably too young to have had his first appointment with a dentist, it might be worthwhile calling and asking a pediatric dentist for information on this topic. What you'll discover will strongly motivate you to put an end to these night feedings. There is a whole class of tooth decay called nursing caries or "baby bottle mouth," referring to cavities in the newly erupted baby teeth caused by milk that the sleepy baby doesn't swallow quickly, the way he would when sucking when fully awake. In some cases children with this syndrome need extensive dental work to repair the damage, and in a few severe cases, the damage can't be repaired at all and the baby teeth must be pulled.

My not-quite-two-year-old daughter Sheila is hard to put to bed—and the situation is getting worse, not better. She's becoming super-demanding: for bedtime snacks, and cups of water, and extra hugs and kisses. She calls me back because there are monsters in her room, or because she's heard a noise, or for any of a thousand reasons. How can I end, or at least cut back on, the number of these "callbacks"?

To be frank, this is a tough problem and one we hesitate to take on as "experts," because we were shamefully miserable failures in the callback department ourselves, when it came to our older daughter. Karen had us well trained: We were back and forth between her room and ours too many times each evening to count. Karen even figured out that she could extend the callback process by first calling specifically for Mommy, then running through the whole process again with Daddy. It's harder not to participate in the callback scam when you're being addressed individually, because the guilt belongs entirely to you. If Karen had simply said, "It's too dark," then we might have been able to ignore her plea. But once she said, *"Daddy, it's too dark,"* that meant Daddy was to blame if he didn't respond promptly. (This is a principle of business that the direct marketers have learned well, and it explains why you receive so much junk mail addressed to you personally, rather than to "Occupant.")

We did figure this out by the time our second daughter was old enough to try it. With two and a half years of experience behind us, we were a little more clever, as well as a lot more tired.

Exhaustion is the mother of invention, when it comes to parenting. Your toddler will discover it's useless to call for you to come if you're perpetually tired and cranky and slow to respond. Chances are good that if you wait till her fourth or fifth round of calls for you, by the time you get to her room, she'll have settled down and gone to sleep. (Okay . . . for the more persistent children, chances of that are fair-to-slim—but at least give them half a chance to quiet down on their own before you come running.)

As always, we urge you to know your child and tailor your solutions to what you think will work with her personality. Some parents have discovered that their toddlers can sleep better in a room with all the lights left on. That seems odd to grown-ups, but children have their own sense of the world, and if darkness has come to be associated with bedtime struggles and a feeling of aloneness, then lights on must mean the opposite—so let them burn! You can tiptoe into her room later and turn them off, if concerns over your electric bill or energy conservation make you feel that you must.

If lighting isn't the issue, then try to figure out what is. Fear is another common theme among children who are reluctant to sleep. Don't just brush off her sighting of a dinosaur under her bed—*she's* convinced it's there. Or maybe there are ghosts who live in the blinds. Take them seriously—just as she does. In this situation, you can really put your adult superiority to use. You tell your child with utter confidence that all monsters and bad things are afraid of you, for you have the power to make them go away. You can blow them away with a few huffs and puffs. Or you can wave a wand (every parent ought to own a wand) and utter a few well-chosen magic words. One parent told us about creating an "antimonster spray." Take an ordinary can of spray air freshener and cover the brand name over with a label of your own devising. You can glue on a label that you've hand-lettered and colored, or you can use a computer program and color printer to design a realistic brand logo, but however you do it, your new label should have some kind of indicator that it's formulated to defeat all kinds of ghosts, goblins, and evil creatures. Try drawing a picture of the thing your child fears inside a red circle with a red diagonal slash through the center. Then explain what the product is and how it works—"It vaporizes all bad things, whether visible or invisible to adults or children"— and cover all corners of the room, spraying any possible monster hiding places. (If you don't like to use chemical sprays for health reasons, then buy a plant mister and fill it with water.) It helps to have watched a lot of *Dragnet* and absorbed the deadpan manner of Sergeant Joe Friday when going after your child's worst (but invisible) enemies. Your cool certainty that you've eliminated the bad guys translates to her sense of peace and an end to her nervous resistance to the idea of sleep.

One good way to provide reassurance without continuing nighttime parental visits is through a two-way intercom. Baby monitors that allow you to hear your child's cries but don't allow you to talk back are of limited use once your child can talk and understand your words. Much better is a radio system with two or more units that you can take with you from room to room. You leave the one in your toddler's room in the "on" position, so that she doesn't have to push any buttons to talk. The unit that you keep with you has a "send" or "transmit" button, and you press that before you say anything to your child.

What you say is not: "I'll be right there," but: "You already had your last drink of water. Good night!" or "I'll come and give you another hug and kiss, but I can't come just this minute. I'll be there in five minutes." Then you keep on reading your book or doing whatever you were doing before, and conveniently "forget" to watch the clock to see when the five minutes are up. Your toddler usually has no idea, anyway, how long five minutes are, and with any luck, will fall asleep on her own before she realizes that the allotted time has gone by.

But in case she does figure out you're taking longer than you said, she'll yell again for you—and in the interim you've had maybe ten or fifteen minutes of peace and quiet. Some parents work the two-way intercom like a snooze button: They ask for ten more minutes each time, and soon their toddlers get conditioned to getting no more than a verbal response, and so no actual parental appearance is ever needed.

One modification of the above strategy is to use a home business telephone system in place of a set of two-way intercoms. Installing business-style phones is an expensive proposition, but we've found it's one of the best things you can do to improve communication among the members of a family living in a large house. With such a system, any phone can act as a direct intercom to any other phone in any specific room. So, for example, if you're monitoring the baby's room from your bedroom, your spouse could be roaming the

Internet from his computer in the family room undisturbed, or he could even talk on the phone (since the internal intercom feature doesn't tie up the outside phone lines). Depending on how you have the system hooked up, you can connect it to a front door unit, so that you can find out who's at your front door, just by picking up the phone and asking. If you want to alert everyone in the house of something, you can page all phones at once: ("Attention, shoppers! Today we're featuring our wonderful fish sticks and tartar sauce for dinner. So everybody go wash up!") The main advantages at bedtime are that you never have to move the monitor around and you don't have to worry about batteries. Imagine: Your child was put to bed a half an hour ago but you think you hear a wheezy, snuffling noise coming from her room. You could peek in, but if she's awake and sees you, GAME OVER. How much better it would be if you could secretly and silently turn on a monitor to find out if this is just a noise she's making in her sleep, or if there's actually something wrong with her (like nasal congestion) that's keeping her awake.

One thing we found that helped is to preempt, as much as you can, your toddler's callbacks. If you know you're going to get a callback (or two or three), take care of the problem before you're asked. Go into her room and say, "Here's a quick story for you," or "I came to give you one last hug and kiss." This helps to put you in charge of organizing the callbacks.

Then when she does call you, you say, "I've already done that, remember?" When she insists she needs it done again, you say, "Once is all you get. It's too late for me to do it again."

This last bit of advice is one of the keys to successful bedtime. You make it clear that *you* have needs. It's past *your* bedtime. And you are not some superhuman who is always strong and always on the go; you are an ordinary person who won't be able to do a good job the next day (as a Mommy or Daddy or anything else) without a full night's sleep.

It's also important for your toddler not to get the sense of being the one in charge of bedtime for everyone else in your household. She actually doesn't *want* this much power, but may be testing you to see what happens when your bedtime rules are challenged. You rise to the challenge by telling her firmly, "I'm done taking care of things for you. You are all set for bed now, so that's it. I'm going to sleep myself. Don't call me again."

Of course, firmness needs consistency. When you've gone back to your room and left her yelling and screeching, what should you do? Consider soundproofing, perhaps? That's one way to deal with the problem, although all you might really need to do is to shut her door and your door to keep the decibel level tolerable.

This isn't as cruel as it sounds—in fact, it's not mean, or dangerous, or even harmful at all. Once you've checked to be sure your toddler's not calling out of pain or illness or for anything else that requires parental intervention, you can rest assured that she can't hurt herself by screaming for a while. She won't damage her own eardrums or wear out her voice. In all likelihood, she will tire herself out, and you'll hear her cries gradually getting weaker and weaker, until she drops the volume to an intermittent grumble before she actually falls asleep.

Yes, it may take as long as a couple of hours that first time you stand firm—but there's no law that says you have to listen to her yell for all that time. You could rent an Arnold Schwarzenegger video with a lot of loud explosions, or listen to rock music turned up to a level at which her wails sound like those of a tone-deaf member of the backup band. You still may not be getting her to bed as early as you'd like, but you'll at least have been passably entertained while you're waiting for your toddler to fall asleep and restore peace to your nighttime household.

THREE THINGS EVERY TODDLER SHOULD BE TAUGHT ABOUT SLEEP

1. Parents need to sleep as much or more than children do. When you keep Mommy and Daddy up, we get cranky and irritable. It's no fun to be up with sleepless parents.
2. Sleep is what everyone does at night. You're not missing out on any fun or excitement when you go to sleep. The whole world over, people like to sleep at night.

3. Nighttime isn't for eating or drinking or anything else. There's plenty of time during the day for those things—so if you get hungry toward the end of the day, be sure to ask before you start getting ready for bed. Once you've brushed your teeth, that's it—no more snacks!

My three-year-old gets in bed promptly at eight—his bedtime— but the bedtime ritual has then just begun. He has to have three different bedtime stories, followed by a couple of lullabies, followed by a back massage that can take up to twenty minutes before he finally falls asleep. I'd like to be able to speed things up . . . but anytime I try to cut back on any of the elements, he cries and cries. I wouldn't mind if he cried himself to sleep, but instead, he works himself into a frenzy. Sometimes I think I should just cut out the ritual altogether, rather than try to cut back. Is that a good idea?

It's a radical one, and if that's what you think it would take to get your son to bed on time, then you might want to try it out. But first we think it might help to think a little about what a bedtime ritual is for, and what elements contribute to the process, and then limit yourself to what's essential, before you try throwing it out entirely.

A bedtime ritual, most parenting experts agree, is extremely useful in helping a child to wind down at the end of a busy day. Each of the ritual's elements should therefore be geared to helping the child get ready for bed, or in some way reinforce the idea that daytime is over and that sleep time—a time of quiet and inactivity and rest—is at hand.

A bedtime ritual should *not* include any elements that stimulate, create excitement or curiosity, or lead the child to want to continue an activity. Each ritual element should take a set amount of time and then be over, at the same, predictable time each night. The adult, not the child, should be the one in charge of the ritual's schedule.

Before we get into any specifics about the elements that fit these purposes and those that do not, it might be helpful to consider briefly why children want to draw the ritual out—that is to say, why they want to avoid sleep.

Sleep is often scary for small children. They frequently are afraid of the dark. And even if they're not, they tend to dislike being alone without their parents for long. Who knows what could happen to them during that mystery time of sleep (or so the child wonders)? Maybe he'll wake up one day and they'll be gone! Most children experience some form of this fear, well before they have the words to explain what they're afraid of. There may be monsters in the dark—who knows? Children have great imaginations, which can be a bad thing as well as a good thing. And then there are those brave, hardy types who, right from the start, seem to fear nothing at all. But they hate to sleep, too, because they're so bold and curious about everything, they think they must be missing out on some fun and excitement that goes on after dark. Sleep is boring! They'd like to stay up just once and find out what Mommy and Daddy are up to after they say good night.

Some, but not all of these reasons for bedtime resistance can be reduced or even eliminated by properly chosen elements of the bedtime ritual. Once the bedtime ritual has become something a child can count on, it provides a sense of order and security to a toddler's confusing and chaotic world. Good bedtime rituals get the tasks done in a logical and efficient order: for example, use the toilet, have a bath, get into pajamas, brush teeth, get in bed, hear a story, get a final hug and kiss, get tucked in with a special stuffed animal, have the night-light put on and the big light put out—then sleep. Good bedtime rituals are relatively short, and are kept that way by firm parental management. For example, you say: "No, I can't sing the lullaby again. You know I only sing it once each night. It's too tiring for me to sing the song twice."

Since children invariably try to prolong the ritual, you will need to work from the very start to get them to understand your inflexible attitude about sticking to the time frame. We see three important concepts every parent should try to get his or her children to understand about the world at nighttime which, once learned, will help your toddler to accept your bedtime authority. You will notice that whenever we suggest a line for the parent to use to reinforce the bedtime rules, it's basically one of the "Three Things Every Toddler Should Be Taught About Sleep" (see page 240). As is always necessary to get an idea to sink into a toddler's head, repetition is the key.

Keeping these principles in mind, now let's consider what elements are generally useful parts of a toddler's bedtime ritual:

- *Cleanup routine.* Many parents want their toddler to put things away to signal the end of playtime. It also starts a neatness habit that you'll be grateful for if it lasts into adolescence. A toddler is seldom able to handle much more than putting a few blocks away or tossing stuffed animals into a toybox, but it's the idea of doing so at the end of the day that's important, not getting the job done perfectly.
- *Bath and toilet time* (or diaper change time, for toddlers who are not yet trained).
- *Getting into pajamas or nightgown.* To the extent possible, the toddler should be allowed to pick out sleeping clothes and put them on unassisted.
- *Toothbrushing and flossing.* Even if the primary teeth are not yet all in, it's important to practice good dental hygiene. Somewhere in late middle age your child will thank you for having insisted upon learning these skills well.
- *One last drink of water.* Give your child a sippy cup or a paper cup with no more than a couple of ounces in it. (Exclude this from the bedtime ritual if your child is in the middle of toilet training and is having trouble keeping dry at night.)
- *A short prayer or expression of thankfulness* for all the goodness in the child's day. A good bedtime prayer, many parents report, is a simple one in which the child names the members of his household and asks God's blessing for each.
- *Tucking in with a special bed object.* Favorite blankets, special pillows, special stuffed animals, and the like, are all a tired parent's friends, as much as they are the child's. Some parents advise making a distinction between toys that the child especially cherishes in the daytime, and the one special toy that the child holds at night. The

special bed toy cannot be taken out of the house (it's too precious to risk being lost if it's let outside) so that the child has to go to bed to be with it.

• *One story or one book.* It's important that you limit the length of the story or the book, and choose one with a theme that in some way relates to going to bed. *Goodnight Moon* is a perennial best-seller among parents of young children for a very good reason—it's a wonderful bedtime book. So is a newer book, like *Guess How Much I Love You,* or *Can't You Sleep Little Bear?* For stories that you tell, "Goldilocks" is our own favorite, because after the three bears come home and discover Goldilocks fast asleep in the baby bear's bed, we say that the Mama and Papa Bear pick her up and carry her gently back to her own house, to her own crib in her own room, where she sleeps peacefully the rest of the night. Of course, there are many such modifications you can make in classic fairy tales to make them more sleep-friendly (and also, less scary!).

• *One lullaby.* As with books and stories, you must hold firm on the amount of time you devote to singing. For children who fall asleep best to music, consider as an alternative setting up a tape or CD player to play a favorite singer's recording of lullaby music. But if it's the sound of the parent's voice your child craves, consider our own humble invention, the Mommy Tape (see page 247).

• *One last hug and kiss* and a whispered "good night."

• *Lights out*—or turning on lights to achieve your child's preferred level of nighttime lighting.

You may choose some, or all, or even none of these, but whatever you end up adding to your ritual should be designed to move your child closer to the goal of a sound night's sleep. Anything that could possibly detract from that goal should be kept out of the ritual. What should you leave out? Here's our advice:

• No *active games and roughhousing.* Anything that requires a high energy level should be avoided near bedtime. It's sometimes the case that one or the other parent must work late, and won't get home until the child has begun the bedtime ritual. That parent may need to be reminded not to initiate any sort of new activity, and may complain that he or she is being deprived of active playtime with the child, but if that's the case, the parents may need to work together to come up with a mutually agreed-upon change in the child's bedtime—or else work out some way for that parent to get home earlier from work.

• *No snacks.* This is many a parent's downfall—they give in to their children's demands for food and drink after the bedtime ritual has started. We've met parents who were cooking grilled cheese sandwiches regularly at ten o'clock at night. Don't go there! Make an inflexible rule while your children are still young that once the bedtime process has started, the dining process is over and done with. (If you think your child is legitimately hungry so late in the evening, then plan for a regular snack time *before* the bedtime ritual begins. But once those teeth have been brushed . . . just say no!)

• *No long books,* or books that are exciting or scary or need to be continued another night (and the same for stories). How can you expect your child to get to sleep when he's left hanging about what's going to happen to poor Wilbur the pig? And even though the Sorcerer's Apprentice gets everything put back in order by the end of the story, your child still may brood in his bed about all the black magic that the evil sorcerer has unleashed in the past. So always preview your material for its bedtime suitability, before you read or tell a story to your child.

• *No music from wind-up toys or mobiles.* These typically play three minutes of music or less, and your child ends up calling upon you for another round of winding. You want either a music player with toddler-operable buttons so that your child can work the controls on his own, or music on a system that you can set to play for thirty or forty-five minutes, by which time your child is likely to have fallen asleep.

• *No rocking your child* in a chair or using the rhythmic movement of a vehicle to rock your child to sleep. Some parents get into a pattern of taking a long nighttime walk with a child in a stroller until sleeps sets in; others bundle their child into a car seat and go for a long drive. All three of these sleep-inducing measures are highly addictive, meaning that your child will soon become unable to get to sleep any other way. Then you're stuck having to provide the service for months (possibly years) to come. Now don't get us wrong—we're not saying you can't ever rock a sick child to sleep in your arms. We're just saying save it for special circumstances. Two nights in a row, tops. After that . . . well, we warned you!

• *No answers to deep questions,* or a discussion about some important topic. Why is it always just around bedtime that your child comes up with a question that needs a long answer? "Where do people go when they die?" or "Why are bad guys bad?" or "How do babies get made?" We think you should give your child thorough and thoughtful answers to these questions—but not just that instant. "Let's talk about that in the morning" is a good reply. Or "That's such a good question, I really would like to sit down with you and tell you all about it. So we'll talk about it [name the time when you think you'll be prepared]."

All these things that should and should not go into a bedtime ritual are fine to think about when you're starting from scratch with a baby who's only a few months old, but it's much more difficult when you're talking about transitioning from one long, drawn-out bedtime ritual to a shorter and more efficacious one. You could experiment with gradual phase-outs, or you could try to substitute quicker, more sleep-oriented elements for some of the more parent-intensive ones you're now using. Yes, small children are creatures of habit, and the longer they go with a routine, the harder it is to get them to accept change, but they're also, by and large, pretty resilient creatures, and they *will* adjust in time.

However, some children do better if they just go "cold turkey" from one method to another. Just tell them things are going to be different from now on—and then as the captain of the *Starship Enterprise* likes to say, "Make it so."

FINALLY! THE SOLUTION FOR PARENTS WHO ARE TIRED OF SINGING THE SAME LULLABY EVERY NIGHT!

Invented here: "The Mommy Tape." If you've ever sung a lullaby for your child, you know two things: First, children love their parents' voices, even if VH-1 wouldn't agree. You can sound like an out-of-tune piano or a cat with a broken tail and your kids will still think you're great. (Come to think of it, that's how we sing!) Second, one song is never enough. No toddler is happy with a single rendition of "Hush Little Baby"—like any true fan of a pop star or an opera diva, they want encores! Once a toddler's discovered the joys of a particular activity, they're happy to have that activity performed over and over again. And again. And again.

Still, ten minutes of continuous performance from a non-professional is a lot. And also, ten minutes of singing is ten minutes you could have spent doing something relaxing and enjoyable for yourself—like sleeping. Which brings us to the Mommy Tape. Why not record your child's favorite songs in your own voice? Don't worry too much about the quality of the tape or the conditions under which you record. Just choose a time when no one's around, pop in a blank cassette, hit the "record" button, and let loose. If you can play an instrument and sing along, that's wonderful, but most amateur singers will just have to do it off the top of their head. If you need to have the lyrics written down in advance, then you'll need a bit more preparation before you're ready.

Peggy's note: For my own Mommy Tape, I stuck to songs I knew by heart. I started with "Hush Little Baby," and then did the Barney song, then "Frère Jacques," followed by "Golden Slumbers," and on to "Twinkle, Twinkle," after which came half a dozen other folks songs from around the world that go in a slow, sleepy tempo. Then I started again with "Hush Little Baby" and the Barney song. I managed to fill out a thirty-minute tape, which I then duplicated on the reverse side. That way, if my child didn't fall asleep within the first half hour, all I had to do was appear for just long enough to flip the tape over. (Newer, better cassette players have autoreverse, so you don't even have to do that!)

In the beginning I didn't mind having my baby in bed with me. My husband wasn't crazy about it, but it seemed better than having me get up three times a night to nurse (which used to wake him up, before he agreed to have the baby in bed with us). Now my daughter is nearly two, weaned to a cup, and doesn't wake up at night anymore—but she's still in our bed. My husband definitely wants her out, and I guess I do, too. But I just can't figure out how to do it!

Don't try to move her into a crib at this point—it will seem like a prison to her. Put a regular-sized twin or double bed in her room, with a set of bed rails that you can put down as she gets into bed, but leave up once she's sleeping (to make sure she doesn't fall out). Take her shopping with you and let her pick out the sheets and blankets that she likes best.

Now for the transitioning technique—you start out sleeping in her room, in *her* bed. Leave—but not when she first falls asleep (if she's not used to sleeping on her own, she'll only wake up the instant you go). Wait until she's in a deep sleep, then go. If she wakes up in the middle of the night, do not give in to the temptation to bring her back into your own bed. Go in and sit with her for a few moments before going back to your bed. Never try to explain or reason with a small child in the middle of the night why you aren't staying with her or letting her go back to your bed. The time for talking is before you make the change, and definitely when the child is alert and not fussing about something.

Introduce this change (or any other planned change) with a simple, positive description. "You're getting your own bed! That's so great!" (Note: Don't ever ask, "Isn't it great?" because your toddler will then have the opportunity to supply a negative answer: "NO! I don't WANT my own bed! I won't sleep in it! I won't!")

Go on to add any details you can to make the new bed sound especially appealing to your child: "It will have all your favorite things in it, like Binky [or whatever she calls her special stuffed animal friend] and Blankie and your own little pillow . . ." and so on.

She'll probably like picking out things for the bed and playing in and around it during the daytime, but she'll still hate it when she wakes up in the middle of the night for the first time to discover that you've gone back to your own bed, and she's alone. Then she'll cry for you to come and stay with her the rest of the night.

Here's where you have to decide where to draw your line. During the first week or two that she's in her new bed in her own bedroom, you might start out by agreeing, and you'll lie down with her until she's back asleep. Maybe that will be enough to get her sleeping through the rest of the night. Or you may hold firm and do the following:

You go in for a short visit, but tell her in a soft whisper, "No, I like to sleep in my own room now. You're big enough to have your own bed, too, so go back to sleep. Good night!" Then you leave, whether or not your daughter is still crying.

If there are other calls for you during the night or on subsequent nights, you make your comfort visits even briefer. Perhaps install a two-way intercom. Then when your daughter calls for you to come, you can simply respond over the intercom: "I'm too sleepy. It's too late for me to get up. I'll see you in the morning."

Since your child has already learned to sleep through the night while in your bed, it probably won't take too long for her to start sleeping through the night again in her new bed. Once she's managed that for about five or six nights in a row, it's time for you to try cutting out the part about getting into her bed with her at the start of the night.

First, stop waiting until she is deeply asleep. Leave for your own bed the minute her breathing becomes slow and regular. Once you've done that successfully for a few nights in a row, then the next night, get up and leave as soon as she closes her eyes. If she opens them wide and asks where you're going, you say, "I'm going back to my own bed. You need your own bed for a good night's sleep." Then give her a hug and kiss and leave.

You might have a little trouble getting her to accept that stage, but resist the temptation to run back into her room in response to her pleas.

Once she's learned to live with the idea that you're going to get up and go before she's fully asleep, she's ready to be put to sleep without you in her bed at all. You'll want to institute a bedtime ritual that gives her a liberal amount of your time—in light of the fact that she used to have you all night and has been made to give that pleasure up. Sit in her bed while you tell her a story or read from her favorite picture books. Tuck her in tight and read her a nighttime poem or sing her a song. The last step is that you just lean over her and kiss her good night and then turn out the lights as you head for your own bed.

Voilà, you've done it! Now that wasn't so hard, was it? Okay, it was torture—but you're alive and well, aren't you, and isn't she? And aren't you both finally getting the sleep you need?

We moved our toddler to a "big boy" bed, but he won't stay in it. He just hops out whenever he feels like it and comes into our room to tell us, "I'm not sleepy!"

It's time for a lock on your bedroom door. It's time to teach the concept of knocking before entering (and not just at night either, but anytime he wants to go into a bedroom with a closed door).

One important thing: Don't lock *his* door to try to end these nighttime travels. That could be a deadly mistake, in the event of fire.

Also, don't put up barriers that he would likely crash into as he wanders in the dark to find you. If he gets hurt trying to climb over the barrier to get to you, you'll have no choice but to get up and come to his aid.

Your main strategy should be not to reward him when he's out of his bed by giving him a long process of being put back to sleep.

That's what he's really after, isn't it—more time with you? So when he knocks on your door at night, don't get up and escort him back to his room. Instead, say (sleepily), "Who is it? I'm sleeping." Then tell him to get back in his own bed and leave you alone.

If he's still there, or he knocks again, or calls for you, this time you should say (a lot more grumpily), "What *is* it? This better be important!"

If he doesn't get back in bed after that, but calls for you a third time, you growl, "Don't make me have to come and put you back in bed!"

He'll probably not budge, at least not the first night, because he wants to find out how you're going to make him go back to bed. Whichever parent is the most annoyed and the least patient should be the one to go out and dump him back in his bed. And we do mean "dump him." Do not go out and lead him by the hand nicely back to his own bed. Pick him up, none too gently, and quickly as possible, deposit him back in his own bed, with little or no conversation. You don't want him to think you're interested in engaging in dialogue or that you owe him an explanation when you've been so rudely awakened in the middle of the night.

If you want, before you leave the room, you can scold him in a harsh whisper: "Now this time, you stay in that bed! We need to sleep!" However, some children get a perverse pleasure in arousing their parents' ire. If they can't get the specific response they want (being allowed to enter the parents' room at will), then they'll settle for any sort of attention, even negative attention, as sort of a consolation prize. If you suspect that such thinking fits in with your little wanderer's psychology, then stick to the silent treatment as you move him back to his bed. Silence also serves to reinforce the sense that nighttime is only for sleeping, not for chats or any other interaction.

Sometimes technology can give parents an edge in preventing postbedtime visits. A video monitor system in the hall just outside your son's bedroom can give you advance warning that he's on his way. Video monitor systems are surprisingly affordable (the one in The Right Start catalog costs $199.95), and when your child is past toddlerhood, you can always reposition the camera to let you know who's at your front door.

An even cheaper, but still high-tech, method of getting the same advance notice that a visitor's on his way is through the use of a motion detector. A large, well-stocked hardware store should carry a free-standing, battery-operated detector that will ring or chime whenever someone passes in front of it. For a more sophisticated model that also flashes a light or sends a signal to a remote unit, look in a specialized security products store, or try the Safety Zone (see the Resource Guide for contact information).

Coupled with efforts to prevent your son from these unauthorized visits at night, you might also want to try some measures that reward him for staying put. You might ease up on the after-bedtime rules a bit, so that if he doesn't feel sleepy after bedtime, he still has a few options for acceptable in-room activities. Perhaps you should allow him to look at picture books quietly in bed with a toddler-sized flashlight, or even let him out of bed, as long as he plays quietly with his toys on the rug.

You might hear him moving his stuffed animals around and talking to them. Such imaginative games can go on a long time independently, until he feels tired on his own and actually *wants* to go to sleep. Then he'll just hop back into bed without a struggle, and put himself to bed. Once your child has learned that skill, bedtime in your household will from that point on be a far less parent-intensive activity.

However, if the out-of-bed roaming persists, despite all your efforts against it, you might get better results if you addressed the root cause of the problem, which is his lack of sleepiness at bedtime. Look at his daytime schedule and see what adjustments you can make that would result in a child who is so worn out by bedtime that he's perfectly willing to lie down and stay put. Measures you can take include:

- *Moving bedtime back.* Right now he's obviously still full of energy. Don't even start the bedtime process until you can tell that he's really tired.
- *Cutting back* or *cutting out his daytime nap.* Especially if your

son has passed his third birthday, and doesn't seem cranky or particularly tired by midafternoon, it might be time for him to stay awake the whole day, the better to get to sleep at night.

- *Increasing his physical activity during the day.* Cut back on the amount of time he spends in front of the TV or VCR. Arrange more playdates and increase his playground time. Perhaps enroll him in Gymboree or other some other toddler exercise program to get him tired out by the end of the day.

- *Waking him up earlier in the morning.* Get your child up perhaps as much as an hour to two hours earlier, to achieve a half-hour earlier bedtime. Yes, this could well cut into your own morning sleep time, but consider whether the trade-off is worthwhile when you find out that your son is now able to go directly to sleep at his bedtime.

My child is a pretty good night sleeper and has been from the age of two months. My problem is she's not much of a napper. Even before she turned one, she would resist being put down anytime during the day. But I really need the downtime myself, for at least an hour each day. How do I get her to nap?

Here's our blunt advice: Give up the nap. It's probably not worth the struggle, and some children are just never good nappers. They don't need to be if they get enough sleep at night. Pediatric manuals generally note that it's the total number of hours of sleep in a twenty-four-hour period that matters, not how that sleep is divided up. If your daughter sleeps twelve or more hours at night, she's probably getting all the sleep she needs—especially if you add in the occasional catnaps that she most likely takes here and there during the day. Most toddlers fall asleep easily in moving conveyances, and she's undoubtedly getting in some Z's during the day when she's in the stroller or in her car seat for a longish outing. Twenty minutes of sleep here and there might be her preferred resting style.

But as you pointed out, you need rest, so even as you agree to end the nap, you can and should still enforce a "quiet time" for an hour or so in the afternoon. Be clear when setting the rules for her behavior during this period that the purpose is so that *you* can get some needed rest. Tell her that adults are not like children, and that they just don't have the energy to be on the go all day long, and she needs to respect that about you.

Good "quiet time" activities are things she can do in her own room (or in some other playroom of the house) without your help. She might be allowed to watch a video for an hour—so long as you aren't required to fast-forward through the scary parts, or change tapes for her. She could color in coloring books or play with Play-doh or do other art projects that need no parental supervision. She could make up her own puppet show using her stuffed animals as characters. She could play with her dolls. If you think she's mature enough to play with another child without fighting over toys, then she could have a friend over for the time. Try her out with various activities to see what works best, and needs the least intervention from you.

But if this doesn't provide the rest you need, then we have a very different sort of solution for you to consider: preschool, for at least part of the day. There will be a nap period for the children, and the effect of seeing other children lying on their mats should be enough to prompt your daughter to follow along. And even if she doesn't sleep there, but only rests, at least you will be getting the break that you need.

FOUR DADS TALK ABOUT SLEEPING . . . AND SLEEPLESS NIGHTS

In the beginning when I wasn't a pro at getting by on just a few hours' sleep at a time, I was . . . well, to be honest, a complete basket case. One night I was so groggy and confused upon waking to the sound of my baby's cry, that I picked up the cat and tossed it out the window. Fortunately, we live in a first-floor apartment. Even more fortunately, I didn't mistake the baby for the cat and toss *her* out the window!

—Edward R.
Jacksonville, FL

I woke up at 3 A.M. to change my one-year-old's diaper. I put on the little nightstand lamp, put the baby on the changing table, pulled down his PJ bottoms, untaped the dirty diaper, cleaned him up with a few quick wipes, and then hastily pulled up his pants and put him back in the crib. All without waking my wife. I felt proud of myself for moving so quickly and efficiently, and I went happily back to sleep. It wasn't until the next morning that my wife pointed out one crucial step I missed: I forgot to put on a new diaper! Ooops! (And she's never let me forget it!)

—Rob P.
Washington, DC

Our nighttime troubles usually started when we went to put Peter into his crib. It was like trying to put a cat in a cat carrier before a trip to the vet! Quickly, this twenty-pound toddler would become very strong. His arms and legs would flay out in all directions. It felt like he could expand to twice his normal size, like one of those fish that puffs itself up to scare off its enemies. But we ultimately did find a technique that worked to outwit him: Each night we would put some new and interesting object in his crib, and that would make him want to be put down to see what it was. He would play with this new toy or game or stuffed animal until he was tired and bored, and then finally he would fall asleep. The only downside to this technique was that it was very expensive to buy so many new toys!

—Gary S.
Los Angeles, CA

Here's my best trick for getting my daughter to sleep. I give her a "good dream," and this is how I do it: I come to her in her toddler bed when she's having trouble falling asleep, and I put my hand to her forehead and then I begin to describe the dream she's supposed to have once she falls asleep. I use lots of different good dream images. I talk about flying unicorns that live in the clouds, or the merry-go-round horse that leaps free of the carousel to take her on a magical ride through fields of colorful flowers. I tell her about the dream fairies who carry her off to their fairy kingdom and have a tea party for her in their castle. The queen of the fairies serves her tea in acorn cups and then afterward sprinkles moondust on her so that she can fly back home to her bed, safe and sound. And she stretches and yawns and falls right to sleep, eager to dream one of the dreams I've "transmitted" into her head.

—Don T.
Great Neck, NY

CHAPTER

11

Maintaining Parental Sanity

You've read all the preceding chapters and now you've got your kids to sleep, and they're not throwing tantrums (at least, not very often), they can cope with separation, they can sit in restaurants and not scream at the top of their little lungs, and all in all, you've done a good job of civilizing them . . . but what an exhausting job it is. You need a break! How to get it? Some thoughts and suggestions follow.

I'm a working mom with three children, age five and under. Will I ever have peace and quiet?

Yes, and you shouldn't have to wait ten years to get it. Here are some things you might consider doing right now:

Take turns with your spouse so you each will have some time for yourselves on a weekend afternoon, and maybe one or two evenings a week, as well.

If you're a single mom, look into having some other close relative or friend come in to give you some "time off." You need a break more than married mothers do.

If you and your spouse or partner both hold down full-time, demanding jobs, sit down together and hash out a schedule that divides up the childcare duties fairly, during the times that you each are home. All too often, we've observed, the mother ends up doing the lion's share of the work, even though her job may be as demanding as her husband's. The exercise of writing down schedules and assigning blocks of time may be all you need to demonstrate that you've been taking on more than your fair share of the laundry, cleaning up, chauffeuring, and other duties.

If you can afford help that comes into your home, by all means avail yourself of it. There's no need, in our view, for any parent to feel guilty about leaving children in the hands of a good, loving sitter. The presence of another responsible, caring person adds to your child's quality of life, rather than taking something away. Your child is certainly better off in the long run to spend stress-free time with someone else than with a parent who is being dragged down by the burdens of parental responsibility, twenty-four/seven.

If you can't afford outside help, given your present budget, we'd go so far as to recommend that you reexamine your finances and cut back in some other area, so that you can use that money for high-quality childcare. We think you'd be far better off keeping your beat-up but still-reliable car or putting off that trip to Europe if the money you would have spent can buy you some needed time to yourself.

We feel very strongly that the key to maintaining your sanity and peace of mind is having children who respect your "space." You'll do yourself a favor to start teaching your children from the very start that you are not their servant. You are not constantly at their beck and call. You love them all day and all night, but that doesn't mean you drop everything and sacrifice all for their comfort or convenience.

Children don't take to this idea naturally. In fact, just the opposite, they are programmed from infancy to expect their parents to be their constant, unwavering suppliers of everything—food, shelter, clothing, knowledge, and protection against all bad things. But growing up means discovering that parents are not these godlike creatures. Growing up means learning that you can't have everything you want, exactly when you want it. This learning should start soon after birth, when the baby discovers that when she cries out of hunger or distress, sometimes it takes a while before a parent will come to her rescue. They don't just magically appear on command.

Some parents don't take to this idea naturally either, and this is a lesson some parents fear to teach. They somehow get the idea that their baby's needs come first, overriding everything, even if it means that the parents get little rest. They tend to their babies at every peep. They have no faith that their babies will ever learn to calm themselves, and drift back to sleep.

They end up with children who can't sleep anywhere but in their own crib or in their parents' bed, or who need to be rocked to sleep every night. Their children typically have no patience, but make demands of their parents all day long—and the parents get conditioned to respond and keep responding to put an end to their children's cries.

Once the child is conditioned to expect each demand to be met with a parental response, it's extremely difficult to bring about a change in the pattern. So preventive steps are in order. Before your children are fully old enough to understand the words, let them know you will not always be willing or able to do what they want. To help you get started, we're providing some useful ways to phrase this idea. Repeat any or all of them whenever they seem appropriate, and eventually the meaning will sink in, and about the time your children are entering kindergarten, they will be conditioned to accept reality, to understand your limitations, and realize it does no good to whine or demand too much. (Note: We don't promise that they will *never* whine or make demands—just that they may do so a lot less frequently than children whose parents do not follow this advice.)

SANITY SAVERS
(USE THESE LINES EARLY AND OFTEN TO LET THE MESSAGE SINK IN!)

"I'm not the waitress!"

"Hold your horses!"

"How many things do you think I can do at once?"

"I only have two hands."

"Just be patient. I will get to it when I have time."

"Now is not the time."

"Excuse me . . . that is *not* the way to ask for something."

"You can ask . . . but you're not going to get it until I hear a nicer tone of voice."

"What's the magic word?" (The correct response is *not* "abra-cadabra"—it's "please.")

"Who died and made you king [queen]?"

"Not in *this* house, you don't."

"When you own the house, you can make the rules."

"I need five minutes of peace. I don't want to hear any noise from either of you until you see that hand"—point to the big hand on the clock—"move to that number." Then point to the number of the time desired.

"Knock before you enter this room." (It's a good idea to teach siblings to knock before they enter each other's room, too.)

"I'm taking a half-hour nap. You can play quietly or I will put on a video for you, but I don't want to hear anything from you until I come out. Is that clear?"

"Wake me only in case of an emergency."

"What's an emergency? It's when the house is on fire or if you fall down and break a bone. Anything less important can wait till later."

Can we—and should we—travel without our small children?

If you can do it, by all means, go for it! We've found that travel under these circumstances requires just two things:

1. Top-notch childcare provided by someone in whom you have complete confidence
2. The means to stay in close contact so that you can deal with any difficulties that may arise while you are away

For the first requirement, grandparents or other close relatives tend to be the best choice. Your child already knows them and loves them, and they're familiar with your child's personality and perhaps her routine as well. More importantly, they have the sort of love and commitment that only in the most exceptional cases can be equaled by a paid childcare provider. However, if you have had a nanny or babysitter working for you for a long time and you know she's got the maturity and experience to be left in charge of your child or children for an extended period of time, you might prefer her as the primary parent substitute—especially if your relatives are for any reason less than ideal for the job.

Even the best babysitter (whether related or hired) needs the right information to take on the job of full-time parent, so be sure before you leave that your substitute has the following:

- Your child's usual schedule written down on a clear, easy-to-follow chart, including normal nap times, meal times (plus suggestions for favorite foods) and any other instructions you think would be helpful (on bathing, bedtime ritual, friends to meet at the playground, and other details)
- Notations for any special events (birthday parties the child is supposed to attend, dental appointments, and so forth)

- Health insurance cards or policy numbers
- Information on any medications your child is taking
- A letter signed by you, authorizing your childcare provider to bring your child to the hospital or take any other steps you wish to authorize in the event of an emergency
- A list of important telephone numbers: pediatrician, dentist, neighbors, preschool teachers, and others that your childcare provider may need to call
- Your complete itinerary for the trip, including the telephone numbers of any place you expect to be for more than a few hours. (A cellular phone that can be programmed to have calls forwarded to you, wherever you may be, provides even greater assurance that you can be reached in an emergency. For those without a cell phone or for those who will be traveling beyond the reach of their current cell phone service, it makes good sense to rent a cell phone that works in the area of your destination for the duration that you'll be there.)

Before you go, arrange for your child's caregiver—even if it's your own mother—to sit down with you and talk about things that may come up while you are away. These things can be very mundane ("Where are the circuit breakers?" or "How do I program the microwave?") or they may be things that do not lend themselves to a simple answer ("What should I do if Kaylie refuses to nap while you're away?").

It's best to hash out any potential problems you can think of ahead of time, rather than get a panicky call from your sitter that can wreck your vacation completely. You don't need (and can't expect) a guarantee that your substitute will do everything exactly the way you would do it yourself, but you do need a heads-up about any unresolved "issues" that could all too easily lead to a conflict. For example: It's fine if your mother is going to let your child stay up later than you usually do, or if she bans video games that you think are fun and harmless—as long as you know ahead of time which of your usual rules she's planning to change, and you have no immediate safety concerns about the change.

It's *not* fine, however, if she says she doesn't want to bother with all those straps and buckles on the toddler car seat, and that your child can simply use the adult seat belt. You need to feel confident, too, that she wouldn't think of waiting until you're gone to try to "correct your childrearing mistakes" behind your back. If, for example, you suspect that the minute you are away, your mother would yank the pacifier out of your toddler's mouth or force him to eat the one vegetable he hates, you need a different sitter. Far better, in our view, to spend the money on a paid professional nanny than to leave your child with a relative, however loving, who can't be trusted to take care of your child according to the basic guidelines you put forth.

Concerning differences of a trivial nature: Just tell your child (if she's old enough to understand) that when Grandma is in charge, she gets to have things done the way *she's* used to.

In general, we think it's easiest for your child to cope with your absence if she can stay in her own home, with minimal changes to her routine; on the other hand, there are certain advantages to sending the child to stay in the home of the relative or other caregiver while you're away. Your child may pine for you less if she doesn't pass by your empty bedroom, and she may have an easier time accepting rules imposed by someone else when she's in their "territory."

How long a time you can leave your child with a sitter depends in large part on your child's age and personality. The younger the child, the longer the separation will seem. A weekend away will feel like an eternity to a one-year-old, but just a year later, it's a comprehensible (and relatively short) block of time. An outgoing child who's used to playgroups and a variety of evening babysitters will adjust with far less difficulty than a quiet, introverted sort who has little experience of sitters. We usually advise taking a short trip of three days or fewer when going away with your spouse for the first time, regardless of your child's age.

Somewhere around age three most children start to develop a sense of how long a day is and so can follow along with some understanding when you explain about your planned trip. You tell your child, "Mommy and Daddy are going to [name of your destination] and that's a long way from here. We will stay there for four [or however many] days, and then we'll come back home."

You can point to the calendar and show what the date is now. Then, each day, you put a bright, red "X" over the calendar date, until the date of your departure, which you may prefer to mark with a little stick figure drawing of an airplane. Your nanny or caregiver can continue the countdown of dates until the day of your return, which you may want to mark on the calendar with a star or a smiley face.

Each day that you are away, you should phone home and check in with the caregiver to find out how things are going. Some children love to hear their parents' voices over the phone; others just become anxious and cry for them to appear. You and your sitters are the best ones to gauge whether or not your child would enjoy speaking to you over the phone.

If you do speak to your child, keep your conversation centered on your child, not on you and your trip. Your child doesn't understand much about travel and probably won't understand you when you explain that the weather or the time of day is different where you are. Focus instead on your child's day. Ask specific questions, because children are seldom good at remembering details, unless prompted. (That's why the answer to "What did you do at school today?" is always "Nothing." Next time try asking, "Did you play tag on the playground? Who was 'it'?")

Perhaps a better way to communicate with your child while you're away is by postcard. Even two-year-olds love to get colorful postcards with animals or strange sights on them. Don't send photos of architectural or historic sights—the Bilbao Museum means nothing to a toddler. A picture of a woolly lamb or a downy duckling is much more interesting. You may well be home before the postcards arrive, but your kids will enjoy looking at them even more when you're there to describe the sights in person.

While you let your child know you are having a good time on vacation, you don't want to leave her thinking that you're having all the fun while she's doing the same-old-same-old. So work out a plan with your caregiver to allow your child to have as fun-filled a time as possible. Ask your parent-substitute to do things with your kids that you haven't done: Go to a fair, visit a petting zoo, try the paddleboats at a nearby pond. Since the week is going to be abnormal in at least one important respect—Mommy and Daddy aren't there—you might as well make it different in some other ways— good ways—at the same time. Just make sure that your child knows that, on such-and-such a date, everything is going to go back to the way it used to be.

We've listed a lot of things to do and say so that your child and your sitter will be well prepared for your absence; it may seem like a lot of trouble to go through, but speaking as parents who traveled extensively from the time our eldest child was one, we think you'll find that good planning pays off, in terms of a more relaxing experience for all concerned. And getting to relax is the main point of a vacation without the kids. Here are a few other good reasons for traveling with your spouse alone:

- It's a great way to keep the spark in your marriage. (You probably have learned by now that it's hard to keep things hot when there are toddlers underfoot.)
- It gets you away from the day-to-day burden of parenthood, making you miss them—and that's good!
- It makes your children less likely to view you as a godlike provider of everything. In your absence they see that others also love them and care for them and that being without you for a short time is not the end of the world.
- It starts your children looking at you and your spouse as separate individuals, who have personalities and interests besides being Mommy and Daddy.
- You know you will be a better parent for having had a respite from the daily grind. So go, enjoy! And don't forget to drop us a postcard, too!

It's been raining all week and we're running out of things to do. What's the cure for "cabin fever"?

Get out of the cabin! Go for a walk in the rain. Or go someplace interesting and exciting, but indoors. There are children's museums, libraries, skating rinks, indoor playgrounds. You may not think of the zoo as a rainy-day sort of outing, but some of the most interesting and kid-appealing exhibits are indoor ones, like the reptile house, the insect house, and the small mammal house. (Ever see the tiny elephant shrew? It looks like a mouse with a trunk! Your toddler will be fascinated!)

To find out about places to go, when, and how to get there, first visit your local bookstore and pick up a copy of a tourist guide written specifically for families with young kids and covering your local area. For example, if you live in the New York metropolitan area, get Frommer's *New York City with Kids*. Fodor's publishes a series of family-friendly city guides called *Around the City with Kids*. You should be able to find a helpful guide for every major city in the country. Also, take a look at books of day trips that are available, usually from smaller, regional publishers in your own area.

Wherever you go, you needn't all cram into a car; for a change, try public transportation for your outing. Subways are especially good on rainy days because you can travel the length of an entire city underground. Also, find out whether there are any short scenic rail trips you can take. A train ride through mist-covered hills can be an enchanting experience.

Another strategy we like is to try activities outside of their normal season. Why not go ice-skating in July? At a year-round indoor rink the temperature outside doesn't matter—except that fewer people think of going to skate when it's broiling outside, and so the rink will be less crowded. The same for swimming in the wintertime. There's something extra special about bundling yourselves up to go out in below-zero weather, to end up basking in 85-degree water of an indoor pool (but if there are any children still in diapers in your family, be sure to call ahead to find out whether there are any restrictions on their use of the pool before you go).

When our kids were toddlers, they particularly liked to visit conservatories and butterfly museums. These enclosed exhibits typically provide a lush, green, jungle-like environment inside a greenhouse or other large, well-heated but airy enclosure.

There are also plenty of games, crafts, and other activities that you can do in your own home. We'll take this opportunity to plug our own book of ideas for family fun, *365 Things to Do with Kids Before They're Too Old to Enjoy Them*. In it you'll learn, for example, how to make a "tent" out of kitchen chairs draped with a blanket. Or roll your own pizza dough and let every member of the family create their own toppings. Or run "Raindrop Races"—a game so simple you need nothing but a rainy day and a little imagination in your sportscaster's voice as you describe which raindrop is leading the race down a windowpane in your house. In addition to these activities, you'll find 362 other things to do while your kids are still young.

And then there's always TV. We're not enemies of the TV set, so long as it's not overused. Kids' videos, especially. In fact, we wish we'd been able to watch some of our favorite childhood movies whenever the mood struck, when we were young. *The Wizard of Oz* is such an incredibly rich story, it practically begs for repeated viewings (although we don't recommend it for children much below age four, except for those few brave souls who really aren't afraid of witches). To name just a few other movies, we think the whole family can enjoy together: *Pinocchio, Dumbo, Beauty and the Beast, Milo & Otis, The Rescuers Down Under,* and *The Little Mermaid* (with Peggy's expressed reservations about the theme that the mermaid needs to marry a prince to be happy).

For a good toddler TV show, there's nothing to hold their interest like those roly-poly Teletubbies ("Again! Again!" your toddler will say). *Blue's Clues* really does promote attention to detail, and your toddler will feel smart as he shouts out the answer to the generally bewildered Steve. Now as to Barney . . . like a lot of our generation, we were once disposed to make fun of that big, purple dinosaur with the annoying voice . . . until the day our toddler came home from a playdate singing the "Clean-Up Song" she heard while watching a Barney tape at another child's house. That song actually got our child to want to pitch in and help! Suddenly we saw Barney in a whole new light. What a clever propagandist he was for our parenting agenda! He had our children singing about "please" and "thank you." And he taught them to brush their teeth without letting the water run. They parroted Barney's lines happily, and did just as he asked. We went out and bought a half-dozen Barney videos and never objected when on a rainy day our kids wanted to watch a couple of hours' worth of them back to back.

Of course, reading is still most parents' first choice for a rainy day pastime. When buying or borrowing read-aloud books from the library, try to gauge how well you think they'll suit your child's interests and attention span. Our older daughter could sit and listen to chapter books at age three and four, following the story from day to day—even in books that were sparsely illustrated. She loved *Charlotte's Web*, *Mr. Popper's Penguins*, *My Father's Dragon*, *Mrs. Piggle-Wiggle*, and *Pippi Longstocking*.

Our younger daughter was quite different. She never liked the idea of having to wait till the next day to hear what would happen in a story—at least not until age six—so when she was a toddler, we stuck to short picture books and rhyming books. She loved Dr. Seuss—*Horton Hears a Who* and *Horton Hatches the Egg*, *Green Eggs and Ham*, *The Cat in the Hat*, *If I Ran the Zoo*, and many others. They're good for all ages and both genders, and if you keep on reading the same book over and over, your child will end up memorizing most of the lines and will then be able to "read" the book on her own.

I'm so sick of the "Farmer in the Dell" tape I could scream! Isn't there any music that both kids and adults will like?

There is. Folk music fits the bill. Try Peter Paul & Mary—their CDs *Peter Paul and Mommy* and *Peter Paul and Mommy, Too!* were made with kids in mind, but most adults, we think, will find them quite tolerable. There are also CDs by groups and individual singers not specifically aimed at the kids' market that all ages can enjoy. Go to a record store that carries a good selection of Irish, Scottish, Appalachian, and other traditional music groups and ask to listen to some samples. The Clancy Brothers, Clannad, Capercaillie, Pete Seeger, the Poor Clares, Six Mile Bridge, and the Chieftains are all worth checking out.

Then there's Raffi. Yes, he's specifically a kid's audience singer—but we know lots of adults who like him, too. Okay, we'll admit it, we're among them. Once you've heard "Baby Beluga," how could you not sing along? And he does do that very hilarious Bob Dylan impression on his *Raffi in Concert* tape.

Back to the folk music suggestion: We've also discovered that music in other languages has lots of cross-age appeal, plus it avoids the problem of having your child ask questions about the lyrics of the many English and American folk songs that deal with sex or death or both. (Quite a few of those old traditional folk songs tell gruesome or ribald stories. It's a good idea to screen any CD before you play it for your children, so that you don't have to explain to your three-year-old, for example, why that girl in the song killed her baby and then herself). "Guantanamera" is a lovely Spanish song that you and your children can enjoy for its lilting melody, without translation of its lyrics (about a dying poet). There seems to be a practically unending supply of bouncy, rhythmic Caribbean calypso tunes. Traditional African music can also have toddlers drumming happily along.

But what if you're a rock 'n' roll sort of family? There are plenty of good groups out there today making music that's fun and singable, but you may well hesitate to bring home a CD that features a portrait of the music makers. You definitely don't want your four-year-old daughter to think it's cool or pretty to have a metal stud stuck in her tongue or wear a spiked dog collar around her neck. A young child can't help but see as a role model anyone her parents consider talented, and so you need to consider the group's image as well as their sound before you buy.

If you don't want your child imitating anything about the Spice Girls, Britney Spears, or Christina Aguilar, then you had probably best stick to the oldies. Compared to most groups today, the Beatles are squeaky clean. Play "Yellow Submarine," "Octopus's Garden," "She Loves You," and "Please Please Me" for your kids. Go back to the fifties for an even simpler, sunnier sound, in songs like "Rockin' Robin" or Richie Valens's "La Bamba." Then there are the funny, novelty hits that kids then and now love: "One-Eyed One-Horned Flying Purple People Eater" and "Does Your Chewing

Gum Lose Its Flavor on the Bedpost Overnight?" (Both can be found on the CD *The Dr. Demento 20th Anniversary Collection: The Greatest Novelty Records of All Time.*)

Most kids love dance songs that have them moving in time to the beat. Let them learn the Locomotion, the Limbo, the Twist, the Peppermint Twist, the Swim, the Mashed Potato, the Monster Mash, Mickey's Monkey, and lots more. Three good dance music CDs for kids are: *Kids' Dance Party; 20 Jukebox Party Dance Favorites;* and *Hot, Hot, Hot* (the Sesame Street characters' dance CD). And don't forget the "Macarena."

Our final and perhaps best recommendation for listening pleasure for all ages comes from the Great White Way. A good collection of showtunes from a variety of different stage hits is *The Broadway Kids Sing Broadway.* Original cast albums are great, especially if your kids are familiar with the story or have seen a kids' theater production of the show. Some of the shows that are easiest for young kids to follow are: *Cinderella, Peter Pan, Once Upon a Mattress* (the "Princess and the Pea" fairy tale), *The Lion King, Beauty and the Beast, The Sound of Music,* and *Annie.*

In some cases, the tone of the play overall may be too dark, or the main plot line may be too complicated for young children to follow, but there are still quite a few songs they would very much like to learn. *The King and I,* for example, has far too much about the cultural and sexual tension between the Englishwoman and the Asian monarch in the 1860s to be comprehensible to a three-year-old, but a child of any age would like to "Whistle a Happy Tune" or sing "Getting to Know You" along with the Siamese princes and princesses. From *My Fair Lady* kids generally love "Wouldn't It Be Loverly?" and "I Could Have Danced All Night." With a CD "burner" or a dual-head tape deck, it's relatively easy to pick and choose cuts from various CDs to make a recording of just those songs your whole family likes best.

Another solution entirely—and one that is a good deal less work for the parents—is simply to get each child his or her own portable music player with its own earphones. Set the volume knob for them and insert cassettes, CDs or minidisks with just the music that your child prefers. You can buy a special child-sized set with color coded buttons for PLAY, REWIND, and FAST FORWARD, or you can buy an ordinary player and make your own little stick-on button labels with symbols that even a toddler can understand. We did this on two small, simple cassette recorders that we bought for our children before they knew how to read. On the PLAY button, we put a musical note symbol; on the REWIND button, a backward-facing arrow; and on the FAST FORWARD button, a forward-facing arrow. On the STOP button we made a label showing a tiny, red stop sign.

Once your child knows how to press the PLAY button, then the STOP, and can rewind the tape and play it again, she can play "Farmer in the Dell" a hundred times if she likes, and you won't mind a bit!

Conclusion

To paraphrase one of Abe Lincoln's wiser sayings: "You can fool some of the toddlers all of the time, and all of the toddlers some of the time, but you can't fool all of the toddlers all of the time." To which we append our own observation, "Two out of three ain't bad."

We think if you're managing to outwit your toddler with two out of every three strategies you try, you are doing all right. Even when a strategy hasn't worked to gain your toddler's cooperation, you very likely can learn something from figuring out why it failed that will be helpful the next time around. Your effectiveness as a parent should grow with each additional year of experience you and your toddler share. Take it from us, it *does* get easier, and will continue to get easier year by year—at least until the problems of puberty start to kick in.

In the meantime, these are the fun years—so enjoy them to the fullest. And try your best to keep at least a few steps ahead of your fast-thinking offspring! We know you can do it!

Resource Guide

The world is so full of resources for parents these days, we hardly know where to stop when drawing up a list. There are literally thousands of good books, catalogs, childrearing institutions, and retailers of toddler products. And when it comes to on-line resources—we're talking in the millions.

So we have decided in the interest of simplicity (not to mention saving book pages—and conserving trees) to limit the listings here to sources we have already mentioned in the body of this book. For example, in Chapter Seven we suggested "Prop-O's Head Support" for traveling and noted that this product is available through the One Step Ahead catalog. You will find contact information here.

General Toddler Product Sources

One Step Ahead	800-274-8440	www.onestepahead.com
The Right Start	800-LITTLE-1	www.rightstart.com
Pottery Barn Kids	800-430-7373	[no online ordering]
Babes and Kids	770-564-1420	www.babesandkids.com

Anything Joe's   877-279-0606   www.anythingjoes.com
Fisher-Price   800-747-8697   www.fisher-price.com

Safety, Health, and Hair Products

Lice detection and treatment information: The National Pediculosis Association, 617-449-NITS, www.headlice.org.

Home hair-cutting information: www.cuttinghair.com or 800-671-HAIR or HairOutlet.com.

EMLA prescription anesthetic disk: www.emla-usa.com.

The Safety Zone: 800-999-3030, www.safetyzone.com.

The National Safe Kids Coalition: 877-348-4254, www.safekids.org.

Fit for a Kid (jointly sponsored by DaimlerChrysler, Fisher-Price, and The National Safety Council): www.fitforakid.org. This web site is a tremendous source of car seat safety information because it has an on-screen video you can play right on your computer about installing a car seat, plus Top Ten tips about children's auto safety, as well as a locator index of sites for free inspection of your car seat installation.

Huggies Pull-Ups Training Pants: 800-990-4448, www.pull-ups.com. Register at this web site for a free toilet-training read-aloud coloring book, personalized with your child's name and using your family's preferred terms for urine and feces.

For bulletins on the safety of infant and toddler equipment:

The American Academy of Pediatrics
141 Northwest Point Boulevard
Elk Grove Village, IL 60007-1098
847-434-4000
847-434-8000 (fax)
www.aap.org

For information on toddler product recalls and many other topics:

The U.S. Consumer Product Safety Commission
Office of Information and Public Affairs
Washington, DC 20207
301-504-0580
800-638-2772 (toll-free)
800-638-8270 (toll-free—TTY)
www.cpsc.gov (From the home page, go to CATEGORIES and click on
INFANT/CHILD.)

Suggestions for Further Reading

Books about Childrearing

Adler, Bill Jr. *365 Things to Do with Your Kids Before They're Too Old to Enjoy Them.* Contemporary Books, 1999.

Azrin, Nathan A. and Foxx, Richard M. *Toilet Training in Less Than a Day.* Pocket Books, original edition 1974, revised edition 2000.

The Best Travel Activity Book Ever. Rand McNally, 1993.

Bickart, Toni S. and Dodge, Diane Trister. *Preschool for Parents: What Every Parent Needs to Know About Preschool.* SourceBooks, 1998.

Borden, Marian Edelman. *Start Smart: The Parent's Complete Guide to Preschool Education.* Facts on File, 1997.

Brazelton, T. Berry. *Touchpoints: Your Child's Emotional and Behavioral Development.* Addison-Wesley, 1992.

Derosa, Laura. *How to Cut Your Child's Hair at Home*. Avery Publishing, 1994.

Eisenberg, Arlene; Murkoff, Heidi; and Hathaway, Sandee E. *What to Expect the Toddler Years*. Workman, 1994.

Ezzo, Gary and Bucknam, Robert. *On Becoming Babywise: Parenting Your Pre-Toddler Five to Fifteen Months*. Multnomah Books, 1995.

Ezzo, Gary and Ezzo, Anne Marie. *Growing Kids God's Way: For No Excuse Parenting*. Growing Families International Press, 1990.

Ferber, Richard. *Solve Your Child's Sleep Problems*. Fireside paperbound edition, 1986.

Freymann, Saxton and Elferrs, Joost. *How Are You Peeling?: Foods with Moods*. Arthur A. Levine Books, 1999.

Herman, Doris. *Preschool Primer for Parents: A Question and Answer Guide to Your Child's First School Experience*. Tarcher/Putnam, 1998.

Leach, Penelope. *Your Baby and Child from Birth to Age Five*. Alfred A. Knopf, 1990 paperbound edition.

Robin, Peggy. *The Safe Nanny Handbook: Everything You Need to Know to Have Peace of Mind While Your Child Is in Someone Else's Care*. William Morrow, 1998.

Rosemond, John. *Making the Terrible Two's Terrific*. Andrews and McMeel, 1993.

Rosemond, John. *Parent Power: A Common Sense Approach to Parenting in the Nineties and Beyond*. Andrews and McMeel, 1990.

Sears, William. *Nighttime Parenting: How to Get Your Baby and Child to Sleep*. La Leche League International, original edition 1985, revised edition 1999.

Spock, Benjamin and Rothenberg, Michael B. *Dr. Spock's Baby and Child Care*. Dutton, 1985 edition.

White, Burton L. *The First Three Years of Life*. Prentice Hall Press, 1985.

Wilkoff, William G. *Coping with a Picky Eater: A Guide for the Perplexed Parent*. Fireside, 1998.

Books to Read to Your Toddler

Atwater, Richard and Atwater, Florence. *Mr. Popper's Penguins*. Little Brown & Company, originally published 1938. Also available as a pop-up book, Little Brown & Company, 1993.

Berenstain, Stan and Berenstain, Jan. *The Berenstain Bears Go to the Doctor*. Random House, 1981.

Brown, Marc, *D.W. the Picky Eater*. Little Brown, 1995.

Brown, Margaret Wise. *Goodnight Moon*. HarperCollins, original edition 1947, available as a cloth-, paper-, or board-bound book.

Frankel, Alona. *Once Upon a Potty*. HaperCollins, 1984.

Gannett, Ruth Stiles. *My Father's Dragon*. Alfred A. Knopf, original edition 1947.

Kennedy, Anne. *A Visit to the Doctor*. Golden Books, 1996.

Kids Travel: A Backseat Survival Guide. Klutz Press, 1994.

Lawson, Robert. *Rabbit Hill*. Penguin Books, 1978, originally published Viking Press, 1944.

Lewison, Wendy Cheyette. *The Princess and the Potty*. Simon & Schuster, 1994.

Lindgren, Astrid. *Pippi Longstocking*. Viking Books, 1999. Originally published in English, translated from the Swedish by Puffin Books, 1950.

McBratney, Sam. *Guess How Much I Love You*. Candlewick Press, 1995.

MacDonald, Betty. *Mrs. Piggle-Wiggle.* HarperCollins, 1989. Original book of the series first published in 1947.

Malfatti, Patrizia. *Look Around the City.* Grosset & Dunlap/ Putnam's, 1992.

Mayer, Gina. *The New Potty.* Western Publishing Company, 1992.

Miller, Virginia. *On Your Potty.* Greenwillow Books, 1991.

Peterson, John. *The Littles.* Scholastic Books, 1967.

Pienkowski, Jan. *The Toilet Book: Don't Forget to Flush.* Price Stern Sloan, 1994.

Ross, Tony. *I Want My Potty.* Kane/Miller, 1986.

Dr. Seuss. *Horton Hears a Who. Horton Hatches the Egg. Green Eggs and Ham. One Fish Two Fish Red Fish Blue Fish. The Cat in the Hat.* Plus many, many more. All Random House, various years.

Waddell, Martin. *Can't You Sleep, Little Bear?* Candlewick Press, 1992.

White, E. B. *Charlotte's Web.* HarperCollins, paperbound edition 1999, originally published 1952.